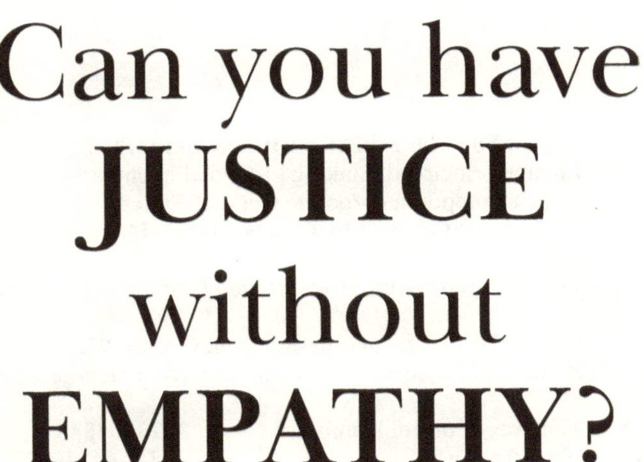

Can you have JUSTICE without EMPATHY?

Engage principled thinking grounded in empathy to support a corporate Code of Ethics

Otto B. Toews, Ph.D.

SO YOU THINK YOU CAN THINK[1]

Thinking through moral dilemmas in pursuit of justice by Otto B. Toews

KIRKUS REVIEW[2]

A debut work of psychology recommends a system to make readers more adept at solving moral dilemmas.

Morality is a deceptively basic concept. Often invoked but rarely defined, morality is something that becomes increasingly subjective, particularly when personal interest is involved. Toews offers a new procedure for teaching morality that he calls the Principled Thinking Model: "The Principled Thinking Model presented in this book does not guarantee right answers but serves as a way of thinking through different situations involving moral dilemmas." By considering the duties, rights, and motives of individuals as well as the merits and justice of a given situation, Toews proposes not only an approach to conflict resolution, but also a method of teaching people to respect objective parameters during the process.

Citing his own research as well as thought experiments and hypothetical scenarios, the author guides readers away from selfish instincts and toward a shared experience based on empathy. The author dramatizes his ideas through dialogues between two fictional teachers, Bill, and Mae, who explore the Principled Thinking Model through the lenses of their students and the pupils' parents. Toews writes in a dense, scholarly prose that makes frequent reference to the work of his predecessors in the field and the relevant terminology. The Bill and Mae dialogues offer a change in tone, but they are nevertheless somewhat wooden and didactic: "Now Bill is struggling...it will not be easy to answer Mae's question. He tried, 'Having a right means that it is not wrong for a person to pursue a specific interest; nor would it be wrong not to pursue it."

The volume is a bit too dry and academic for a general readership. That said, Toews' in-depth work delivers an insightful take on the way individuals approach morality, and the tests he recommends to shape moral understanding are specific and comprehensive. It is hard to argue that society is not in need of better moral standards—standards built on empathy, not simply religious or cultural values.

The Principled Thinking Model provides one possible way forward.

An ambitious, though specialized, treatise on how to improve moral understanding.

Pub Date: Oct. 30th, 2017
Page count: 208pp
Publisher: FriesenPress
Program: Kirkus Indie
Review Posted Online: Feb. 22nd, 2018

Dedicated to my soulmate and wife,
Edna Joan McCreath
June 28, 1933 – May 12, 2022

CONTENTS

CHARTS

PREFACE

This book is for business students, employers/employees, entrepreneurs, and lawyers to expand their understanding of justice/fairness and to challenge them to pursue it in the workplace with empathy. Although companies are encouraged to develop a customized code of ethics, everyone needs to be able and willing to discuss controversial and important company issues and concerns. To that end, employees need to be able to exercise empathy to address the emotional stress in conflicts as they apply principled thinking. **Can you have JUSTICE without empathy?** is designed to provide a working-knowledge of principled thinking grounded in empathy which can lead to justice.

My emphasis is on the *pursuit* of justice because I acknowledge that pursuing justice is a process. At best we can strive for justice without any certainty of achieving it in every instance.

To that end, I applaud you for your commitment and determination to engage with empathy as you pursue justice. I wish you much success.

INTRODUCTION

Thrusting a news clipping at me, Trump said, "Did you say that?"

"Yes, I did, Mr. President," I responded. "The reporter asked me what the department had found to date, and I told him."

"Why would you say that?" he barked. "You could have just said, 'No comment'... You must hate me."

After an extensive review of the allegations of voter fraud, Bill Barr tried to bring the conversation to a conclusion ...

... "I am willing to submit my resignation. But I have ..."

Bang.

"Accepted!" the President yelled.

The President had slammed the table with his palm. "Accepted!" he yelled again.

Bang.[4]

Was this Trump's gut reaction to Bill Barr's offer to resign? Probably. Whether or not Barr should be retained by Trump in his cabinet, my question is, 'Was this intuitive response appropriate on a weighty matter like firing a newly appointed Attorney General?'

Read the following scenario.

> As a dad of a 16-year-old daughter and the CEO of a software company, KnowledgeBuilder Software Inc[5], I remember rescheduling a management meeting so that I could watch my daughter play in her final basketball playoff game. Since some staff members objected to my decision, I reviewed my line of thinking with them.
>
> I asked myself, 'Do I have a primary duty to my company or my daughter? Do I honor my promise to my daughter or concentrate on my obligation to lead and protect my company?
>
> When challenged, I was protective of both, my rights as a parent and my shareholder's rights in my company. I reflected on questions like, 'When is the right time to do one or the other? Do I have time to see my daughter play in her final playoff game?'
>
> I imputed a motive to my team leader, Peter, who insisted that my first obligation always must be to my company, but I did not acknowledge my own motive for wanting to see my daughter play in her final game. That led me to take defensive action sub-consciously – like being dismissive about what Peter had to say.
>
> On the other hand, I felt that my Communications Director, Betty, deserved approval for standing up for my decision to see my daughter's final basketball game.
>
> Unfortunately, I was quick to judge Peter unfairly for criticizing my decision to take the time to see my daughter's final game.

There are an endless number of questions that could have been triggered by this line of thinking which could take hours to resolve.

Did I really need to 'overthink' the issue of taking off a few hours to attend my daughter's final game?

These two scenarios offer ways of addressing the moral question, 'What is the just or fair thing to do?' The first illustrates a gut feeling or intuitive response and the second illustrates overthink. Most often, we use our intuition to make decisions which demand immediate resolutions. That is what Trump did in response to Barr. Sometimes we need to think through decisions which might have short-term or long-term consequences. That is what I demonstrated in the second scenario.

In this book I focus on issues which require careful reflection where people feel uneasy about the decisions they face. They are uneasy about whether the decision they are about to make is right or wrong.

All decisions involve emotions; they serve as the foundation of decisions. They can help to transform thinking into action as you will see in Part IV. With the use of scenarios and conversations, I show the impact of different emotions. Not all of them lead to just and fair resolutions of conflicts. That is why it is important to know which ones can lead to the pursuit of justice. No guarantees.

But emotional intelligence by itself is not sufficient to lead to just or fair resolutions of conflicts. If that were not the case, then there would be no difference between 'love' which is a good motive and 'empathy' which is a morally good motive. I illustrate the need for principled thinking' as a necessary follow-up on emotional intelligence. Hence, this book addresses the need for both emotional intelligence, and principled thinking (cognitive intelligence).

We face moral questions daily with family, but employers and employees face them as well. It probably is not easy for companies to be 'just' all the time. I put the following question to CEOs: **As the CEO of a company, would you hire an employee who follows a corporation's code of ethics, OR someone who cares about the welfare of everyone affected and exercises principled thinking based on both, the company code of ethics and justice with empathy for all?**

Principled thinking driven by empathy in pursuit of justice adds to the daily challenge facing CEOs. Maybe their Boards want them to focus only on the bottom line. Or they might take a 'do or die' attitude about the life of their companies. Some CEOs might see that the life of a CEO is so overwhelmingly busy that they cannot find time to attend to the ethical matters such as being just towards colleagues or competitors. I draw your attention to an article on the daily life of a CEO. In this article, Bret[6] chronicles the difficulties in a 20-hour day where he waits for feedback on a proposal just to discover that more modifications must be added to the proposal before it will be accepted. I have been through this back-and-forth many times and appreciate Bret's frustration.

Tom Nault, Managing Partner at Middlerock Partners LLC (2016-present) tells a similar story about the life of a CEO.[7]

That a CEO lives a hectic life is an understatement. Many employees have a similar hectic pace though their responsibilities differ significantly. Never-the-less, in an increasing age of transparency, for a company to function in a fair and just way is not an option. So how can a CEO manage a company in a fair and just manner? Although there are many and varied factors involved, I focus on one basic factor – principled thinking driven by a sense of fellow-feeling (empathy). Read on to see 'why'.

This book is based on the following sources.

I developed the framework for principled thinking in my doctoral dissertation, *Discretion and Justice in Educational Administration: Towards a Normative Conceptual Framework*[8] under the guidance of Dr. Tony Riffle, my thesis advisor. This philosophical inquiry was developed to enable educational administrators to resolve ethical and moral issues in a just and fair way. It classifies and illustrates essential moral terms – duty, rights, motive, desert, and just - used in principled thinking that may lead to justice.

Justice has an objective basis and a subjective basis. Principled thinking forms the objective basis, and a sense of fellow feeling is the subjective basis. My thesis concentrated on the objective basis in pursuit of justice. The objective framework evolved in a graduate seminar conducted by Dr. Glassen, Philosophy Professor at the University of Manitoba. I tested the framework in sessions for aspiring educational administrators.

The persistent criticism of my objective basis was that it addressed the cognitive aspect of making decisions almost exclusively. Little attention was paid to the subjective basis (empathy) when the subjective basis should serve as the foundation for objective basis. My first book, *SO*

YOU THINK YOU CAN THINK[9], did not address the subjective basis (empathy) adequately. That failure to address empathy is dealt with in this book so that it could assist CEOs in building a durable foundation for companies.

Second, I needed scenarios about dilemmas/violations occurring in companies to apply principled thinking grounded in empathy. Through an on-line search, several major conflict issues surfaced which I used to I create scenarios about moral dilemmas arising in companies. I refer users to *INTENTIONAL INTEGRITY*[10] by Robert Chesnut for his Code Moments for additional scenarios.

Third, I created hypothetical conversations involving collage students which deal with an imminent crisis affecting everyone – companies, governments, non-profit organizations, and private citizens. The topic is Climate Change.

Here is a brief introduction to each chapter in Part I – V.

Part I: Recent history This story begins in the late nineteenth and early twentieth century when companies were free to dismiss employees when it was assumed that the market is best capable of regulating itself. This practice was challenged, during the depression in the thirties, by Maynard Keynes[11]. His view was challenged by Milt Freedman[12] in the nineteen seventies when he insisted that a company's exclusive obligation is to its shareholders.

In the twenty-first century, Robert Chesnut developed standard elements for a basic code of ethics. He set the stage for the evolution of the code of ethics to 'create a better world for everyone.'[13] This leads to the primary purpose of my book, to customize a company's code of ethics so that a company is driven by principled thinking grounded in empathy in pursuit of justice.

Part II: Emotional Intelligence. Conflicts in the workplace create stress which must be dealt with through emotional intelligence. I identify four common forms of distress in Chapters 1-5 which I call dissonance: experiential dissonance, logical dissonance, cultural dissonance, and cognitive dissonance. In Chapters 6-9, I suggest ways of addressing the dissonance that lowers the stress to a point where a fair and just resolution can be considered. These moral values principle tests are: universal consequences test (consider the consequences of a resolution), subsumption test (prioritize the values involved, new cases test (applicability of a resolution in new cases), and role exchange test (invite people to put themselves in the shoes of another person). Most important, I stress that the emotion, empathy, can lead to the pursuit of justice.

Part III: Principled thinking. Principled Thinking, which offers a deeper level of thinking, is possible only after the stressful situations identified above are addressed. Then the emotional energy that is released can be used to engage principled thinking in pursuit of justice by considering the following concepts discussed in Chapters 10-14 – duty, rights, motive, desert, and just. In Chapter 10, three concepts of 'duty' are applied. It is pointed out that it would be difficult to determine through a code of ethics when to apply each. Chapter 11 addresses the category 'rights'. The correlative relationship between duty and rights is explored. Chapter 12 introduces the concept of 'motive' and addresses the question, 'Must an action which is right be done from a morally good motive to be a morally good act?'. Chapter 13 is focused on 'desert'. An interesting connection is discovered between 'desert' and 'motive'. Finally, we get to Chapter 14 which addresses the category 'just' where all the categories - duty, rights, motive, desert - are included. That makes 'just' a pivotal category in pursuit justice.

Now, for the important question, 'How can principled thinking energized through emotional intelligence be transformed into moral action? To find out, go to Part IV.

Part IV: In pursuit of justice. The primary purpose of Part IV is to illustrate how the emotional energy of empathy can address the emotional stress generated by conflict to enable companies to engage in principled thinking in pursuit of justice. Principled thinking is applied to the following key categories: duty, rights, motive, and just in Chapters 15-19. The key categories are applied to the following hypothetical conflict scenarios: HIV positive, a Chocolate factory, Toxic emissions, Dealing with staff performance, and I Promised. The scenarios are analyzed and reviewed on how emotional intelligence can provide the energy necessary to apply principled thinking in pursuit of justice.

In short, I demonstrate ways of transforming a feeling of discomfort (dissonance) into empathy, so that a person might engage in principled thinking in pursuit of justice. However, there are situations where a transformation does not occur.

Part V: Practical learning activities. Now for some practical learning activities to challenge students and employees to apply emotional intelligence (empathy) and cognitive intelligence (principled thinking) to resolve conflicts in pursuit of justice. Learning Activity A and My response focus on conflicts of interest that arise in companies. Learning Activity B and My response engages college students in conversations on ways of addressing problems caused by Climate Change. Learning Activity C and My Response addresses Code Moments developed by Robert Chesnut in INTENTIONAL INTEGRITY[14] based on his experience as Chief Ethics Officer with Airbnb. Students will need access to Chesnut's book to do these learning activities.

Conclusion. In the Conclusion, I raise several questions that have not been addressed which stress the need for on-going research on the role of emotional intelligence to facilitate principled thinking.

Postscript: Transparency. I maintain that the current demand for more transparency could lead to increased effort by companies to focus on justice for all.

This concludes a summary of how the book is organized.

Empathy is the first step in moral thinking. It will be to the 21st century what 'rights' was to the 20th century and 'equality' was to the 19th century.[15]

PART I: RECENT HISTORY

Before the 1930's, companies in North America saw little need for a code of ethics. Management would simply fire employees for a variety of reasons from not meeting expected performance levels to personal reasons. Debates about the function of companies focussed on major principles based primarily on current cultural values. No attention was paid to a corporate code of ethics to promote best ethical behavior.

In the depth of the 1930's depression, John Maynard Keynes[16] challenged the current understanding of economics that the free market was perfectly capable of generating full employment. Consequently, it was argued that there was no need for government-initiated stimulus programs. Keynes, however, maintained that in times of dramatic down-turns in the economy, the government has a critical role in stimulating the economy. Many countries, including the US and Canada, followed this revised thinking about the role of government.

After Maynard Keynes, along came another giant in economics, Milton Freedman. He revived the reliance on free markets to address the difficulties of the market in his famous 1970 address, *The Social Responsibility of Business Is to Increase Its Profits*.[17] The popular slogan of the day was 'Greed is good.' The sole purpose of a company was to generate profits which meant higher returns for the shareholders. Again, there was no perceived need for a code of ethics.

An increasing number of knowledgeable people were discouraged by the outcome of successful companies who had adopted the shareholder model. Here is how one American put it:

I need only look out the window to see the results of libertarian economic ideology. A pall of grayish-orange smoke lies over my neighborhood near Seattle, as it does along the entire West Coast. Fed by the hot, dry air of climate change, unprecedented wildfires rage across our landscape.[18]

Not until 10 years later, in the '80's, did society and hence companies see the need to demand ethical behavior from companies, due to an awareness of unethical behavior by some companies. Was this concern about the unethical behavior of employees in part due to the influences of 'free markets' ideology? Who knows?

In the 1990's, corporate leaders' thinking evolved from Friedman's original shareholder primacy philosophy to an emerging stakeholder value model. The stakeholders of a company should include employees, customers and, of course, shareholders. When employees are well-served, it can lead to increased revenue and potentially increased profits. Likewise, when employees serve their customer well, that can lead to increased profits from increased sales. The challenge for management is to balance the interests of all stakeholders. This provided an expanded view of Freedman's original philosophy.

In the past 20 years, Robert Chesnut has led an ethical revolution in companies.[19] He maintains that the purpose or interests of a company should be stated in a code of ethics. In *INTENTIONAL INTEGRITY*, Chesnut presents a critical review of the shareholder model and outlines a convincing framework for the stakeholder model. He developed this Model through an analysis of Code Moments he constructed based on the numerous cases he dealt with as the Chief Ethics Officer at Airbnb.

He maintained that 'stakeholder value' should be the basis for companies to develop their own code of ethics. To that end, he named five basic elements for a standard code of ethics.[20]

1.   **Mission**
     The CEO lays out company's mission and purpose.
2.   **Core values and principles**
     Deliberate, affirmative commitment to values such as
          honesty, fairness, respect for the law
     as well as values related to the business mission:

excellent customer service
low prices
maximum shareholder value
respect for and empower employees
commitment to ethically sourced ingredients
or materials

3. **Specific rules and practices for each specific workplace**
Bring life to core values and principles
include examples

4. **Detailed consequences**
How the code will be enforced
Resources available to employees
How to report an infraction

5. **Employees expected to read, understand, and sign a pledge to follow the code.**
Report violations
It is a code violation to retaliate because of a report
It can be a code violation to fail to report a code violation
Source: Robert Chesnut, *INTENTIONAL INTEGRITY*[21]

Chart 1: Chesnut's Code of Ethics

However, an increasing number of knowledgeable people were still discouraged by the outcome of successful companies who had adopted the stakeholder model. As one observer wrote:

> … the wealthiest 1 percent of people in this country have 40 percent of the wealth. And the number of people finding themselves food and housing insecure is out of control. Our national debt is now more than sixty times higher than it was 50 years ago. We have the most advanced medical care in the world, yet it is inaccessible to many.[22]

On the other hand, some economists drew attention to the positive steps taken by many companies. Here is one response to an editor:

> The notion of linking corporations to explicit social goods is resurfacing. Nine countries now require greater gender equity on corporate boards. About

fifty countries require some sort of environmental and social sustainability reporting. International anti-money-laundering rules have grown far more stringent. Numerous countries, the United States among them, restrict corporate use of conflict mineral.[23]

By the 21st century, Chesnut acknowledged the limitations of transitioning from the shareholder model to the stakeholder model. He maintains that in the 21st century, companies need to take another step forward by adopting the goal of 'creating a better world for everyone'. His account of this goal could coincide, I think, with my understanding of 'justice for all'. To be consistent with his framework for a code of ethics, this expanded goal would have to be translated into rules for everyone to follow. Chesnut has not attempted to generate a necessary set of rules to include 'justice for all'; nor can or should I because it cannot be done (as we will see later). I conclude that since this goal cannot be reduced to 'rules', everyone in a company needs to understand and exercise principled thinking and be sensitive to a sense of fellow feeling (e.g., empathy) for a company to act morally responsible.

Chesnut goes on to elaborate on a code of ethics for the 21st century. But he misses an opportunity to present what is involved in generating ethical/moral behavior by companies accepting this broader 21st century view. I maintain that if a code of ethics is designed to promote ethical/moral behavior in all circumstances by everyone in a company, then everyone must have a good command of principled thinking with empathy necessary for moral action. If front-line workers simply follow rules and do not consider the implications of rules or directives, they might take action that is immoral in certain circumstances. More on this later.

Chesnut acknowledges that everyone in a company needs to engage in principled thinking with empathy at the end of his Postscript in response to the COVID 19 pandemic where he describes the following independent action taken by employees at Airbnb:

> Several employees surfaced the idea of donating their credits to hosts, and on their own, unprompted by management, over two thousand employees donated over $1 million to hosts in need.[24]

Employees started this action and management did not interfere with it. In other words, not only senior management but also employees can and need to exercise sound moral judgement. This action by the employees reflects the following features which, I maintain, need to be added to Chesnut's framework for a code of ethics designed to promote justice for all:

> Empathic emotions that drive people to moral action
> Principled thinking to pursue justice for all

By adding these two features (empathy and principled thinking) to Chesnut's framework, I offer a more comprehensive and just framework for addressing moral dilemmas.

Of course, this addition to Chesnut's framework raises questions particularly as it relates to the place of 'emotions' in making company decisions. Why include a sense of fellow feeling along with principled thinking? What is involved in enabling shareholders, employees, and all levels of management to think and act based on a sense of fellow feeling? These questions demand answers.

While Chesnut was wrestling with what companies need in the 21st century, psychologists were exploring what they called 'emotional intelligence'. Says Chignell[25], "As we will see, this approach provides the necessary foundation for moral action."

In the early 20th century, the father of emotional intelligence, Goleman[26], stated, "The interest in emotional intelligence in the workplace stems from the widespread recognition that these abilities – self-awareness, self-management, empathy, and social skill – separate the most successful workers and leaders from the average." Hence, EI has developed distinct components applicable in the workplace. Employers and employees need to be able to recognize, discuss, and manage their own emotions; only then can they deal with the emotions of others.

For example, how might a director manage an employee who has a moody day at work? If the Director expresses his impatience with the moody employee and demands the usual outstanding performance from everyone, including the employee who is having a dreadful day, the Director displays a low level of emotional intelligence. On the other hand, if the Director takes the time to have a thoughtful conversation with the employee, he might help the employee overcome his moodiness and return to his usual excellent performance. In this case, the Director would display an elevated level of emotional intelligence because he understood his own emotions and that of the employee. That made it possible for the Director to regulate the performance of one of his employees.

The empathic relationship of the Director towards his employees enabled him to solve the problem of one employee arriving at work in a moody state of mind. That is why I stress 'justice with <u>empathy</u>' in this book.

That takes me back to the significance of intuitive thinking and deep thinking I presented in the Introduction. The most used of these two approaches to making decisions is the former. It has been convincingly presented by Daniel Kahneman in THINKING, FAST AND SLOW where 'fast' refers to intuitive thinking and 'slow' refers to deep thinking.[27] My focus in this book is on how we might exercise deep thinking in pursuit of justice grounded in empathy. I refer to this thinking as 'principled thinking'.

The focus on principled thinking presents a special challenge for companies. Read what David Brooks[28], columnist for the *New York Times*, reported in 2011 on how young people answered questions about "right" and "wrong."

[Brooks] based the article on a study conducted in 2008 by the Notre Dame sociologist Christian Smith[29] that involved in-depth interviews with 230 young adults from across America. Smith's research team asked the young adults open-ended questions about "right" and "wrong" moral dilemmas and the meaning of life.

Brooks reported that … "when asked to describe a moral dilemma they had faced, two-thirds of the young people either could not answer the question or [shifted to describe] problems that were not moral at all.[30]

When asked about wrong or evil, the respondents agreed that rape and murder qualified as such. But, aside from agreeing on these two extreme examples, moral thinking (e.g., thinking about right and wrong) did not enter the picture for them, even when they considered issues like drunk driving, cheating in school, or cheating on a partner.

The default position, that most of them came back to repeatedly, was that moral choices are just a matter of personal viewpoints. "It's personal," the respondents typically said. "It is up to the individual. Who am I to say?"

Brooks concluded that "they [the young people] don't have the categories or concepts to answer questions about right and wrong".[31] This inability to think about moral issues can have major implications, because moral issues are part of daily living, including corporate living.

That is why I have included learning activities to support necessary on-going training for students in business colleges and management/employees on principled thinking in the context of a sense of fellow feeling. The first set of learning activities concentrates on the kinds of conflicts of interest that occur in a company. The second set applies principled thinking to a world-wide issue which affects all companies albeit in diverse ways: Climate Change. The third set targets 'code moments' presented by Robert Chesnut based on his experience as Chief Ethics Officer at Airbnb.

In short, this book is organized around three goals: Emotional Intelligence with an emphasis on empathy, Principled Thinking in pursuit of justice, and Learning Activities on the first two goals. I begin with the first goal, Emotional Intelligence – Empathy. Remember, emotional intelligence is the foundation of all decisions – intuitive and deep thinking.

PART II: EMOTIONAL INTELLIGENCE

Part II identifies the tension or dissonance we often face when we make decisions. It also identifies four strategies that could be used to address the emotional stress or dissonance. Most important, Part II emphasizes the power of empathy which can enable or urge employers and employees to look at conflicts through the eyes of the aggrieved. Without this emotional energy, principled thinking is not likely to be tried. In other words, Part II is the pre-condition for Part III.

Let me illustrate this with the following scenarios involving two parents who express their views or planned to express them to their respective Principal on the following question:

> Should access to the search functions of the Internet be restricted at the high school level?

This is how Parent One dealt with this issue.

> *Mr. Brown, an irate parent, burst into the Principal's office and dove into his objections, "Why do you permit your English teacher to insist that her class read Of Mice and Men by John Steinbeck … (he paused for a moment to catch his breath) … when you know the book is not on the required reading list of the State Education Ministry? That is wrong", he went on to say before the Principal could say a word, "Morally wrong! The language used in that book utterly offensive … all that cursing! I repeat," he stressed, "That is morally wrong. You have a responsibility to remove that book from the school curriculum immediately!"*

"What's more, it is wrong to require my daughter to read a novel which is offensive to me whether she agrees with me or not", he asserted.

All the while, the Principal was wondering how she might respond as she listened to Mr. Brown. Even though she suspected that the parent's motives were self-serving, she respected his moral indignation. She agreed that it would not be wrong to offer his daughter an option to study an alternative novel.

However, the Principal felt she could not ignore the way Mr. Brown had verbally accosted her. Hence, she said to him, "I will review the situation with my staff at the next Department meeting. In the meantime, your daughter is required to stay in the class where students study Of Mice and Men."

She considered this action to be an appropriate way of expressing her disapproval of the Mr. Brown's action because she felt he deserved this response. Never-the-less, she viewed him as a just person because she agreed that the action he demanded was the right action for his daughter. At the same time, she was troubled at the thought of requiring the English teacher to individualize the English course to meet the demands of every parent. How could the English teacher teach such a fragmented course? This raised another perplexing issue – should she prioritize the demands of the parent or the teacher's workload or the education of the students? This posed a difficult moral dilemma.

What chances did this parent have in getting what he wanted? Did he consider how the Principal might feel about the way the parent accosted her? The Parent expressed himself with anger towards the Principal and his daughter's teacher. He used the terms – duty, rights, motive, desert (deserve), and justice to present his case but displayed no understanding of expressing empathy towards the Principal who was expected to follow through with her expectations. Nor did he consider the implications of his demand on the teachers. There is no indication that the Parent was empathetic towards the Principal, teacher, or other children in the classroom.

What did the Principal do to address the angry emotions of the Parent? Could a discussion about resolving the issue be possible without first resolving the anger? Not likely. The Principal realized that an understanding and appreciation of the 'other' point of view is a prior condition to resolving a conflict in pursuit of justice or fairness. Justice was not possible if the parent remained angry.

Let us look at the following scenario involving Parent Two who faced the same problem as Parent One.

This is how Parent Two dealt with this issue.

> *Mrs. Jones, whose daughter attended another high school, was anxious about what to say to the Principal, Mr. Anderson, about her objection to the use of John Steinbeck's novel, Of Mice and Men in English classes. Adolescents hear enough bad language on the street and in public places. Moreover, she felt she had a duty to raise her objections because she had a right to defend her daughter's rights. She simply had to make her case, first to the Principal and if the Principal failed to act on her objection, then to the School Board.*

> *Mrs. Jones really wanted to do what is right ... her motives were noble. That is why she kept thinking about what she should say to the Principal.*

> *When she had asked her husband for his opinion, he replied with a question, 'Are all right acts also considered just?' As if that was not confounding enough, he went on to ask, 'What if not all right acts are just? Are all just acts right? Are all wrong acts unjust? Are all unjust acts wrong?' This was quite confusing for her and certainly not helpful.*

> *She felt that she should present her concerns with respect. Putting herself in the Principal's place, she was certain that the Principal did not do wrong for wrong's sake. This is no time to be critical of him personally ... he did not deserve that.*

> *'Why was the Principal condoning the use of this novel?' she wondered. Maybe the teacher randomly assigned Steinbeck's novel to her daughter's class. That might be wrong, but not necessarily unjust. On the other hand, if the teacher had picked her daughter's class for some reason to read a novel containing foul language, that would have been unjust.*
>
> *She picked up the phone to make an appointment with the Principal. Justice had to be done, she felt.*

What do Parent 1 and Parent 2 have in common? Both claimed that they tried to do the right thing by considering their duty, the children's rights, what the parent deserved, and how to be just/fair to the children. Where do they differ? Parent two put herself in the shoes of the Principal. She expressed *empathy* for the Principal by being concerned about the challenge he might face. Her planned response pointed out the importance of addressing emotional tension and draw on the power of empathy to resolve conflict.

These scenarios emphasize the condition that must be met before attempting to resolve a conflict – attempt to understand and appreciate the point of view of the 'other' person.

Parent One technically followed principled thinking, but he did not pay any attention to the way he presented his case to the principal. He ignored the emotional intelligence needed to set the stage his presentation.

Suppose Trump's response to Bill Barr's offer to resign had been,

> Bill, do not rush your decision to resign; it has big implications not just for my administration but for the whole country.

This response would have given both men time to think about Bill's offer to resign. That would have shifted Trump's response from an intuitive response to deep thinking. It might not have changed the ultimate outcome but would have changed the decision from a 'gut reaction' to a thoughtful decision. Trump would have reflected at a higher level of emotional intelligence which was needed to respond to the emotionally charged event. In other words, Trump would have had to deal with the emotionally charged event (the exchange with Barr); what changed was how he would have dealt with it – by deep thinking.

In short, emotions are present in all decisions; how they are managed is what makes the difference. This book is focused on deep thinking, even though it is used less frequently than intuition (gut feeling).

There are ways of resolving emotional distress but no assurances. First, there are two steps every company should take. Every company should have a customized code of ethics and an HR department. A code of ethics sets out the basic rules, which reflect the company's goals and principles. HR can apply the necessary skills and has the time to deal with any conflict of interest as quickly as possible – to relieve the CEO of this challenging and time-consuming process.

Second, everyone in a company must become sensitive to the feeling of discomfort when a specific action seems wrong or inappropriate. This feeling is called 'dissonance'. People can encounter a variety of feelings of dissonance when they face moral dilemmas including logical dissonance, cultural dissonance, experiential dissonance, and cognitive dissonance. Employees/employers must be able to recognize the differences among these emotions. Specifically, they need to be able to recognize the significance of one kind of dissonance - cognitive dissonance which is driven by a sense of fellow feeling called empathy.

Dissonance generation

To understand the central role of emotions in dealing with dilemmas, we need to consider two factors – a feeling of dissonance, which has been addressed above, and moral values principle tests. The tests are designed to reduce the stress or dissonance. A sense of follow feeling (empathy) can prompt people to question their own emotions. Replacing negative emotions with empathy, can urge people to exercise principled thinking prompted by empathy.

First, let us look at the feeling of dissonance. 'Dissonance' refers to a psychological state of discomfort which needs to be resolved. People try whatever it takes to get out of this uncomfortable state because it can increase a feeling of anxiety, fear, etc. To resolve the problem that created the feeling of distress, CEO's might try to avoid the problem, or deny it. Festinger identified four types of dissonance[33] - logical dissonance, cultural dissonance, experiential dissonance, and cognitive dissonance. I explain and illustrate them by applying them to scenarios. Chart 2 lists the types of dissonance and several approaches to resolve dissonance.

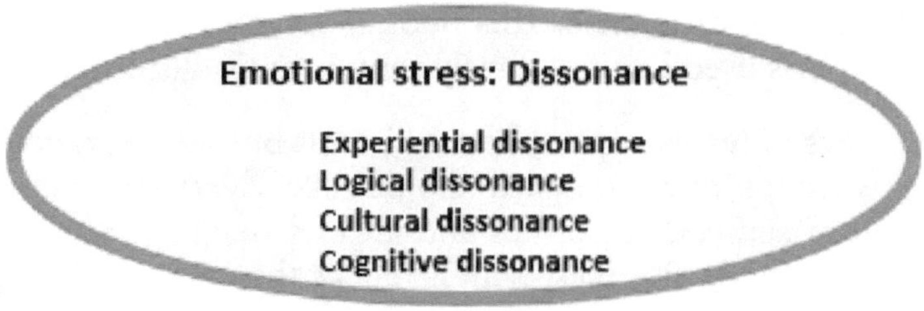

Emotional stress: Dissonance

Experiential dissonance
Logical dissonance
Cultural dissonance
Cognitive dissonance

Chart 2: Resolve emotional distress

I begin with Experiential distress or dissonance by applying it to *HIV positive*.

As I mentioned in the Introduction, the events and persons in these scenarios are mostly fictional based on reading a wide variety of scenarios and case studies. Any similarity to real persons or companies is accidental, though hopefully instructive.

CHAPTER 1: EXPERIENTIAL DISSONANCE

Experiential[34] dissonance is felt when past habits or relationships do not align with a current incident or when two similar events seem to result in different outcomes. It increases the intensity of feelings with no apparent way out of it. Let us observe the experiential dissonance experienced by Flo.

HIV positive - Duty

As the nurse of an international wholesale company, Flo encountered a wide range of health-related problems. Recently David brought a new case when he admitted to her that he is HIV positive. When she asked about his partner, Jack, David insisted that he was not ready to share this information with his partner.

Word gets around; Jack became uneasy about his relationship with David and wonders where he might share his unease. The company nurse of course; everyone goes to her when they need someone to talk to!

When he finally had the courage to talk to the nurse about what he regarded as an overly sensitive and personal topic, he blurted out his concern about his partner, David. He suspected that David may have been unfaithful and consequently may be HIV positive.

Now, what should the nurse do with the information she received from both, David and Jack? She felt that she was morally obligated to client confidentiality. On the other hand, the company's Code of Ethics clearly states that as the company nurse, she has an obligation 'to protect the health and safety of the employees.' Is she caught in a conflict of interest? She decides that, no, she is not in a conflict of interest because the company Code of Ethics states very clearly that her responsibility is to protect the health and safety of the employees. What is more, Flo is part of the company's three member HR team which interprets and applies the Code. She followed the company Code of Ethics.

As a veteran nurse, Flo felt she had encountered every health-related problem – till David showed up at her office. He announced that he was HIV positive. But he was not ready to share this information with his partner, Jack. No sooner had he left Flo's office, his partner showed up at Flo's office. Immediately upon entering her office, he blurted out his concern about his partner, David, whom he suspected of having been unfaithful and consequently probably contracted HIV.

These two visits, which are related to each other, created considerable distress for Flo. When David first arrived, she had no difficulty assuring him that she would keep his information confidential. He left her office peacefully with this assurance.

When David's partner, Jack, shared his fears about his partner possibly having contracted HIV, she realized her potential challenge. She recalls that the company Code of Ethics states very clearly that her responsibility is 'to protect the health and safety of the employees.' In the past she has had no difficulty complying with this clause. Now what should she do – break the confidentiality she promised David or confirm to Jack that David has admitted that he is HIV positive? Should she follow the Code of Ethics or make an exception? Her experience did not seem to fit with her current situation. This generated a feeling of experiential dissonance for Flo. How might she deal with it so that she can do what is right?

Emotional Distress (dissonance)
Experiential dissonance – HIV positive
Logical dissonance – Chocolate factories
Cultural dissonance – Toxic emissions
Cognitive dissonance A – I Promised
Cognitive dissonance B – Dealing with staff performance

Chart 3. Experiential dissonance

Let us turn to logical dissonance to see how it can block the resolution of a conflict of interest.

CHAPTER 2: LOGICAL DISSONANCE

Logical inconsistencies can create dissonance when what appears to be logical is not.[35] Let me illustrate this with the following scenario.

Chocolate Factory

Since 'rights' have come to mean human rights in the 20th century, every major violation of people's rights alarms consumers, CEOs, and politicians. When Jane, CEO of a major chocolate factory in Atlanta, was tipped off that the evening news would report on the widespread use of child slave labor in the production of cocoa in several African countries, she knew she had a major problem on her hands. Consumers would be incensed, and politicians would demand immediate action. As president of the American Chocolate Association and as the CEO of a chocolate producing company, much would be expected from her. What should she do?

First, she thought, the industry needs time – time to develop and promote a sound course of action. Through her leadership, they got four years of grace in which to develop and test a plan to eliminate the use of child slave labor. Jane and her research team soon encountered several obstacles that defied any implementable solution. First, cocoa was produced on countless small farms across eastern Africa. Who could ensure that the production in these farms would never involve child slave labor? Second, the cocoa from these farms was collected by large foreign companies. How could you make sure that a shipment did not include some cocoa produced involving child slave labor?

Politicians demanded a solution. What should Jane do – pursue a human rights plan of action to be developed by the government at potentially huge losses of revenue for her company or manage to delay any action by the government if possible?

Jane no doubt meant well (wanted to be fair to everyone including the children) when she requested time to develop and test a plan for eliminating the use of child slave labor in the cocoa industry. Unfortunately, there appeared to be insurmountable obstacles blocking this objective. Jane could not find a way of monitoring all the farmers who were involved in producing cocoa and the large marketing companies could not guarantee that their huge shipments did not include some cocoa production involving child slave labor.

Jane concluded that there were only two options. Cut back on the number of farmers from whom companies like hers would purchase cocoa or ask the governments to assume the responsibility of enforcing the prohibition of using child slave labour. She chose the latter. As part of that decision, she made every effort to delay if possible any government action so that her company could maintain or increase the volume of cocoa sales.

Jane's decision was flawed logically. There were not only two either/or options from which she had to choose one. In fact, there were several options in no order. First, she could consider a delaying strategy. Second, the purchase of cocoa could be limited to farmers who had a consistent reputation of not using child slave labor. This option might reduce the availability of marketable cocoa and hence reduce sales volume in the short run. The result would be lower returns for the marketing companies like Jane's. Third, private for-profit companies could cooperate with government where the government could gradually increase the number of farmers who would not use child slave labor and hence increase the volume of sales. I can think of more options, and you probably can too.

If Jane had considered more options, she might have arrived a better solution. That might have triggered the adoption of a solution to the problem of using child slave labor that could be fair for all parties involved – children, farmers, marketing companies, and the government. Since Jane did not consider other options, her feeling of dissonance was not resolved; she remained in a state of logical dissonance which blocked her from applying principled thinking.

Emotional stress (Dissonance)
Experiential dissonance – HIV positive
Logical dissonance – Chocolate factory
Cultural dissonance – Toxic emissions
Cognitive dissonance A – I Promised
Cognitive dissonance B – Dealing with staff performance

Chart 4. Logical dissonance

Let us move on to another example of dissonance, cultural dissonance, to observe how it can block resolving solutions.

CHAPTER 3: CULTURAL DISSONANCE

A clash of cultural mores can generate dissonance which prompts people to try to reduce or block the uncomfortable feeling created by the incongruity between conflicting cultural mores or customs.[36]

Toxic emissions

Betty is the quality control supervisor for AGInc, a thriving midsize plastics company which meets all the local toxic emissions regulations. She knows of innovative technology which can reduce the current emission level even more to protect the fish in local rivers and lakes. This would save the local recreational and commercial fishing industry for years to come.

When Betty expressed her concern about the current toxic emissions of her company at a shareholder's meeting, where the Press was allowed to attend, the shareholders reminded her that AGInc was following local limits. Hence, there was no need for the innovative technology. Of course, the Press put a different spin on Betty's concern; it expressed alarm at the potential consequences of not reducing the toxic emissions. In fact, the reporters suspected the motive of the company – increased profits vs. installing expensive technology to reduce emissions beyond current local regulations. The companies preferred the former option.

Although Betty took issue with the Press for imputing that the company was driven by profits, she decided not to invest in the new costly technology that might risk the profitability of the company. She argued that AGInc should delay acquiring the innovative technology till the government changes the toxin emission regulations.

Changing her position from recommending the installation of innovative technology to delaying the installation till the government introduces legislation that reduces toxic emissions caused an elevated level of cultural dissonance for Betty. Having grown up in the community, she was fully aware of what the current level of toxicity did to the local rivers and lake. Her family and neighbors used them for recreational fishing and boating. She was concerned about their long-term health.

"So, why wait for the government to act?" she wondered.

Emotional stress

Dissonance
Experiential dissonance – HIV positive
Logical dissonance – Chocolate factory
Cultural dissonance – Toxic emissions
Cognitive dissonance A – I Promised
Cognitive dissonance B – Dealing with staff performance

Chart 5. Cultural dissonance

That leaves the fourth and final form of dissonance identified by Leon Festinger – cognitive dissonance. Can it generate opportunities to resolve conflicts of interest?

CHAPTER 4: COGNITIVE DISSONANCE A

Cognitive dissonance refers to a situation where two cognitive elements do not fit together – they may be inconsistent or contradictory.[37] For example, suppose John knew there were only friends at his birthday party, but he still felt afraid. He was caught between two cognitive elements – friend and fear – they do not make any sense together. Cognitive dissonance creates a feeling of discomfort. As I mentioned before, people try to resolve the feeling or avoid it. In 'I Promise', note how I considered 'duty, rights, motive, desert, and just' to justify my decision to attend my daughter's final game.

You might ask, "Why am I using this scenario to demonstrate the feeling of cognitive dissonance when I maintain in the Introduction, that this scenario illustrates overthink?"

I maintain that one can be caught in a situation where one needs to walk directly through the process of principled thinking in pursuit of justice. *I Promise* is one of them. Based on my team's commitment to empathy when they solve conflicts, I did not see the need to walk them through other forms of dissonance and procedures for transforming them into cognitive dissonance which includes the urge to be empathetic.

In all other feelings of dissonance, I would have walked my management team through emotional intelligence till they were open to understand the current situation with empathy.

Here is the background for this scenario. As a dad of a 16-year-old daughter and the CEO of a software company, KnowledgeBuilder Software Inc., I remember rescheduling a management meeting so that I could watch my daughter play in her final basketball playoff game. When this decision created discord in my leadership team, I walked them through the principled thinking process of resolving conflicts. Here it is:

I Promised

I asked myself, 'Do I have a primary duty to my company or my daughter? Do I honor my promise to my daughter or concentrate on my obligation to lead and protect my company? I concluded that my decision would have no effect on company, but it could affect my father/daughter relationship.

When challenged, I was protective of both, my rights as a parent and my shareholder's rights. Questions came to mind, 'When is the right time to do one or the other? Is this the time to see my daughter play in her final playoff game?'

I imputed a motive to my team leader, Peter, who insisted that my first obligation always should be to my company, but I did not acknowledge my own motive for wanting to see my daughter play in her team's playoff game. That led to defensive action done consciously or unconsciously – like being dismissive about what Peter had to say.

On the other hand, I felt my HR team leader, Betty, deserved approval for supporting me for deciding to see my daughter's final basketball game.

Unfortunately, I was quick to judge Peter unfairly for criticizing my decision to take the time to see my daughter's final game. I had no reason to judge Peter; there is nothing unfair about Peter's advice.

What are the cognitive elements in this scenario that do not fit together? They are my promise to watch my daughter play her final basketball game and my commitment to my shareholders to manage the company. My leadership team was split on these two options.

My management team created the feeling of discomfort. My team leader, Peter, insisted that my first obligation always must be to my company. I imputed a motive (make money) to him for saying this. I felt my HR team leader, Betty, deserved approval for supporting me.

The dissonance generated by these two cognitive elements challenged me to work through the principled thinking process in search of a fair and just resolution of the cognitive dissonance. It involved considering my duties, the rights of people affected by my decision, my motive, what my daughter and shareholders deserved, and finally, what is the just and fair to do.

My team was ready to address the dissonance because they were experiencing a cognitive dissonance which could be addressed by engaging in principled reasoning in the context of empathy. As the CEO of the company, I cared for them. That is how cognitive dissonance is different from the other forms of dissonance – experiential, cultural, and logical dissonance.

I assumed that my team could exercise emotional intelligence to address the emotional tension generated the two points of view. That probably was a mistake.

Emotional stress

Dissonance
Experiential dissonance – HIV positive
Logical dissonance – Chocolate factory
Cultural dissonance – Toxic emissions
Cognitive dissonance A – I Promised
Cognitive dissonance B – Dealing with staff performance

Chart 6. Cognitive dissonance A

CHAPTER 5: COGNITIVE DISSONANCE B

As I mentioned above, cognitive dissonance can be created when two cognitive elements do not fit together – they may be inconsistent or contradictory. When the inconsistency is recognized and addressed, it can be dealt with. That opens a way for a person to exercise principled thinking which enables a person to pursue justice. However, there are no guarantees that this will happen. How is dissonance addressed in the following scenario?

Dealing with staff performance

"A woman's place is in the home," chuckled Bill as he saw Sadie racing back to her desk 42 minutes late. Not only had arriving late become a common occurrence, but she had been seen leaving her desk early rather frequently. Coming in late was of particular concern to management because by arriving late, she missed several team meetings which were scheduled at the beginning of each day. In addition, Sadie had taken a leave of absence to take care of her elderly father. Suitable homes for seniors were at a premium and difficult to get especially for seniors of limited income as was the case with her father. In fact, Sadie had to work not only to support herself but also her father.

As the Department Manager at NEWTECHInc, Nancy appreciated Sadie's work ethic and performance. At the same time, she was concerned about the undue stress imposed on Sadie's overworked colleagues due to her frequent 'lates' after her prolonged absence. One or two colleagues were undermining Sadie, thus creating even greater stress not only for Sadie but also for management.

"Is it time for management to intervene? If so, how?" mused Betty. "First, I will have to talk to Bill."

Dealing with staff performance is always difficult. Frequently it involves at least two views of the performance driven by competing motives. Sadie hoped that her manager and colleagues would understand her demanding situation of finding affordable accommodation for her aging father. She felt she was meeting expectations at work even though she came in late and sometimes had to leave early. The occasional snide remark from one or two colleagues reflected the view of those who made them and probably a few of their male colleagues. These men were prone to make nasty remarks about anyone, especially women at work.

As Department Manager, Betty took a different view. She was not only concerned about Sadie's performance but also about her Department working as a team. To do so required that everyone support each other and consider the challenges everyone faced at work and at home. Comments like the one made by Bill interfered with this objective.

Having allowed the situation at work to deteriorate to the point where people made snide remarks about their colleagues created a difficult challenge. It led in the opposite direction of trusting each other and being empathetic towards each other. Being fair did not only mean sharing the workload evenly. It included respecting each other's duty, acknowledging everyone's rights, not imputing motives to colleagues, being careful about what a person deserves (i.e., approval or disapproval), and finally, remaining focused on fairness. On top of that, it requires an empathetic attitude towards each other. That is a huge order! How can that become a reality in the current toxic workplace? Can Betty turn that around? That seems doubtful because the atmosphere seemed too toxic for the emotional conditions necessary for engaging in principled reasoning. If Betty cannot create a situation where the toxic dissonance can be changed into cognitive dissonance, principled reasoning remains remote.

Emotional stress

Dissonance
Experiential dissonance – HIV positive
Logical dissonance – Chocolate factory
Cultural dissonance – Toxic emissions
Cognitive dissonance A – I Promised
Cognitive dissonance B – Dealing with staff performance

Chart 7. Cognitive dissonance B

What can be done to overcome the kinds of dissonance presented in the five scenarios above? That is our next challenge. To that end, I introduce Leon Festinger's moral values principle tests.

Moral Values Principle Tests

1. Universal consequences test
2. New cases test
3. Subsumption test
4. Role exchange test

Chart 8. Moral values principle tests

Moral Values Principle Tests

According to Leon Festinger[38], moral values principle tests (see Chart 8) can assist in reframing dilemmas and possibly changing the dissonance into cognitive dissonance. The tests can activate the emotional energy that can transform the dissonance. Without that emotional energy, principled thinking can remain quite passive. I use scenarios to illustrate how these tests can transform dissonance into cognitive dissonance thus opening a way to exercising principled reasoning.

Before I proceed, I want to reinforce two points Chesnut makes in his book *INTENTIONAL INTEGRITY*. He emphasizes the importance for a company to develop a customized code of ethics based on a framework he developed which I presented in the Introduction. Second, I acknowledge and agree with Chesnut's emphasis on the need of every company for a chief ethics officer or its equivalent.

I begin the moral values principle tests with the Universal consequences test by applying it to the scenario, *HIV positive*. The key question is, 'How can the moral values principle tests transform dissonance into a situation where people can exercise principled thinking in pursuit of justice?'

CHAPTER 6: UNIVERSAL CONSEQUENCES TEST

Can applying the universal consequences test[39] create the situation where the people involved are prepared to exercise principle thinking? Can the test generate empathy?

HIV positive

As the nurse for an international wholesale company, Flo encountered a range of health-related problems. Recently David brought a new case when he admitted to her that he is HIV positive. When she asked about his partner, Jack, David insisted that he was not ready to share this information with his partner.

Word gets around; Jack became uneasy about his relationship with David and wondered where he might share his unease. The company nurse of course; everyone goes to her when they need someone to talk to!

When he finally had the courage to talk to the nurse about what he regarded as an extremely sensitive and personal topic, he blurted out his concern about his partner, David. He suspected that David may have been unfaithful and consequently may be HIV positive.

Now, what should the nurse do with the information she had from both David and Jack? She realized that she was morally obligated to client confidentiality. On the other hand, the company's Code of Ethics clearly states that as the company nurse, she has an obligation 'to protect the health and safety of the employees.' Is she caught in a conflict of interest? She decides that, no, she is not in a conflict of interest because the company Code of Ethics states very clearly that her responsibility is to protect the health and safety of the employees. What is more, Flo is part of the company's three member HR team which interprets and applies the Code. She followed the company Code of Ethics.

We have seen that Flo avoided any dissonance by trying to resolve the conflict of interest through literally applying the company's Code of Ethics. This effectively closed any chance of considering any other paths to fairness – she would 'protect the health and safety of the employees.' But what course of action does that statement in the Code of Ethics expect? Should she tell Bill what Jack told her? Should she maintain client confidentiality? The Code does not seem to answer these questions.

What if Flo had considered the consequences of these questions. Might that have made her more open to the implications of the Code? In fact, what might be the consequences of breaking her confidentiality with Bill? What might the consequences be of disclosing what was shared with her in confidence to comply with the company Code of Ethics? Reflecting on these questions might open her to exploring resolutions by applying principled thinking with empathy. Principled thinking includes considering the duty, rights, motive, desert, and just applicable in this scenario. Empathy refers to a commitment to care about all parties involved in the scenario. Combining principled thinking with empathy could lead to a just and fair way of addressing the current issue and possibly future issues. What if Flo had applied this process?

Moral Values Principle Tests
Role exchange
New cases
Subsumption
Universal consequences

Chart 9. Universal consequences test

Let us look at another scenario where the subsumption test might apply.

CHAPTER 7: SUBSUMPTION TEST

How can applying the subsumption[40] test create the situation where the people involved are prepared to exercise principle thinking? First, can the test generate empathy?

Chocolate factory

Since 'rights' have come to mean human rights in the 20th century, every major violation of people's rights has alarmed consumers, CEOs, and politicians. When Jane, CEO of a major chocolate factory in Atlanta, was tipped off that the evening news would report on the widespread use of child slave labor in the production of cocoa in several African countries, she knew she had a major problem on her hands. Consumers would be incensed, and politicians would threaten immediate action. As president of the American Chocolate Association and the CEO of a chocolate producing company, much would be expected from her. What should she do?

First, she thought the industry needed time – time to develop and promote a sound course of action. Through her leadership, they got four years of grace in which to develop and test a plan. They soon encountered several obstacles that defied any implementable solution. First, cocoa was produced on countless small farms across eastern Africa. Who could ensure production on these farms would never involve child slave labor? Second, the cocoa from these farms was collected by large foreign companies. How could you make sure that a shipload of cocoa did not include some cocoa produced by child slave labor?

Politicians demanded a solution. What should Jane do – pursue a government initiated human rights plan of action at potentially a huge loss of revenue for her company or manage to delay any action by the government for as long as possible?

How might moral values principle tests assist in resolving the issue of using child slave labor to reduce the cost of producing cocoa? Of the four tests recommended by Festinger, let us apply the 'subsumption test'. Here is why. The subsumption test explores the interrelationship of values such as the value of a person's life to that of the life of a dog. When there is a strong disagreement on principle, it may be helpful to prioritise them using the subsumption test. So, what are the values imbedded in this scenario?

The values in this scenario center on 'rights' – the rights of children to get an education, the farmers' rights to produce cocoa using child slave labor to reduce costs so that small farms in remote villages can produce enough to feed and clothe their children, and the rights of international corporations to find markets for the cocoa produced in Africa.

Children cannot work on local farms and attend school at the same time. Small farms may not be able to compete with large farms to produce cocoa if child slave labor was prohibited. Hence, some small farms would have to drop out of the cocoa industry. How will these farmers feed, clothe and send their children to school?

Does John Rawls offer a way of solving this challenge? Here is what he has to say. He identified the fundamental meaning of justice as 'the tension between liberty and equality.' He put it this way.

- Society should be structured so that the greatest possible amount of liberty is given to its members "limited only by the notion that the liberty of any one member shall not infringe upon that of any other member."

- Inequality should be allowed "provided that the worst off will be better off than they might be under an equal distribution"[41.]

Based on Rawl's understanding of liberty and equality, children's right to attend school should be prioritized. Only then will a new generation have the opportunity for a better life. Maintaining child slave labor would infringe on the liberty of the children. Hence, maintaining the practice of child slave labor, as Jane proposed after they were unable to arrive at a way of ending child slave labor, would be wrong.

Could the farmers together with international marketing companies determine the outcome of this dilemma by simply continuing the use of child slave labor? Probably. But that does not address the dilemma for the children. Applying the subsumption test could convince people to apply principled thinking grounded in empathy for the children.

That did not happen in this scenario. Hence, no path to justice became available to allow children to get an education.

Moral Values Principle Tests

Role exchange
New cases
Subsumption
Universal consequences

Chart 10. Subsumption test

Let us look at a scenario, which might address the dissonance, using the new cases test. By applying this test, management can consider whether a decision in one case also applies in a similar new case. If so, that might confirm a decision. It does not guarantee that a decision is right even if it confirms the decision. The scenario chosen for this test is *Toxic emission.*

CHAPTER 8: NEW CASES TEST

How can the new cases[42] test create the situation where the people involved are prepared to exercise principle thinking? How can the test generate empathy?

Toxic Emission

Betty is the quality control supervisor for AGInc, a thriving midsize plastics company which meets all the local toxin emissions regulations. She knows of innovative technology which can reduce the current emission level more to protect the fish in local rivers and lakes. This would save the local recreational and commercial fishing industry for years to come.

When Betty expressed her concern about the toxic emissions at a shareholder's meeting, where the Press was allowed to attend, the shareholders reminded her that AGInc was following local limits. Hence, there was no need for the innovative technology. Of course, the Press put a different spin on Betty's concern; it expressed alarm at the potential consequences of not reducing the toxic emissions. In fact, they suspected the motive of the company – preferring increased profits vs. installing expensive technology to reduce emissions beyond current local regulations.

Although Betty took issue with the Press for imputing that the company was driven by profits, she decided not to invest in new and costly technology that might risk the profitability of her company. She argued that AGInc should delay acquiring the innovative technology till the government changes the toxin emission regulations. Why? Might she be motivated by the excessive cost of the innovative technology? Did she give any thought to potential benefits of installing the innovative technology to reduce emission levels?

Why are motives so important in making decisions?

As we can see in the scenario, Betty listened to the shareholders' advice and followed it. What if, in preparation for the shareholders' meeting, she had presented case studies that projected the implications of introducing the innovative technology. She could have presented a case where the innovative technology, which reduces toxicity, had been in place for three years and another case for five years. In both cases the toxicity of the rivers and lakes was reduced substantially, and the cost of the innovative technology was fully recovered. How might the shareholders have responded to these actual case studies? Might they have recognized the importance of introducing the innovative technology sooner rather than later? Might they have felt an emotional tug to do the right thing?

In fact, the media might have been convinced about the merits of introducing the innovative technology immediately instead of speculating about the company's motivation. As for Betty, she might have presented a more convincing story if she had presented new cases for implementing the innovative technology. Presenting new cases, which are less toxic, prompted the emotional feeling to do the morally right thing which created the urgency to apply principled thinking in pursuit of justice.

Moral Values Principle Tests
Role exchange
New cases
Subsumption
Universal consequences

Chart 11. New cases test

Let us turn to a scenario using the role exchange test. How could its application address dissonance?

CHAPTER 9: ROLE EXCHANGE TEST

Can the role exchange[43] test create the situation where the people involved are prepared to exercise principle thinking? How can the test generate empathy?

I Promised

As a dad of a 16-year-old daughter and the CEO of a software company, KnowledgeBuilder Software Inc., I remember rescheduling a management meeting so that I could watch my daughter play in her final basketball playoff game. Since there was discord or tension in my management team, I decided to walk them through the principled thinking process while at the same time, apply one of Festinger's moral values principle tests – role exchange test. I felt confident that my team was sufficiently familiar with principled thinking that I could use this event to reinforce the principle thinking process. I took my team through the following process.

I asked myself, 'Do I have a primary duty to my company or my daughter? Do I honor my promise to my daughter or concentrate on my obligation to lead and protect my company?

When challenged, I was protective of both my rights as a parent and my shareholder's rights. Questions came to mind, 'When is the right time to do one or the other? Is this the time to see my daughter play in her final playoff game?'

I imputed a motive to my team leader, Peter, who insisted that my first obligation always is to my company, but I did not acknowledge my own motive for wanting to see my daughter play in her team's playoff game. That led to defensive action done unconsciously – like being dismissive about what Peter had to say.

On the other hand, I felt my HR team leader, Betty, deserved approval for supporting me on deciding to see my daughter's final basketball game.

Unfortunately, I was quick to judge Peter unfairly for criticizing my decision to take the time to see my daughter's final game.

With this scenario, I would like you, the reader, to personally engage in a role exchange on a subject of concern to you. That can be a promising way of understanding and appreciating putting oneself in the shoes of another person. Here is one of my experiences where role exchange offered me insights about how to pursue justice or fairness in a personal situation. I have altered some of the details to protect the privacy of the people identified.

First, to appreciate what my attendance at her final game meant to my daughter, I found it helpful to put myself in her shoes. I recalled my final concert in high school singing in the school ensemble. It was important to me emotionally that my parents attend (which they did) just as it was important for my daughter for me to see her play in the final game.

Second, I had to understand why some shareholders felt I should not allow my motive for watching by my daughter's high school basketball game distract me. "Don't waste your time," they said. To appreciate their perspective, I had to walk in their shoes. That helped me to understand especially my team leader, Peter, who was most vocal about my planned absence to attend the game. I realized how counterproductive it was for me to impute that Peter was driven by a particular motive. In contrast, I commended Betty, my HR team leader who, I felt deserved approval for her support. Doing a role exchange with Peter exposed my closed mind about passing judgement on Peter. To think that I was trying to pursue justice; this certainly was not the way to pursue justice or fairness in my company. My conduct was not likely to generate cognitive dissonance; instead, it was likely to create discord.

In this scenario, I used role exchange to show how important it was for my daughter that I attend her final game, and why my reaction to Peter's response was not appropriate.

Moral Values Principle Tests
Role exchange
New cases
Subsumption
Universal consequences

Chart 12. Role exchange test

This concludes the discussion of the four moral values principle tests - role exchange test, new cases test, subsumption test, and universal consequences test. The application of these tests to scenarios shows that they might help to resolve conflicts of interest by first addressing the feelings created by each scenario. This in turn, could open the possibility of resolving the conflict of interest, which created the moral dilemma, with principled thinking.

A word of caution about emotional intelligence – it can be used for good and bad. Although studies since the 1990's have shown the benefits of exercising emotional intelligence, it can have negative consequences. In the article, *The Dark Side of Emotional Intelligence*, Adam Grant[44] points out some of the abuses of emotional intelligence. First, it can be used to manipulate others to engage in ethical or unethical acts. Second, hyper-emotionally intelligent people may treat other's emotions too personally. This may lead to inappropriate reactions. Third, logically, people with higher emotional intelligence would be better at delivering criticism or identifying inappropriate behavior. But it can be used to manipulate people, especially, people with lower levels of emotional intelligence. Fourth, emotional intelligent people are so aware of the emotions of people around them that they might be reluctant to call other's actions or decisions. Most important, as I see it, there may be the temptation to resolve conflicts by using emotional intelligence without exercising principled thinking on the assumption that once the tension is resolved, all is well.

Let me explain with reference to the scenario, *Dealing with staff performance*. Nancy, the Department Manager, had to attend to the increasing emotional tension created by Sadie's frequent absence, but also the stress level of the staff who had to cover for Sadie. Most immediately, she had to contain the emotional stress caused by the inappropriate remarks tossed at Sadie by staff members like David. Nancy concluded that first she had to get David to agree not to engage in name calling to reduce the tension on staff. Suppose she managed to accomplish this and consequently was able to reduce the tension by everyone being understanding and empathetic towards Sadie. That is great and certainly needed to be done. But this sets the stage for the heavy lifting – Sadie's frequent absence and the subsequent load that the rest of the staff had to carry must be addressed. To resolve these two issues required Nancy and her staff to resolve these to issues in a fair way. This requires that staff be engaged in principled thinking which includes considering everyone's duties, rights, motive, desert, and just treatment. Without resolving the two issues in a fair and just way, the tension will surely return.

In short, emotional intelligence should be exercised in balance with other decision-making skills. In Part III, I stress that it be applied together with principled thinking strategies.

Let us move on to see how to apply principled thinking grounded in empathy to resolve moral dilemmas.

Chart 13: Principled Thinking Model

PART III: PRINCIPLED THINKING

With emotional intelligence as a prior condition, let us have a look at what deep thinking grounded in empathy, can do to resolve issues.

My formal background in philosophy was on deep thinking in moral philosophy where the focus was on five concepts – duty, rights, motive, desert, and just. For an example, a professor would pose a question like

'Is morally bad simply the converse of morally good?'

[My response: An act is morally good if it is right and done from a desire to do what is right. If a morally bad act is the converse of a morally good act, it would read, 'an act is morally bad if it is wrong and done with a desire to do wrong.' To test this definition, I apply it to a specific case. Suppose a student is absent from school (truant). Did he choose to be truant from a desire to do wrong? Or did he want to be somewhere else to do something different? Why would he choose to do wrong for the sake of doing wrong? What is in it for him? He probably chose to be truant because he wanted to be somewhere else or do something different. That is not the same as saying that 'he did what is wrong with a desire to do wrong.]

The philosophy professors reinforced a focus on thinking. For example, a professor would typically call on a student to respond to a statement like this one:

> All just acts are right but
> Not all right acts are just.
> What would you say?

> [My response: 'All just acts are right.' For an act to be just, it must meet two conditions: a) it must be done from a morally good motive; and b) it must be right. For example, a police officer would act from a morally good motive if she refused to shoot the burning truck driver caught in the cab on fire because it is wrong to kill a person. I was also right because it allowed her to use a device to make the burning driver instantly unconscious of his pain. The police officer's action met the two conditions for her action to be just.

> 'Not all rights are just.' For an act to be right, it must comply with the regulations of a particular organization. For example, if a company welcomes the practice of displaying personal items in the office, it would be a right act. However, it would not be a just act because it does not include one of the conditions of a just act – doing an act for a morally good motive such as empathy – it was simply a welcoming act.

As a student was struggling to respond, the professor would pose follow-up questions or make comments on the student's response. This mode of teaching reinforced sound logical thinking. There was no attempt to address the emotional aspect of issues or responses. If anything, this teaching strategy added stress to the students involved.

This kind of philosophical inquiry could lead to what I call principled thinking[39] about moral dilemmas. By wrestling with the issues related to duty, rights, motive, desert, and just, we view moral dilemmas through the question 'What is the just or fair thing to do?

John Rawls, a moral philosopher, identified the fundamental meaning of justice as the tension between liberty and equality which he maintains are primary properties of moral action. I repeat how he put it:

> Society should be structured so that the greatest possible amount of liberty is given to its members, limited only by the notion that the liberty of any one member shall not infringe upon that of any other member
>
> Inequalities either social or economic are only to be allowed if the worst off will be better off than they might be under an equal distribution.[45]

Companies are quick to agree with Rawls on the concept of liberty till they see the clause – "limited only by the notion that the liberty of any one member shall not infringe upon that of any other member." Rawls' second statement also creates a challenge for companies which concentrate only on profits or returns to shareholders. I maintain that all companies should include the pursuit of justice in their goals. Or as Robert Chesnut says, a twenty first century company needs to contribute to "creating a better world for everyone"[46].

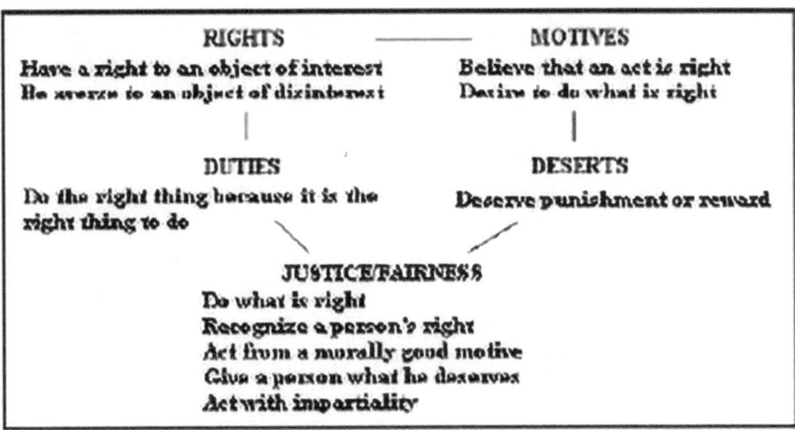

Chart 14. The meaning of each category

Chart 14 captures the essential meaning of each category of principled thinking – duty, rights, motive, desert, and just. I illustrate how the categories of principled thinking could be applied in five scenarios (one scenario for each of the five categories – duty, rights, motive, desert, just). I conclude with explaining and illustrating   why and how only a few principled thinking strategies are used to resolve a controversial issue in any given situation.

Here is a quick review of each of the five categories: duty, rights, motive, desert, just.[47]

Duty. Here are a few key issues it addresses:

- Duty means doing the right thing because it is the right thing to do.
- Can one put someone under an obligation but not under a duty?
- Does ought imply can?
- Are there degrees of rightness?
- Are there degrees of wrongness?
- Are people's acts determined or done from free will?
- Are judgments about beliefs, attitudes, feelings, emotions, and thoughts moral judgments?

Rights. Most people tire quickly when someone keeps reminding them of their duties or responsibilities. Before long, they shift the conversation to their rights. In other words, we tend to be quite defensive about our rights and object to being reminded of our duties. It addresses many questions and claims we make about our rights. Here are a few examples of the questions raised:

- What does it mean to say that 'John has a claim to X'?
- How do we distinguish between moral rights and legal rights?
- What does it mean to have a prerogative?
- Is it true that for every duty a person has a corresponding right?
- Is it the case that to every right there is a correlative duty?

Motive. We are driven by motives; some are morally good motives, and some are not. We address 'motives' when we are committed to act from a morally good motive.

I raise many questions and explanations about motives. Here are a few examples.

1. What is a morally good motive?
2. What if a person does an act which is wrong, but he believes it to be right and he does it from a morally good motive?
3. Are morally good motives the same as good motives like compassion and love?
4. Is morally bad simply the converse of morally good?
5. Does morally bad refer to the desire to do wrong for the sake of doing wrong?
6. What about the motive of a person who is careless?

Desert. We often talk about what a person deserves. Look at this brief story about David Suzuki.

> David Suzuki is a well-known biologist and outspoken environmentalist who was born on March 24, 1936, the eldest son of the Suzuki family. His interest in public speaking developed when he was in Junior High School. He went on to win public speaking contests, often speaking about conserving nature. After teaching in several universities, Suzuki moved to the University of British Columbia where he continued his research in biology. Today, Suzuki shares his environmental concerns with the world through his TV program, The Nature of Things.

We might be inclined to say that Suzuki deserves a public commendation, possibly an honorary degree, for his contribution to making people aware of the need to conserve nature.

On the other hand, look at this story about Thierry Henry.

> Thierry Henry, captain of the French soccer team, has become the subject of international outrage as many from Irish fans and their Prime Minister to French gym teachers condemn the captain's decision not to admit to handling the ball in the build-up to a goal that eliminated Ireland and sent his team to the World Cup finals.

> David McCarthy, an Alberta provincial team soccer coach, has seen 12-year-olds admit to bad plays that referees have missed. But a video showing French Captain Thierry Henry remaining silent about the handling of a ball that led to the game-tying goal has Mr. McCarthy worried. Will he witness less honour among young players on community soccer fields in the future? "What action should have been taken about Captain Henry's conduct?" McCarthy wondered.
>
> Many people insisted that Captain Henry deserved a strong form of disapproval – maybe even some form of punishment. They condemned his decision not to admit to handling the ball.

These two stories highlight the concern and importance placed on what people deserve – also known as desert.

I raise questions and issues about desert. Here are a few:

- Approvals are not wilful; they are psychological states of being.
- A person deserves disapproval for willingly doing a wrong act.
- What if a person planned to commit a wrong act but failed to execute it? What does he deserve?
- Does a person deserve punishment for willing to do wrong?

Just. The concept of *justice* provides a context for integrating the concepts which have been explained so far: duties, rights, motive, and desert. *Justice* refers to the distribution of what people desire or do not want. It integrates the following:

- Act from a desire to do one's *duty* if it is the right thing to do
- Recognize a person's *rights*
- Act from a morally good *motive*
- Give people what they *deserve*
- Act with impartiality in pursuit of *justice*

In the next five chapters, I apply each of the five categories – duty, rights, motive, desert, and just – to five scenarios.

CHAPTER 10: PRINCIPLED THINKING – DUTY

I begin with the category, *duty*[48] and the scenario selected for this analysis is *HIV positive*.

HIV positive

As the nurse for an international wholesale company, Flo encountered a range of health-related problems. One day David brought a new case when he admitted to her that he is HIV positive. When she asked about his partner, Jack, David insisted that he was not ready to share this information with his partner.

Word gets around; Jack became uneasy about his relationship with David and wonders where he might share his unease. The company nurse of course; everyone goes to her when they need someone to talk to.

When he finally had the courage to talk to the nurse about what he regarded as a sensitive and personal topic, he blurted out his concern about his partner, David. He suspected that David may have been unfaithful and consequently may be HIV positive.

Now, what should the nurse do with the information she had from both, David and Jack? She realized that she was morally obligated to client confidentiality. On the other hand, the company's Code of Ethics clearly states that as the company nurse, she has an obligation 'to protect the health and safety of the employees.' Is she trapped in a conflict of interest? She decides that, no, she is not in a conflict of interest because the company Code of Ethics states very clearly that her responsibility is to protect the health and safety of the employees. What is more, Flo was part of the company's three member HR team which interprets and applies the Code. So, she followed the company Code of Ethics.

In this scenario the overriding issue is 'duty' – Flo's duty in her role as the company nurse. Since the company has a Code of Ethics, Flo believes she does not have to decide about what is the right or just thing to do. But does the Code distinguish between different views of duty? Does the Code mean 'if it is her duty to do something, then the act of doing it is morally right and it would be wrong not to do it?' If so, she would simply follow whatever is her duty. Flo would simply follow through with whatever the Code says, she would give no second thought as to the implications of what the Code means. In fact, which is what she did.

Or Flo could interpret 'duty' to mean *wanting to do what is her duty to do.'* I have reason to believe that Flo also wanted to do her duty because she was one of the architects of the company's Code of Ethics as a member of the HR team.

Or Flo could interpret duty to mean 'wanting to do her duty *because it is the right thing to do.'* But is that what the Code says? It does not make a distension between the three options. The Code does not necessarily include the condition 'because it is the right thing to do.' In other words, the Code does not necessarily focus on what is fair or just.

Chart 15 identifies the concept of duty addressed in this scenario.

Duty	Rights	Motive	Desert	Just
if it is her duty to do, then the act of doing it is morally right and it would be wrong not to do it				
Or '*wanting* to do what is her duty to do'				
Or 'wanting to do her duty because it is the right thing to do' – is about justice.				

Chart 15. Principled Thinking about Duty in *HIV positive*

What do these options have to do with justice? How might they lead to justice? Only the last option about duty speaks to the issue of justice - 'wanting to do one's duty because it is the right thing to do.' Suppose Flo wanted to do her duty only if it is the right thing to do? In this case, Flo's decision to do her duty only if it was the right thing to do may have created a moral dilemma for her.

Should these different interpretations of 'duty' be included as rules in a code of ethics? Can they be reduced to rules? If so, how could someone know which interpretation applies in a specific situation? Are these decisions best made by the employees on the ground? Of course.

Flo must remember that 'to do one's duty' is independent of her motive, likes or dislikes. At the same time, she needs to be reminded that she is not obligated to do every morally right act; she is not obligated to do what every employee might ask her to do even when the request is a morally good act. For example, should an employee ask her to donate to a particular cause (e.g., Cancer Society), she is not obligated to make it even though it would be a morally good act.

In short, Flo needs to remember the conditions that must be fulfilled for an act to be right or wrong. They are: distinguish between right and wrong, apply the concept of right and wrong, and understand the meaning of right and wrong.

We will face many issues related to the concerns about justice: duty, rights, motive, desert, and just. In this example, I have selected only a few of the issues that might be raised about duty in this scenario. For a comprehensive list of the issues, go to Chart 16 to see the range of issues that are addressed by duty.

Let us remember, attend to the emotions before applying principled thinking in an attempt to resolve conflicts at home or in the workplace. Only then does one have a chance to apply disciplined thinking through issues related to duty, rights, motive, and just.

Concepts about Duty

1. Duty means:
   - following whatever is one's duty to do
 	
   - wanting to do what is one's duty to do.'
 	
   - wanting to do one's duty because it is the right thing to do

2. A duty is the right thing to do independently of a person's motive or interest.
3. An action is right or wrong independent of a person's likes or dislikes.
4. One can put someone under an obligation but not under a duty.
5. If it is a person's duty to do something, then the act of doing it is morally right and it would be wrong not to do it.
6. A person is not necessarily obligated to do every morally right act.
7. Going beyond the call of duty is called an act of supererogation.
8. Doing one's duty may or may not be an object of interest.
9. Immoral must be distinguished from non-moral and amoral.
10. A morally permissible act is not morally wrong; it could be morally right or morally indifferent.
11. If a person may do an act, it is not wrong to do or not to do it.
12. Are there degrees or rightness? No.
13. Are there degrees of wrongness? Yes, there are degrees of the seriousness of wrong acts.
14. Does it follow from the fact that an act is right that not doing it is wrong? It may be wrong, but it need not be.
15. Are there morally indifferent acts? Yes.
16. What conditions must be fulfilled for an act to be right or wrong? A person must distinguish between right and wrong, have a concept of right and wrong, and understand the meaning of right and wrong.
17. A moral person can distinguish between right and wrong, have a concept of right and wrong, and understand the meaning of right and wrong.
18. Ought implies can.
19. Are people's acts determined or do people act from a free will? This question has no clear answer.
20. Is choosing determined or does it have a cause? This question has no clear answer.
21. Can a person have a conflict of duties? A person can have a *prima facia* conflict of duties but not an actual conflict of duties.
22. What may be proper duties? They must be something a person can do or refrain from doing.
23. Judgments about beliefs, attitudes feeling, emotions and thoughts are not moral judgments.

Chart 16. Concepts about Duty[49]

To illustrate how these concepts about duty might apply in a scenario, I have applied them in another scenario *Company or Family Shares.*

Company or Family Shares

"I will not let them get away with it. That's highway robbery!" exclaimed Jake, the oldest of Len's four sons. Len had been CEO of TOPInc till he suddenly died of a heart attack a month ago. The company had been extraordinarily successful in the Texas oil patch since they drilled the first well seven years ago. The shareholders had enjoyed lucrative dividends for the past five years and were looking forward to many more. Collectively, six minor shareholders owned 10% and Len owned 90% of the company shares.

What will happen now that Len is gone? The company's Shareholder's Agreement states clearly that when a shareholder dies, that person's shares are assigned to the remaining shareholders.

Len's family felt that their father's shares should remain in the family as part of the family estate. Jake, the oldest, felt he had to defend the family rights. Len's shares were worth millions provided that the company could weather the loss not only of its CEO but also of its major shareholder. 'How best to move forward' pondered the remaining shareholders. The dispute about who owns Len's rights must be resolved quickly before the company declines due to lack of leadership.

With the support of this scenario, I illustrate the scope of the category 'duty'.

To begin with, let me point out that 'duty' includes the following concepts some of which, I am certain, you have used many times:

> duty, obligation, right, wrong, responsible, forbidden, ought, prescribe, should, permissible, must, may, bound, correct, sinful, moral, immoral, ethical, unethical.

Wrong acts include words like crime, moral transgression, and moral offence.

I view 'duty' in the moral sense, unless otherwise indicated. Some of the terms can also be used in a nonmoral sense. The term, wrong, is used in the moral sense in the sentence: 'It is wrong for our company to use fraudulent funds to pay for a year-end party.' The term is used in a nonmoral sense in the sentence: 'the media published wrong information'. Other examples of using these terms in the moral sense include: 'responsible' means 'morally responsible' 'incumbent' means 'morally incumbent', 'permissible' means 'morally permissible'.

Let us get started with determining how duty is or could be used in *Company or Family Shares.*

I begin with one of the most basic concepts people face every day – doing one's duty. If it is a person's duty to do something, then the act of doing it is morally right and it would be wrong not to do it. Jake felt it was his responsibility to protect the family's interests. But we will see later the conditions that have to be met for a duty to be 'morally right.' However, the converse – if an act is morally right, it is a person's duty to do it - does not seem to follow. In other words, 'morally right action' does not necessarily mean that it is a person's duty to do the act. For example, if it is morally right for Jake to volunteer to serve on the Christmas Cheer Board, it does not follow that it is his duty.

'Doing one's duty' can refer to several diverse levels of commitment. First, it can mean that a person simply follows whatever is his duty to do. A person simply follows whatever duty has been assigned to him by way of an order or a rule. The shareholders followed through with what the company Code of Ethics stated. They gave no second thought to its implications. Second, it can mean 'wanting to do what is one's duty to do.' The person shows intent - wanting to do what is one's duty to do. This intent reflects a stronger commitment. Jake seemed intent on negotiating the best terms for the family. Third, it can mean 'wanting to do one's duty because it is the right thing to do.' In this case, a person identifies a condition for doing one's duty – it must be the right thing to do. Maybe Jake was concerned about doing the right thing.

Sometimes people engage in acts which are done beyond the call of duty, called acts of supererogation. What might an act done by Jake look like if it was viewed as going beyond the call of duty? He might have challenged the shareholders to double the net profits in the current year. An annual increase could be expected but doubling the increase in a year would be going beyond the call of duty.

We know that sometimes doing one's duty is not an object of interest but an object of disinterest. It was not an object of interest for Jake to challenge the shareholders of his dad's company. The family had had a good relationship with the shareholders.

Did you ever notice that 'obligation' and 'duty' tend to have the same meaning but are used in separate ways? A person can put someone under an obligation but not under a duty. Obligations tend to be incurred as the result of something a person has done. Jake felt obligated to defend family interests in the company because that is what his father had done. On the other hand, he also felt he had a duty as the oldest son to look after the family after his father's death.

Often, we feel a sense of 'responsibility' whenever we have assumed a specific position or career. A responsibility is a duty which a person has by virtue of his/her specific position. The interim CEO felt it was her responsibility to get the best terms possible the under circumstances.

Note the normative and descriptive use of the antonyms of 'moral'. When 'moral' is used in the normative sense, its antonym is 'immoral', but when it is used in the descriptive sense, its antonym is 'non-moral.' The same applies to the antonym of the term 'ethical'.

Morally forbidden simply means it is morally wrong to do a particular act. Notice the flexible use of the term morally permissible. To say that an act is morally permissible means that it is not wrong to do it. It could be a right or morally indifferent act. For example, the statement 'It is morally permissible for the interim CEO to defend the company interests' could be a right or a morally indifferent act. To say that the interim CEO engaged in a morally indifferent act is to say that it is not wrong to do it. The meaning of the term 'may do' is even more flexible.

It is important to be aware of certain issues that arise in the use of the terms right and wrong in moral discourse. For example, 'Are there degrees of 'right' as well as degrees of 'wrong'? The answer to the first part of this question is simple; there are no degrees of rightness. An act is either right or not. For example, 'looking after family interests cannot be half right or partially right or very right. It is simply the right thing to do.

On the other hand, there are degrees of wrongness. One act can be more seriously wrong than another. For example, it is considered more seriously wrong to cheat the family of its rights in the company than to make an error in calculating the final monetary settlement. Both are considered wrong but not to the same degree. This distinction is reflected in ordinary moral conversation as well as in the fact that a person would be punished more severely for the former.

Another issue regarding the use of the terms right and wrong is: 'Does it follow from the fact that an act is right that not doing it is wrong?' The answer to this question is more complicated. It may be wrong not to do the act and it need not be wrong. For example, it may be right for a CEO to pay a bonus for a job well done. However, it need not be wrong not to pay a bonus for a job well done – provided that a company does not pay bonuses to anyone.

Are there no morally indifferent acts? To argue that there are no morally indifferent acts seems contrary to common sense. Some acts are neither right nor wrong; they are morally indifferent. For example, 'Len died of a heart attack' is neither morally right nor wrong – it is a morally indifferent act.

Right and wrong are not contradictory terms but contrary terms. Contrary refers to terms that are opposites or opposed to each other. Right actions and wrong actions are opposites. They can both be true. Contradictory statement cannot both be true ... they cannot both be right and wrong. For example, the interim CEO 'cares' and 'doesn't care' are contradictory. They cannot both be true.

However, the statement 'It is not a question of whether this action is right' leaves open the possibility that the action might be morally indifferent. 'I don't think that's wrong' may refer to an act as being morally indifferent. For example, to say 'I do not think it is wrong to for Jake to defend the family interests' is not saying that 'it is right; it may simply be a morally indifferent act.

A third issue concerning the use of the terms right and wrong is: 'What conditions must be fulfilled for an act to be right or wrong?' The person making the judgment must meet three conditions: a) have a concept of right and wrong, b) distinguish between right and wrong, and c) understand the meaning of right and wrong. A non-moral person does not meet these conditions and therefore cannot judge the morality of an act. Jake had a concept of right and wrong, distinguished between right and wrong and understood the meaning of right and wrong. As the oldest in the family, he simply assumed the responsibility of defending family interests.

Who or what is a non-moral being? A person may be a non-moral person if he suffers from psychosocial pathologies to the extent that he cannot have a sense of right and wrong. In short, 'non-moral beings' refers to people who cannot make moral decisions probably due to a problem in their development. There is no indication that the interim CEO did not have a sense of right and wrong.

You might ask, 'What about amoral people?' He or she is someone who was brought up in total isolation. Again, this does not apply to Jake. There is no reason to think that he does not have a sense of right and wrong.

A fourth issue to keep in mind about duty is: Does ought imply can? A person must be capable of what is morally expected of him. Without the capability, 'ought' simply does not apply. A person cannot be responsible for his actions if he is not in his right mind or incapable of assuming responsibility for his action. I have reason to believe that Jake is capable of what could be expected of him.

What if a person is not in his right mind because of some action he took, such as consuming too much alcohol? The interim CEO would be responsible for her action even if she acted under the influence of alcohol. She put herself out of a state of being in her right mind by drinking too much alcohol. She put herself in a situation where she could not do what she ought to do.

What if a person committed a wrong act in a fit of anger? Whether the person is held responsible for committing a morally wrong act would depend on whether the person had any control or influence over the extraordinary circumstances. If the fit of anger was brought on by a devastating performance report, he would be responsible for his fit of anger. If, on the other hand, the fit of anger was brought on by a malfunctioning of his glands or brain, the interim CEO would have had no control over the exceptional circumstances and therefore should not be held responsible for her action.

Are persons who cause injury and destruction, moral persons? They could be. A person can have the concepts of right and wrong but need not be influenced by them. Such a person is unscrupulous. As I have indicated above, the interim CEO probably had a sense of right and wrong. If she did not apply it, she would be considered an unscrupulous person.

I raise the controversial issue of freedom of will vs. determinism. First, I state the obvious. Not only must a person be a moral person and be in his right mind so that he can assume responsibility for his action, but he must also be free to make moral judgments. Without this freedom he could not be held responsible for his action. That applies to the interim CEO as well as to Jake.

However, the complexity of this issue lingers. Determinism means events have causes. Are 'freedom of the will' and 'determinism' really all that different? The difficulty of this question becomes apparent in the question 'Is the act of choosing determined or does it have a cause?' If choosing is not caused it would be like a 'bolt out of the blue.' If that were so, how could a person be held responsible for what he chose? If 'choosing' is not caused by something, it would be inexplicable.

It might seem then that freedom of will need not exclude determinism. Freedom of will seems to refer to choices determined by reasons rather than by causes. But reasons may be just another set of causes. Even if the distinction between causes and reasons was established, it is not certain that the problem of 'freedom of will' vs. 'determinism' would be solved. This seems to be an intractable problem. People generally assume that they can make moral judgments. In other words, they assume that sometimes people make judgments of right and wrong suggesting that people have, to some degree, freedom of will. In other words, the interim CEO and the shareholders assume that, to a degree, they were free to make judgements. As for the limits set by the company Code of Ethics, they were established by whoever was responsible for them.

Finally, there are two more issues related to the conditions for an act to be right or wrong. First, 'Can a person have a conflict of duties?' A person can have a *prima facie* conflict of duties but not an actual conflict of duties. A *prima facie* conflict of duties is a conflict at first glance or an apparent conflict. However, since a person cannot perform both conflicting duties at the same time, he does not have an actual conflict of duties. The interim CEO did not have a conflict of duties even though he might have felt caught between the shareholders and the family. Difficult as it may have been, he had to decide what to do.

The second issue is: 'What may be proper objects of right and wrong judgments?' In other words, what sorts of things could be judged to be right or wrong? For example, can beliefs, attitudes, feelings, and emotions be judged to be right or wrong?

Beliefs, attitudes, feelings, and emotions are mental states and therefore cannot be judged to be right or wrong. A person cannot cease to have a particular mental state such as a particular feeling or emotion by choosing not to have it. Similarly, a person cannot arbitrarily cease to have a certain attitude although a person can cultivate certain attitudes. It could be wrong for a person to fail to cultivate certain attitudes. For example, it would be wrong for the interim CEO not to cultivate an atmosphere of fairness applied to everyone, including herself. The same applies to thinking certain thoughts and have certain beliefs. A person cannot prevent a certain thought from crossing his mind. Since some beliefs are couched in a person's cultural background, they are inherited. It would be wrong for the interim CEO not to cultivate the practice of carefully reviewing her thoughts. In short, it is problematic to judge thoughts, beliefs, attitudes, feelings, and emotions as being morally right or wrong.

This review of the application of 'duty' as applied to one scenario, shows multiple situations where 'duty' could apply. Later, I will show that practically speaking, only a few issues related to 'duty' are relevant in any given situation.

Let us turn to another key concept commonly used in dealing with moral dilemmas: 'rights'. Look at 'rights' and how it might or can apply in the scenario, *Chocolate Factory*.

CHAPTER 11. PRINCIPLED THINKING – RIGHTS

In the following scenario, *Chocolate factory*, the overriding issue is 'rights.'[50]

Chocolate factory

Since 'rights' have come to mean human rights in the 20th century, every major violation of people's rights has alarmed consumers, CEOs, and politicians. When Jane, CEO of a major chocolate factory in Atlanta, was tipped off that the evening news would report on the widespread use of child slave labor in the production of cocoa in several African countries, she knew she had a major problem. Consumers would be incensed, and politicians would threaten immediate action. As president of the American Chocolate Association and as the CEO of a chocolate producing company, much would be expected from her. What should she do?

First, she thought, the industry needs time – time to develop and promote a sound course of action. Through her leadership, the industry got four years of grace in which to develop and test a plan. However, they soon encountered several obstacles that defied any implementable solution. First, cocoa was produced on countless small farms across eastern Africa. Who could ensure production in these farms would never involve child slave labor? Second, the cocoa from countless farms was collected by large foreign companies. How could you make sure that it did not include cocoa produced by child slave labor?

> Politicians demanded a solution. What should Jane do
> – pursue a human rights plan of action developed by
> the government at potentially a huge loss of revenue
> for her company or manage to delay any action by the
> government?

Quite simply, 'rights' refers to objects of interest - everything a person would like to have, prefer, wish for, or want. Through Jane's skillful negotiations, the industry was granted four years to develop and test a production and marketing proposal. However, Jane's planning committee soon discovered that since cocoa was produced by countless small operators, Jane's planning committee were unable to design a plan that could ensure that none of the cocoa produced involved child slave labor. What are Jane's options? Several questions came to mind.

First, do small farmers have a right to produce cocoa to look after the needs of their families? This leads to the question, 'Is it wrong for anyone to prevent a person from having or enjoying objects of interest if it is their right? Can government or big international companies interfere with that right? Does it apply to all rights a person may want? Can a Code of Ethics restrict a person's personal rights?

Second, 'Is it true that for every right, a person has a corresponding duty?' A right is an entitlement to perform or not to perform certain actions, either legally or morally. In civil cases, for each right that a person has, there is a corresponding duty to allow each to exercise their civil rights. The shareholders have a right to their shares. What corresponding duty do they have? That is not clear.

Third, what about the converse question, 'Is it true that for every right, there is a correlative duty?' For every right, there is a correlative duty is analytically true because 'the duty of everyone who has a right' is part of the meaning of having a right. To deny that would be contradictory. That applies to the stakeholders.

Is it true that for every duty, there is a correlative right? It is not clear why there is a correlative connection between duty and rights. Just because government has a duty to protect farmers does not give farmers the right to produce cocoa. That right would have to be defended on some other basis.

The following Chart identifies the application of the concepts about rights applied in this scenario.

Duty	Rights	Motive	Desert	Just
if it is her duty to do something, then the act of doing it is mor-ally right and it would be wrong not to do it	everything a person would like to have, prefer, wish for, or want			
OR '*wanting* to do what is her duty to do'	Is it wrong for anyone to prevent a person from having objects of interest if it is his or her right?			
OR 'wanting to do her duty *because it is the right thing to do.*'	Is it true that for every right, a person has a corresponding duty?			
	Is it true that for every right, there is a cor-relative duty?			
	Is it true that for every duty, there is a cor-relative right?			

Chart 17: Principled Thinking about Rights in Chocolate Factory

In short, Jane realized that 'having a right' raises several issues in addition to the ones raised by 'duty.' Can the rules in a code of ethics address these issues appropriately or do employees in a company need to think through issues of 'rights' to be fair and just? I have selected only a few of the issues that might be raised about rights. For a full list of the issues, go to Chart 18 below.

Concepts about Rights
1. What is meant by the statement, Paul has a right to X?
2. How are moral rights different from legal rights?
3. What does it mean to say that 'Paul has a claim to X'?

4. Does 'to be entitled' mean the same as 'to be warranted'?
5. Is the word 'legitimate' also used in a moral sense?
6. How does ownership differ from possession?
7. Does the word 'belong' mean the same as 'ownership'?
8. What does it mean to have a prerogative?
9. What are some of the diverse ways we use the word 'have'?
10. What are some diverse ways we use the word 'earn'?
11. Is it true that for every duty a person has a corresponding right?
12. Is it true that for every right a person has a corresponding duty?
13. Is it the case that to every right there is a correlative duty?
14. Is it the case that to every duty there is a correlative right?

Chart 18. Concepts about Rights.[51]

To illustrate how these concepts about rights might apply in a scenario, I have applied them in another scenario, *An Industrial Case Study.*

An Industrial Case Study

Three former employees of an offshore manufacturing company, PRInc, distributed an email online claiming that there were excessive restrictions on employees' behavior in PRInc. These included the need to obtain permission before getting a drink or a snack, and strict limitations on washroom break. While the restrictions were applied strictly to all frontline employees, they were not applied to managers.

The email also claimed that the employees had to pay compensation for any product that was stolen or went missing, even though the losses were insured. Employees had to clock out after eight hours but had to continue to work a few more hours. This created a false electronic record.

Overall, they accused the company of lacking systematic and humane management and complain that their rights and dignity were being violated. The email aroused widespread criticism not only from PRInc employees but also from workers around the world.

This class of terms, of which the word, rights, is a representative term, includes many other terms which have a similar meaning.

> claim, prerogative, justified, warranted, entitled, give, bestow, lend, own, belong, have, own, his, hers, yours, mine, property, sell, purchase, buy, ownership, inherit, confer, legitimate, illegitimate, earn, authority.

The term, right, introduces the notion of someone having a right to do something or having a right to something. This sense of the word 'right' refers to people's objects of interest. It refers to everything a person would like to have, prefer, wish for, or want. For example, the former employees maintained that the restrictions imposed on frontline staff, denied them access to some of their rights.

On the other hand, an object of disinterest refers to anything a person may be averse to, not want, avoid, escape from, or does not wish for. Reference to objects of interest also introduces an element of motives. For example, what were the motives of the remaining shareholders?

The most basic concept of the category, rights, is 'object of interest.' In the statement 'John has a right to do X,' the word right is used in the moral sense as in statements about human rights found in documents like the Canadian Bill of Rights and the United Nations Declaration of the Rights of Man. These documents have been drafted to identify, advocate, and protect the rights or objects of interest of people.

What does it mean to have a right to an object of interest? It means that it is not wrong for a person to pursue it; nor would it be wrong for the person not to pursue it. It would be wrong for someone else to prevent a person from pursuing his object of interest if he has a right to it. For example, if Len's family has a right to own his shares upon his death, it would be wrong for the shareholders to deny them that right.

For 'X' to be a right, it must be an object of interest, either actual or potential. People demand rights and are frequently willing to protect and defend their rights. An infringement of rights sometimes results in anger. Might Jake get angry if the shareholders denied the family the right to own Len's shares?

Although it would be wrong for anyone to prevent a person from having or enjoying objects of interest if it is a right, it does not follow that a person has a right to pursue all his objects of interests. Jake must realize that even if the family has aright to some of Len's shares, it does not follow that they can own as many shares as they want from Len's shares.

People frequently make a distinction between human rights and legal rights. As I have mentioned before, when a right is claimed to be a moral right, it is a right which people claim they have as human beings. Hence, these rights are referred to as human rights. 'Legal rights' refers to rights which people have in law. A human right can be enshrined in law and become a legal right. However, a human right is a right even when it is not established as a legal right. Were the shareholders claiming a human right or a legal right? What about Len's family?

Rights must be distinguished from duties. Duties are regarded as being burdensome or onerous whereas rights are sought after and defended. This distinction is reflected in the fact that a person is sometimes deprived of his rights (War Measures Act in Canada) but relieved of his duties (dismissed at work). At the same time, a person may have a right as well as a duty.

To say that 'John has a claim to 'X' is to say that there are some reasons to believe that John has a right to X. Several people may maintain that they have a claim to X. However, a person has a right to it only if he has sound reasons for making his claim. Did Jake have sound reasons for making the claim on behalf of the family when he claimed that his father's company shares were a part of the family estate?

I need to draw attention to the difference between 'having a claim to X' and 'justifying a right to X' 'Having a claim to X' is to say that there are some sound reasons to believe that a person has a right to X, but 'to justify a right to X' is to say that there are sufficient reasons for a person to have a right to X. More on 'to justify a claim' later.

Some terms are interchangeable. The terms 'to be entitled' and 'to be warranted' basically have the same meaning. For the shareholders to maintain they were entitled to Len's share, they referred to the Shareholders' Agreement. To say that a reward was warranted for a particular performance is to say that someone had a right to receive the award.

We use the term 'authority' frequently in daily conversation. So, let me explain how we use it in the moral and nonmoral sense. In the moral sense of the word, we say that the CEO has the right to make rules and enforce them. The word authority is used in a nonmoral or descriptive sense in, 'John Rawls is a person of authority on ethics.' The word 'authority' in this case, is used in the descriptive sense to refer to a person who is regarded as being knowledgeable in a particular field. The term, legitimate, sometimes is used in a moral sense although it is more often used in a legal sense. To say that the company's HR department is legitimate is to say that it has the right to adjudicate moral controversies within a company. It might also have the legal right if a government has made it a legal right in its jurisdiction.

There are a few more commonly used terms which also convey a moral sense of right. One of the basic terms, at least in the Western culture, is 'ownership' which means the right to use, enjoy or dispose of something. The meaning of this word becomes clear when it is contrasted with the term possession. To say that someone possesses an object is to say that someone has the actual power to use, enjoy, and dispose of that object.

So far, I have referred to a distinction between 'having rights' and 'having a duty'. The relationship between these two concepts raises a few more issues. First, 'Do rights and duties correspond?' It raises two more questions:

1. Is it the case that if John has a right then in virtue of his having that right, he has a certain duty?
2. Is it the case that if John has a duty, then in virtue of his having that duty, he has a certain right?

Let me rephrase the first question: 'Is it true that for every right, a person has a corresponding duty?' At first glance, for every right there is a corresponding duty.

For example, does Jake have a certain duty in view of having a right to represent the family? Would it be his duty to make sure that he defends the family rights? In other words, does he have a corresponding duty? This not clear.

Now let us look at the reverse question. 'Is it true that for every duty, a person has a corresponding right?' The right would have to be something other than the right to do one's duty.

For example, if it is your duty to keep a promise, then you have a right to expect it of others. Does a person have a right to expect it of all others? Second, if you have the duty to obey, what corresponding right do you have? Do you have a right to expect recognition or reward? Not necessarily, recognition or rewards usually are given only under exceptional circumstances.

Let us try another example, 'What are the corresponding rights to the duty referred to in the statement, 'We have a duty to work for the benefit of humankind.' What if this was what prompted Schweitzer to provide medical services to Indigenous people living in the jungles of Africa without the conveniences of a fully equipped and staffed hospital. What would be Schweitzer's corresponding right? Would he have a right to a fully equipped and staffed hospital? The answer is not immediately clear.

I conclude that it cannot be established that duties and rights correspond though I acknowledge that some plausible correspondence is conceivable.

The second major problem raised about the relationship between rights and duties is, 'Are rights and duties correlative?' This raises the following questions:

1. If someone has a certain duty then in virtue of his having that duty, does someone else have a certain right?
2. If someone has a certain right, then in virtue of his having that certain right, does someone else have a certain duty?

The answer to the first of these two questions is as uncertain as were the answers to the questions raised concerning the correspondence of rights and duties. It is not clear why there is a correlative connection between the duty and the rights. If Jake has a duty or obligation to represent his family rights to Len's shares, there is no necessary correlative right for anyone else in the company. In other words, it is not clear that to every duty there is a correlative right.

Let us look at the converse question: 'Is it the case that to every right there is a correlative duty?' The answer to this question is contained in the meaning of the concept of 'having a right.' It was pointed out that to every right a person has, someone else has a duty. The duty of everyone else towards the person who has a right is a part of the meaning of the concept of 'having a right.' Therefore, 'To every right there is a correlative duty' is analytically true. To deny it would be contradictory.

In summary, only one of the questions raised concerning the relationship between having a right and having a duty can be answered conclusively. That is the question concerning the correlativity of rights and duties. The other three questions require more than analytic propositions.

This concludes my account of the category, rights, and how its terms are used to make moral judgments. It is an important class of terms because, as we have seen, so many situations in companies involve rights. It is interesting to observe that many familiar words, which usually are not regarded as moral terms, include a moral sense. More significant, however, is the relationship between duties and rights. That tells us that as we try to resolve moral dilemmas in the workplace, we need to consider both duties and rights. In every moral dilemma situation, we need to select what aspect of 'duty' and 'rights' apply. That suggests that whoever makes decisions about right and wrong needs to be aware of the complexity of the relationship between duties and rights.

Let us move on to another concept, motive, and see how it applies to resolving moral dilemmas. How does it relate to duty and rights? The plot thickens as we need to consider more categories in resolving moral dilemmas.

CHAPTER 12: PRINCIPLED THINKING – MOTIVE

Motive[52] is applied and illustrated in the following scenario, *Toxic Emissions*.

Toxic Emissions

Betty is the quality control supervisor for AGInc, a thriving midsize plastics company which meets all the local toxin emissions regulations. She knows of innovative technology which can reduce the current emission level to protect the fish in local rivers and lakes. This would save the local recreational and commercial fishing industry for years to come.

When Betty expressed her concern about the toxic emissions at a shareholder's meeting where the Press was allowed to attend, the shareholders reminded her that AGInc follows local limits. Hence, there is no need for the modern technology. Of course, the Press put a different spin on Betty's concern; it expressed alarm at the potential consequences of not reducing the toxic emissions. In fact, they suspected the motive of the company – preferred increased profits vs. installing expensive technology to reduce emissions beyond current local regulations.

Although Betty took issue with the Press for imputing that the company was driven by profits, she decided not to invest new costly technology that might risk the profitability of the company. She argued that AGInc should delay acquiring the innovative technology till the government changes the toxin emission regulations. Why? Might she be motivated by the excessive cost of the innovative technology? Did she give any thought to potential benefits of installing the innovative technology to reduce emission levels?

We assume that for an action to be morally good, the action must be right. My question is, 'Must it also be done from a morally good motive?' Had Betty thoughtfully explained why the company should consider the community benefits of installing the innovative technology, her action would be regarded morally good even though the cocoa industry might suffer some short-term losses. Her 'thoughtful explanation' would have shown that she wanted to do the right thing. Hence, this course of action would be regarded as a morally good act because it met both conditions – it was the right thing to do and was done for a morally good motive.

The decision Betty made was morally wrong because she did not consider what is the morally right thing to do.

Friends of Betty might want to help her by saying, "You ought to do what you believe you ought to do."[52] That is a common response suggesting that Betty would meet her duty/obligation by doing what she believes is the right thing to do. But that is misleading because by saying "You ought to do what you believe you ought to do" is simply saying that Betty's action would be morally good if she did it and morally bad if she did not do it which refers to her motive. However, the second part of Betty friend's statement, "what you believe you ought to do" refers to Betty's duty. So, what was Betty's friend referring to – her motive or her duty? Every effort should be made to avoid these kinds of confusing statements. By the way, how could this distinction be captured in a 'rule' in a code of ethics?

What if Betty had made her decision from a good motive such as 'compassion?' Compassion is not considered a morally good motive even though it is considered a good motive. How could Betty's decision be a morally good act if she acted out of a good motive such as compassion?

Suppose as the quality control officer of the company, Betty ensured that the company met local toxic emission standards (which is the right thing to do) while ignoring the destruction of the fishing industry due to the approved level of toxicity (which she does not think it is the right thing to do), and she does it 'to get the shareholders off her back' (not a morally good motive). Is she considered a morally good person? That is doubtful.

How do you think Betty would answer this important question – Is 'morally bad' simply the converse of 'morally good'?[29] How she would answer that question depends on how she defines 'morally bad'. Does she believe 'morally bad' simply means 'the desire to do wrong for the sake of doing wrong'? But that does not square with the reason she gave for accepting the current level of toxicity (i.e., getting the shareholders off her back). There is no reason to think that Betty was motivated by 'the desire to do wrong for the sake of doing wrong.' Could it be that Betty acted from an indifference to do what is right in this case? Possibly.

The following Chart identifies the application of concepts about motive used in this scenario.

Duty	Rights	Motive	Desert	Just
if it is her duty to do something, then the act of doing it is morally right and it would be wrong not to do it	everything a person would like to have, prefer, wish for, or want	for an action to be morally good, the action must be right		
OR '*wanting to do what is her duty to do*'	Is it wrong for anyone to prevent a person from having or enjoying objects of interest if it is his or her right?	Must it also be done from a morally good motive?		
OR 'wanting to do her duty *because it is the right thing to do*.'	Is it true that for every right, a person has a corresponding duty?	Is it a morally good act even though one of the conditions of a morally good act is missing?		

	Is it true that for every right, there is a cor-relative duty?	You ought to do what you believe you ought to do		
	Is it true that for every duty, there is a cor-relative right?	Is 'morally bad' simply the converse of 'morally good - the desire to do wrong for the sake of doing wrong'?		

Chart 19. Concepts about Motive in the scenario

Once again, we have met several thought-provoking issues. Could they be addressed in a set of rules in a code of ethics? Or do they require the knowledge and ability to think through moral dilemmas with empathy? I have selected only a few of the issues relevant to this scenario that might be raised about motive. For a full list of the issues, go to the Chart 20.

Concepts about Motive	Response
1. What conditions must be fulfilled for an act to be morally good?	The act must be right. The act must be done from a morally good motive.
2. What if a person does an act which is wrong, but he believes it to be right and he does it from a morally good motive?	The act is not morally good even though the person would be regarded as a mor-ally good person.
3. What if a person does an act which is right, but he does not believe it to be right and his motives are not good?	The person would not be regarded as a morally good person.
4. What is a morally good motive?	- believe that the act is right. - desire to do what is right.
5. 'Wanting to do one's duty' must be distinguished from 'Wanting to do the right thing.'	
6. Cynics assume that people act only from self-interest.	
7. Morally good motives must be distinguished from good motives.	Good motives include compassion and love.

8. Moral virtues must be distinguished from non-moral virtues.	Moral virtues - propensity to do what is right from a morally good motive Non-moral virtues – intellectual motive like wit.

Chart 20. Concepts about Motive[53]

To illustrate how these concepts about motive might apply in a scenario, I have applied them in another scenario, *Scene of an Accident.*

Scene of an Accident

"SHOOT ME! SHOOT ME," screamed the driver.

Ed, the driver, had just struck a tree as he lost control of his flatbed loaded with drums of explosives. Some of the drums were torn from their mooring and hit the cab. They exploded and burst into a ball of flames engulfing the cab including the driver. Writhing in pain, Ed pleaded with the RCMP Officer on the scene to end his painful death by shooting him.

The Officer, realizing that she could not come close to the burning truck to remove the driver, spontaneously withdrew her revolver from its holster but just as quicky return it. As Ed continued his plea, the Officer again drew her revolver and again returned it. The Officer was caught in a dilemma of choosing between two opposite values: taking the life of a person or ending the pain of being burnt alive. Both options were unacceptable to her because both options required the Officer to shoot the driver.

In a matter of seconds, she recalled a third option. She removed the fire extinguisher from her RCMP cruiser, not to douse the raging flame, but to spray Ed's face which made him instantly unconscious. Seconds later, the cab exploded killing Ed.

The representative terms for this class are 'morally good' and 'virtue' as well as their converse 'morally bad' and 'vice.' Included in this class of terms are the following terms:

> moral excellence, evil, sinful, wicked, (nasty), wanton, nice, morally cleansed, ill repute, awful, corrupt, terrible, decadent, effete, criminal, ethical, unethical, moral, immoral, heinous, atrocious, (gross), depraved, nefarious, inequity, odious, hideous, (repugnant), vile, foul, degenerate, degraded, defiled, (demonic), (unholy), debased, debouched, angelic, upright, upstanding, noble, righteous, dutiful.

The term 'morally good' applies to people, character, and motives. For example, a person who has pejorative moral characteristics is called a scoundrel, wretch, blackguard, cad, villain, heel, or a rat.

The terms about duty, which are described above, refer to judgments of right and wrong without considering the motive of the person who did the act. However, when people make judgments about right and wrong, they also consider the motive of the person who contemplated or consummated an act. This class of terms adds a significant dimension to judgments about duties.

So, what conditions must be fulfilled for an act to be morally good? As has been pointed out earlier, the action must be right. If the Officer does an act which is clearly wrong, the act is not a morally good act. It was right for the Officer to consider a third option.

Second, the action must be done from a morally good motive. The Officer considered a third option from a morally good motive. This act would also strike most people as being the right thing to do. Hence, this course of action is regarded as a morally good act.

What if a person does an act which is wrong, but he believes it to be right and he does it from a morally good motive? What if the Officer did was wrong (shoot the driver), but she believed it was the right thing to do and she did it from a morally good motive (relieve the driver's pain at his request), it would not be a morally good act because one of the conditions of a morally good act is that the act must be right.

What is a morally good motive? It must meet two conditions. First, the person must believe that a certain act is right and second, the person must have a desire to do what is right. Just believing something is not a morally good motive. The Officer met these two conditions.

'Wanting to do one's duty' must be distinguished from 'wanting to do one's duty because it is the right thing to do.' It seems the Officer wanted to relieve the driver's pain without shooting him because she thought relieving the driver's pain was the right thing to do.

How might a cynic respond? Cynics do not believe that people ever act from morally good motives but act purely from a motive of self-interest. When the Officer returned her gun to the holster and did not shoot the driver, she did not look after her own interests. She did not act like a cynic.

There are good motives besides the desire to do what is right or doing one's duty, but those motives are not considered morally good motives. For example, 'compassion' and 'love' are considered good motives. When the Officer refused to shoot the driver, she was not motivated by compassion for the driver, she acted from a morally good motive. Let me explain.

Compassion is a motive from which a non-moral person could also act. Insofar that a moral person acts from this motive, she is no different from a non-moral person. If a non-moral person acted from the motive of compassion, the motive would not be regarded as a morally good motive because a non-moral person is not capable of distinguishing right from wrong, have the concepts of right and wrong, or understands the meaning of right and wrong. If compassion cannot be judged to be a morally good motive for non-moral person, it should not be judged to be a morally good motive for a moral person. In short, compassion is a good motive, but not a morally good motive. Morally good motives must be distinguished from good motives such as love, generosity, kindness, and friendship which sometimes are referred to as naturally good motives.

What is meant by the term 'moral virtue?' Not all virtues are moral virtues. For example, wit (i.e., quickness of thought) is regarded as an intellectual virtue but not a moral virtue. On the other hand, some virtues, like truthfulness, are regarded as moral virtues. It can be regarded as a moral virtue if telling the truth is the right thing to do. It is regarded a moral virtue because it refers to a disposition to do what is the right thing to do. In short, a moral virtue is a disposition to do what is right from morally good motives. A virtuous act is a manifestation of this propensity.

'Morally good' and 'virtuous' are not only applied to action and motives, but also to people. Is a virtuous person the same as a morally good person? This question distinguishes a disposition from doing something. As I pointed out before, 'morally good person' refers to the disposition of the person. A morally good person must have a consistent inclination to do virtuous acts like telling the truth, being friendly, or being generous. 'Virtuous' person refers to someone who is doing what is right. A virtuous person would resist, with persistence, the temptation to do wrong acts such as degrading other people, committing odious or dastardly deeds, or living a degenerate life. So, is the Officer a morally good person or a virtuous person? She probably is a virtuous person because she acted on what she believed was the right thing to do. She would be considered a virtuous person if she consistently acted, from morally good motives.

What if a person is often mistaken about what he believes to be right, but acts from a morally good motive? Clearly the person's action would not be morally good, but the person may not be considered morally bad; she might be misguided. We might say that 'she means well but is misguided.' If the Officer had tried to remove the driver from the burning truck thinking it was the right thing to do, she might be misguided. This does not make her action right. The frequency of being mistaken would affect one's judgment about the Officer. The degree of wrongness is discussed later.

What about the distinction between 'morally good acts' and 'morally bad acts?' Is 'morally bad' simply the converse of 'morally good'? Is an act morally bad because it is wrong and done from a desire to do wrong, just as an act is morally good because it is right and done from a desire to do what is right? Are morally immoral acts done from a bad motive - a desire to do wrong for the sake of doing wrong?

It is doubtful that people commit wrong acts because they desire to do wrong for the sake of doing wrong. Suppose the Officer, knowing it was the wrong thing to do, had shot the truck driver at his request. Why would she do it for the sake of doing wring? She refused to shoot the driver because it was the wrong thing to do. That is not the same as wanting to do wrong for wrong's sake.

Surely, she considered the cost of a court challenge. What would be her object of interest in the desire to do wrong for wrong's sake? It is much more plausible to assume that her object of interest was to reduce the driver's pain. Ironically, when a person does a wrong act, invariably she seems to do it from motives which, in themselves, may not be morally bad. For example, The Officer's motive to relieve the driver's pain is not a morally bad motive.

Do people sometimes do wrong acts for the sake of doing wrong acts in small matters? For example, suppose the Officer took a leisurely trip back to the office just for kicks, thereby suggesting that she did what was wrong for wrong's sake? 'Just for kicks' can just as well mean 'test the system' or 'to show that I can do it.' These motives are not analogous to doing something for wrong's sake. In short, it is doubtful that people act from a desire to do wrong for wrong's sake. There is no reason to believe that such a desire is an object of interest for anyone other than those who possibly suffer from a pathological condition.

What motive might make a wrong act a morally bad act? It is the absence of a certain motive, namely, the desire to do right (or refrain from doing wrong). Had the Officer shot the driver (which is a wrong act), she would have committed a morally bad act.

If a person does something which is not wrong, but he does it despite his belief that it is wrong, he is acting immorally. This simply means that he acted in a way in which an immoral person would act. This manner of action reflects a certain property – an indifference to the wrongness of the act. The Officer certainly did not show a desire to act with indifference to the wrongness of her action.

On the other hand, if the Officer did what was wrong (shoot the driver at his request) but believed it to be the right thing to do and did it from a desire to do the right thing, she would have acted morally. She would have acted in a way in which a moral person would have acted.

Let me summarize. A person is morally bad when the act she committed is wrong and she is not deterred by its wrongness. When an act is very bad, morally, it is judged to be evil, atrocious, wicked, iniquitous, nefarious, fiendish, or demonic. 'Wicked' applies to both the act and the person. 'Nefarious' applies only to the act. 'Heinous' expresses a strong disapproval of both the act and the person. 'Vile' or 'foul' expresses a strong feeling of disgust. What makes an act morally worse is the degree of the seriousness of the wrong act. For example, it is more seriously wrong to murder a person than to steal a car.

Just as 'morally good' can apply to people so also 'morally bad' can apply to people. 'Who, then, is a morally bad person?' A morally bad person is quite prepared to do a wrong act if it suits his purpose. Was the Officer prepared to do wrong if it served her purpose? There is no indication that she was.

It should be noted that a person need not actually do the act. In fact, doing a morally wrong act does not necessarily make a person a morally bad person. I f the Officer did a wrong act but acted from a morally good motive, she would not be regarded a morally bad person. If she did a wrong act reluctantly, she might be regarded as being a morally weak person instead of a morally bad person. She might be regarded as someone who yields to temptation somewhat frequently or succumbs to temptation on a regular basis.

On the other hand, a person who feels no reluctance about doing a wrong act would be regarded as an unscrupulous or unprincipled person. A thoroughly bad person is regarded as a thoroughly unscrupulous person. She would lack all scruples, which is to say, that she would not be deterred by any sense of wrong. The Officer did not act like an unscrupulous person. She did not engage in rationalizing her action.

A lack of scruples could be brought on by certain naturally bad motives like hatred, revenge, jealousy, envy, greed, lust, or malice. These motives can overcome people when they do not make continuous efforts to deter the influence of naturally bad motives. When these naturally bad motives become strong enough in a person, they can blur the person's sense of right and wrong and so the person can become unscrupulous.

Some people seem to have a moral blind spot. They persistently fail to see that what they do in certain areas is wrong.

Sometimes a person commits such dastardly acts that it is felt that the person is not in his right mind. Suppose the Officer shot the truck driver immediately upon arriving at the scene. That could be regarded as suffering from a pathological condition. Her motives would not be viewed in terms of moral goodness or moral badness. She probably would be considered as a person who was not in her right mind.

Issues of moral goodness and moral badness raise questions about conscience. It implies that people have a special faculty called 'conscience' which tells them what is right and wrong. It can motivate people to do what is right and deter them from doing what is wrong.

What about the person who is not indifferent to the wrongness of an act and who desires to do his duty but who is careless? This might be viewed as negligent behavior. It is frequently said of such a person that 'he meant no harm.' There is no reason to suspect the Officer of being careless about her responsibilities as an officer of the law. Nor was she careless in the crisis of the moment.

I need to draw attention to the use of the word, ought, which can be used in two different moral senses. The problem is illustrated in the following example:

- John believes that he ought to do X.
- But in fact, it is not the case that he ought to do X.
- Ought he then do X?

This dilemma frequently evokes the following response: 'A man ought to do what he believes he ought to do' or 'since he thought it was the right thing to do, he ought to do it.' At first glance, these responses seem to imply that one's duty is determined by what one thinks to be one's duty. However, in this case 'ought' is used in two moral senses. In the saying 'A man ought to do what he believes he ought to do.' The term 'ought' is used to say that his action would be morally good if he did it and that it would be morally bad if he did not do it. 'Ought' refers to the **motive** of the person. In 'what he believes he ought to do,' the term 'ought' is used to say that 'he believes that it would be the right thing for him to do X and it would be the wrong thing for him not to do X'. In this case 'ought' is used in the moral sense in that it refers to the person's **duty**. Therefore, to say 'A man ought to do what he believes he ought to do' does not necessarily mean that one's duty is determined by what one thinks is one's duty. How might this concept be captured in a 'rule' in a code of ethics? It is, I believe, too complex to be expressed in the form of a rule.

In summary, I need to emphasize two observations. First, it is apparent from the analysis of the word 'ought' that some moral terms can be used in more than one sense. Hence, we need to be able to determine the moral sense not only from the choice of moral terms but also from the context in which the terms are used. This is illustrated in the use of the word ought.

Secondly, with each additional class of moral terms and reasoning, a greater variety of moral judgments can and should be made. Since moral judgments affect the lives of people, it is important that moral judgments be articulated and differentiated as much as possible.

I have introduced three categories with their respective concepts for addressing moral dilemmas. Two more to go – desert and just. You can imagine how complex the process of resolving moral dilemmas can be. At some point, I illustrate how taking these five categories can be used to resolve moral dilemmas. How is it even possible without breaking down the process of resolving moral dilemmas? You can see that it seems more practical to declare a list of duties which apply to specific situations. I have acknowledged the challenge of thinking through moral dilemmas. I will address it after I have dealt with the two remaining categories – desert and justice. So, bear with me.

Let us move on to desert. What does it have to offer to the process of resolving moral dilemmas?

CHAPTER 13: PRINCIPLED THINKING - DESERT

Desert[54] can take one of two forms: approval or punishment.

Dealing with staff performance

"A woman's place is in the home," chuckled Bill as he saw Sadie, racing back to her desk late. Not only had arriving late become a common occurrence, but she had been seen leaving her desk early rather frequently. Coming in late was of particular concern to management because by arriving late, she missed team meetings which were scheduled at the beginning of each day. In addition, Sadie had taken a leave of absence to take care of her elderly father. Suitable homes for seniors were at a premium and difficult to get especially for seniors of limited income as was the case with her father. In fact, Sadie had to work to not only to look after herself but also her father.

As the Department Manager at NEWTECHIC, Nancy, appreciated Sadie's work ethic and performance. At the same time, she was concerned about the undue stress imposed on Sadie's overworked colleagues due to her frequent lates after her prolonged absence. One or two colleagues were undermining her, thus creating even greater stress not only for Sadie but also for management.

"It is time for Management to intervene. But how?" mused Nancy. "First, she would have to talk to Bill."

"If only the company had a Code of Ethics which would lay out the number of lates and early leaves an employee could take. It would also identify the escalating forms of punishment. Then I would know exactly what to do with Sadie," Nancy thought. "Then she could be fair to everyone. Bill would have no reason to make his snide remarks about Sadie's lates." Now she felt she had to start with Bill.

Although Bill insisted that he meant no harm with his comment, there should be some consequences for him. The question then becomes, what consequences? Should an expression of disapproval be right for Bill's conduct, or should he receive some form of punishment? But here is the problem with this option. Punishment can be given or withheld at will, but disapprovals are not wilful.[30] An attitude of approval or disapproval is a psychological state; one either has it or does not have it. Does that make 'expressing disapproval' inadequate for Bill's action?

Some people would argue that Bill deserved some form of punishment because he acted in a manner that probably hurt Sadie. Did Bill plan to say what he did so that Sadie would hear him say it? Planning and organizing deliberate harm are part of the process of executing a harmful act. Does a person who acts with intent to harm someone deserve some form of punishment?

I discovered an interesting connection between *desert* and *motives*. I have described different situations where a person might deserve approval for wanting to do what is the right thing to do (motive) and disapproval for being indifferent about doing the right thing (deserve). This shows that judgments about desert considers the motives of the person as well as what he deserves. For example, what motivated Bill to say about Sadie what he did? What did he deserve for saying what he did? This combination of questions about motive and desert needs to be answered before Nancy should determine what form of punishment is appropriate.

The following Chart identifies the application of some concepts about desert used in this scenario.

Duty	Rights	Motive	Desert	Just
if it is her duty to do something, then the act of doing it is morally right and it would be wrong not to do it	everything a person would like to have, prefer, wish for, or want	for an action to be morally good, the action must be right	deserves some form of punishment because he acted in a manner designed to inflict harm on other people	
OR '*wanting* to do what is her duty to do'	Is it wrong for anyone to prevent a person from having or enjoying objects of interest if it is his or her right?	Must it also be done from a morally good motive?	judgments about desert consider the motives of the person and what he deserves	
OR 'wanting to do her duty *because it is the right thing to do.*'	Is it true that for every right, a person has a corresponding duty?	Is it a morally good act even though one of the conditions of a morally good act is missing?	Does a person deserve punishment for willing to commit a harmful act but not doing it?	
	Is it true that for every right, there is a correlative duty?	You ought to do what you believe you ought to do	Should expression of disapproval be appropriate, or should he receive some form of punishment?	
	Is it true that for every duty, there is a correlative right?	Is 'morally bad' simply the converse of 'morally good - the desire to do wrong for the sake of doing wrong'?	Punishment can be given or withheld at will, but disapprovals are not wilful	

			An attitude of approval or disapproval is a psychological state; one either has it or does not have it.	

Chart 21. Principled Thinking about Desert in Dealing with staff performance

For a full list of the issues on desert, go to the Chart 22. Can the various questions triggered by *desert* be answered through a set of rules in a code of ethics? Nancy hoped. I doubt that it can. Hence, I see the urgent need for employees and employers to be able and willing to think through these and other related questions about desert.

Concepts about Desert	Responses
1. Standard form for desert: Z deserves X on account of Y.	'Z' is the moral agent 'X' is an object of interest or disinterest 'Y' provides the reasons for allocating an object of interest or inflicting an object of disinterest.
2. Objects of disinterest	acts of disapproval or punishment.
3. Objects of interest	acts of approval or reward.
4. Awards	can be given or withheld at will.
5. Approvals and disapprovals	psychological states of being that are not wilful.
6. Acts of disapproval include the following:	a frown, words of disappointment, mild censure, or mild criticism.
7. Acts of approval include the following:	a smile, words of praise, a nod, slap on the back.
8. For what does a person deserve approval?	doing one's duty, and for doing a morally good act from a morally good motive.
9. For what does a person deserve a reward?	performing a challenging task or going beyond the call of duty – called an act of supererogation.

10. Normally, a person is not rewarded for:	- morally good action - morally good motive - not doing something wrong - being a moral agent - doing one's duty
11. A person deserves disapproval for:	- willingly doing a wrong act - being a morally bad person
12. On account of what does a person deserve punishment?	committing a morally wrong act with indifference as to the wrongness of the act.
13. Do all terrible acts deserve the same degree of punishment?	The punishment should be in proportion to the seriousness of the wrong act.
14. Does a person deserve punishment for willing to do wrong?	deserves some form of disapproval.
15. What if a person planned to commit a wrong act but failed to execute it?	deserves some form of punishment.
16. Does a person deserve punishment for failure to do his duty?	Possibly, though sometimes an expression of disapproval may be appropriate.

Chart 22. Concepts about Desert[55]

To illustrate how these concepts about desert might apply in a scenario, I have applied them in another scenario, *Allow a low-cost generic for Zerit.*

Allow a low-cost generic for Zerit

HIV/AIDS had ravaged the world, rich and poor alike. The only difference was wealthy people could afford Zerit as a treatment for HIV/AIDS; the poor could not.

Yale had developed Zerit and formed a partnership with a for-profit company, BMS, to market the product. This partnership was a win-win-win situation for Yale, BMS and the wealthy. The poor in places like South Africa were left to die.

Doctors Without Borders (DWB) appealed to Yale and BMS to provide a low-cost generic Zerit for poor countries but they would have none of it. Yale quickly realized that they could not afford the negative publicity for supplying Zerit at a cost which only the rich could afford. So, they acknowledged the human need for a low-cost generic Zerit. For Yale, this had the appearance of a humane gesture. Was it?

What does Yale deserve for having formed a partnership with a for-profit company which priced Zerit out of reach for millions suffering from HIV/AIDS? Does it deserve approval for lowering the price after widespread protests? But approval is a state of being that is not wilful. One either has it or does not. Is that sufficient for someone who is willing to do a wrong act? Did Yale enter the partnership knowing that they committed a wrong act? Did they commit a wrong act with indifference as to the wrongness of the act? Do they deserve some form of punishment? If punishment is appropriate, what form should it take?

Should universities like Yale enter partnerships with for-profit companies to support and generate innovative research projects? Might it change their community-based mission?

I raise questions and issues about desert. Here are a few:

- Approvals are not wilful; they are psychological states of being.
- A person deserves disapproval for willingly doing a wrong act.
- What if a person planned to commit a wrong act but failed to execute it? What does he deserve?
- Does a person deserve punishment for willing to do wrong?

For a complete list of the questions and statements discussed on desert, go to Chart 22.

Key words

This class of terms and judgments is made up of the representative term, deserve, plus at least two more terms: worthy and merit. Deserve is used most often. For example, "Doctors without Borders deserved a commendation for forcing BMS to provide a low-cost Zerit for poor people. Worthy is used mainly with reference to. For example, Yale was worthy of a commendation for developing a low-cost Zerit as motives a treatment for people with HIV/AIDS.

Although I focus on the use of terms in the moral sense, deserve is frequently used in a *non-moral sense*. The non-moral sense is used in this sentence: "Yale deserved the respect of the government." The moral sense is used in this sentence: "When Doctors without Borders appealed for lower prices for poor people, they deserved respect."

Moral judgments are not only made about the act, the actor, and the interrelationship of the two, but also about the consequences of moral or immoral acts. DWB deserved commendation for getting the for-profit company to lower the price for Zerit for poor people.

Judgments about whether a person deserves something usually take the following form:

> Z (moral person) deserves X on account of Y.
>
> Z - is the logical subject even though it is not always the grammatical subject. In the sentence, "The President of Yale deserves respect for reducing the cost of Zerit." 'President' is the logical and grammatical subject.
>
> X - is an object of interest or disinterest. In the example cited above, X is an object of interest. When X is an object of disinterest, it means that Z deserves an expression of disapproval or punishment which is inflicted by someone. When 'X' is an object of interest, it means that Z deserves an expression of approval or a reward which is bestowed by someone.
>
> Y - provides the reasons for stating that Z deserves an object of interest or disinterest.

When a person claims that a certain person deserves punishment or reward but does not offer a reason for the judgment, people usually retort by asking 'Why?' This typical response suggests that a person is expected to offer reasons, implicitly or explicitly, for making the claim that someone deserves a punishment or reward.

People frequently take issue with the reasons offered. For example, Doctors without Borders might disagree that a reprimand is an appropriate punishment for Yale; the punishment should be more severe as in the payment of a fine. On the other hand, the President of DBS might insist that both options are inappropriate because the protesters were led by professional disrupters. In short, Y is an important aspect of determining whether Z deserves punishment or reward and what form it should take.

DWB insists that Yale deserves something, either an object of interest or an object of disinterest. Objects of disinterest take one of two forms - *disapproval* and *punishment*. Disapproval is a mild form which is frequently expressed in the form of a frown, words of disappointment, mild censure, or mild criticism. Although an attitude of disapproval is not something one has wilfully, often a person can choose what form the feeling of disapproval should take. When disapproval is expressed in a stronger form, it is usually referred to as punishment. Punishments include an expression of disapproval, but a feeling of disapproval does not necessarily involve punishment.

Objects of interest can take one of two forms – approval or reward. Mild forms of approval include a nod, words of praise, or a pat on the back. Mild forms of approval are commonly expressed for a person who has done his duty. When approval is expressed in stronger terms, it is usually referred to as a reward, which includes an approval, but takes on a more substantial form such as a gift. Rewards are usually reserved for two kinds of occasions. A person may deserve a reward when he has completed a challenging task which many people may not even try or which they frequently fail to complete. For example, a research team at Yale invented Zerit which saved many lives. For this Yale received a major research grant.

Second, a person is frequently rewarded for doing something which is beyond the call of duty. Many Yale students spent hours on the picket line protesting the high price of Zerit.

I need to mention an important distinction between *approval* and *reward*. Rewards can be given or withheld at will, but approvals are not wilful. An attitude of approval is a psychological state; one either has it or does not have it. A person may choose to hide it so that other people cannot detect it or choose to give expression to it through words of praise or some other form. For example, when the President of Yale was informed of the invention of Zerit, he chose to commend publicly the research team which invented it.

That leads me to the question, "On account of what actions judged morally, does a person deserve approval?" As was pointed out earlier, a person probably deserves some form of approval for doing his duty from a sense of duty or for doing what is right for right's sake. People deserve approval for having done morally good acts, acting from morally good motives, and deliberately refraining from doing wrong acts.

Ordinarily, *a person does not deserve a reward* for *having done a morally good act*, that is, for an act which is right and was done from morally good motive or from a desire to do one's duty. A person does not deserve a reward for acting from morally good motive alone. For example, if the President of Yale would have cooperated with DWB to show the world Yale's interest in helping poor people, Yale would not have done it for a morally good motive because its motive would have been self-serving. If the President had intended to serve the poor but had not acted on the intention, he would not have deserved a reward. Finally, a person does not deserve a reward for not doing something that is wrong. Had the President refused to endorse the high price for Zerit, he would not have deserved a reward.

In short, people *deserve rewards* only for the two kinds of actions mentioned earlier, namely, when a person performs a challenging task which many people frequently fail to perform or when a person does something which is beyond the call of duty. In most situations people do not deserve anything more than approval. A person deserves disapproval for being willing to do a wrong act. For example, Yale was willing to partner with a for profit company which put a high price on Zerit which was wrong.

Yale deserved disapproval for willing to do a wrong act. This should not be confused with maintaining that people do wrong for wrong's sake which I explained before. The same applies to doing a morally wrong act. A morally bad person might do what is right but engages in it for self-serving reasons.

A *person deserves punishment* for the following action. A person should be punished for committing a seriously wrong act with indifference to its wrongness. For example, Yale should be punished for partnering with a for-profit company which put a high price on Zerit.

A person *does not deserve the same degree of punishment* for all morally bad acts. The magnitude of the punishment inflicted upon a person should be in proportion to the seriousness of the wrong act committed. The more seriously wrong an act is, the more severe the punishment should be. Take, for example, the issue of "life" vs. "property." Since it is more seriously wrong to take the life of a person than destroying property, the former is considered a more serious crime and therefore should be punished more seriously.

A person may not deserve punishment for *willing to do wrong but not doing it*. As a rule, such a person would only deserve an expression of disapproval. Had Yale been willing to enter a partnership with a for-profit but declined the partnership, it would not have deserved punishment, only an expression of disapproval.

If a person *planned to commit a wrong act, such as robbing a bank, tried to execute it, but failed to do it*, the person deserves to be punished. The person deserves some form of punishment because he acted in a manner designed to inflict harm on other people. For example, conspiracy is not just a matter of being willing to do wrong; it is an act of planning and organizing steps to inflict harm on other people. Planning and organizing deliberate harm are part of the process of executing the harmful act and therefore deserves some form of punishment.

Does a person deserve *punishment for sins of omission* such as failure to do one's duty? Possibly, for it is wrong not to do one's duty. Of course, it would have to be established clearly that the person had a duty to do the act in question. In some instances that is easy. For example, if Yale had a policy which prohibited it from entering a partnership with a for profit company, it could be determined whether Yale had entered into that kind of agreement. In other situations, it is much more difficult to determine one's duty. For example, how can a fair market value be established when a product, like a drug, takes a decade to develop? At the same time, which does not make the question concerning sins of omission irrelevant.

There is a connection between *desert* and *motives*. I have described different situations where a person deserves approval or rewards for wanting to do what is the right thing to do (motive) and disapproval or punishment for being indifferent about doing the right thing (motive). In other words, *judgments about desert consider the motives of the person as well as what he deserves*. For example, what motivated Yale to enter the partnership? What did it deserve for agreeing to enter the partnership? This combination of questions about motive and desert needs to be answered before it is determined what Yale deserved.

That the question of desert is taken very seriously by people of all ages, is evidenced by the fact that people have strong feelings about rewards and punishment. This is apparent in the day-to-day interaction at home, in school, in the community, in the legislature, the courts, and certainly also in companies. CEOs and department managers must frequently make discretionary decisions about what punishments or rewards are deserved. What people deserve is a fundamental part of resolving moral dilemmas.

For the final category, **just**, we observe how all the categories – duty, rights, motive, desert and just work together to determine just action. Although the immediate application of principled thinking in situations like *I Promised*, would be replaced with intuitive thinking (gut reaction), it offers a way of showing how all the criteria in principled thinking work together.

CHAPTER 14: PRINCIPLED THINKING – JUST

To illustrate how the concepts about just[56] might apply in a scenario, I have applied them in another scenario, *I Promised.*

I Promised

As you no doubt have experienced many times, whenever you are confronted with right and wrong situations, your attention is quickly drawn to several concerns. It happened to me many times. For example, as a dad of a 16-year-old daughter and the CEO of a software company, KnowledgeBuilder Software Inc., I remember rescheduling a management meeting so that I could watch my daughter play in her final basketball playoff game.

To justify my decision to my team, I applied principled thinking WITHOUT first addressing the emotions generated by my decision.

I asked myself, 'Do I have a primary duty to my company or my daughter? Do I honor my promise to my daughter or concentrate on my obligation to lead and protect my company?

When challenged, I am protective of both my rights as a parent and my shareholder's rights to make money. Questions came to mind, 'When is the right time to do one or the other? Is this the time to see my daughter play in her final playoff game?'

I imputed a motive to my team leader, Peter, who insisted that my first obligation always must be to my company, but I did not acknowledge my own motive for wanting to see my daughter play in her team's playoff game. That led me to do defensive actions, consciously or unconsciously, like being dismissive about what Peter had to say.

On the other hand, I felt my HR team leader, Betty, deserved approval for supporting me on deciding to see my daughter's final basketball game.

Unfortunately, I was quick to judge Peter unfairly for criticizing my decision to take the time to see my daughter's final game. I had no reason to judge Peter; there is nothing unfair about Peter's advice.

This scenario takes us to the last and toughest questions in pursuing justice. What makes justice the most difficult challenge? To address it fully, it requires that we consider all the concerns raised so far - duty, rights, motive, and desert. And we need to do it under 'vailed ignorance'[40] as John Rawls put it. In other words, we need to do it without being influenced by our own values and preferences or those of any other person. How?

First, I discovered that 'justice' as applied to a person refers to motive. When justice is used in a subjective sense, it is used in a way "good" or "virtuous" are used to refer to the motive of a person. For example, what was my motive for promising to attend my daughter's final basketball game?

Second, the objective sense of the term *just* refers to whether an act is right. When 'just' is used with reference to the distribution of goods, it is used in a way that 'right' refers to 'duty.' Hence, *just* is frequently treated as being interchangeable with *right*. For example, 'Was it right to take time off from work to watch my daughter play basketball?

Third, the rights of a person must be acknowledged and respected. Did my team respect my right to take time off to see the game?

Fourth, justice also raises the question of what a person deserves. For example, did I deserve to take time off?

Some other significant issues need to be considered in deciding whether an act is just. For example, are all right acts considered just? Suppose it was right for me to take time off to see the game? Does that make it just? Not necessarily.

What about the converse? Are all just acts also right acts? Since one of the conditions for an act to be just is that it must be right, it would be contradictory to say 'no.' If it is just for me to keep my promise to my daughter, it would also be right. And all unjust acts are wrong.

There is one more condition that must be addressed to make a just decision – make the decision in 'veiled ignorance'[40] as John Rawls would say. In other words, decisions should be made without appealing to any personal values and preference or that of any other person. Could a set of rules in a code of ethics resolve this dilemma?

Once again, we have met many thought-provoking issues. Could they be addressed by a set of rules in a code of ethics? Or do they require the knowledge and ability to think through moral dilemmas? As I have said repeatedly, that is the central question.

I was reminded, while writing and discussing this book with colleagues, that the purpose of companies is to generate profits for shareholders. The question put to me was, 'How can a company be profitable when it is expected to pursue justice?'

John Rawls offers a concept of justice which offers a framework for companies to do both, make a profit and pursue justice. It is captured in the following two statements:

> Society should be structured so that the greatest possible amount of liberty is given to its members, limited only by the notion that the liberty of any one member shall not infringe upon that of any other member.

> Social or economic gains are only to be allowed if the worst off will be better off than before.

I ask again, **would you hire an employee who follows the corporation's rules OR someone who cares for the welfare of everyone and exercises principled thinking and acting based on company rules and justice for all?**

The following Chart identifies the application of some concepts about just as used in this scenario.

Duty	Rights	Motive	Desert	Just
if it is her duty to do something, then the act of doing it is morally right and it would be wrong not to do it	everything a person would like to have, prefer, wish for, or want	for an action to be morally good, the action must be right	Punishment can be given or withheld at will, but disapprovals are not wilful	Justice requires that we consider - duty, rights, motive, and desert
OR '*wanting* to do what is her duty to do'	Is it wrong for anyone to prevent a person from having or enjoying objects of interest if it is his or her right?	Must it also be done from a morally good motive?	An attitude of approval or disapproval is a psychological state; one either has it or does not have it.	vailed ignorance - without being influenced by our own values and preferences
OR 'wanting to do her duty *because it is the right thing to do.*'	Is it true that for every right, a person has a corresponding duty?	Is it a morally good act even though one of the conditions of a morally good act is missing?	Doses a person deserve punishment for willing to commit a harmful act but not doing it?	'justice' as applied to a person refers to 'motive'
	Is it true that for every right, there is a correlative duty?	You ought to do what you believe you ought to do	he deserved punishment because he acted in a way to do harm to other people	When justice is used in a subjective sense, it is used in a way "good" or "virtuous" are used to refer to the motive of a person
	Is it true that for every duty, there is a correlative right?	Is 'morally bad' simply the converse of 'morally good - the desire to do wrong for the sake of doing wrong'?	judgments about desert includes the motives the act.	the objective sense of the term *just* refers to whether an act is right.

				When 'just' is used with reference to the distribution of goods, it is used in a way that 'right' refers to duties
				the rights of a person must be acknowledged and respected
				justice also raises the question of what a person deserves
				are all right acts considered just?
				Are all just acts also right acts?
				decisions should be made without appealing to any personal values and preference

Chart 23. Principled Thinking about Just in *I Promised*

The Chart below summarizes the concepts about just.

Concepts about Just	Responses
1. Justice refers to the distribution objects of interest or disinterest.	
2. Justice is administered by people who exercise authority	
3. 'Fair' may be used in the objective and subjective sense	
4. What is the relationship between right acts and just acts?	- Not all right acts are just but all just acts are right - Not all wrong acts are unjust, but all unjust acts are wrong
5. On what basis is a distribution just or unjust?	The basis is how the distribution affects the interests of the recipients relative to each other.

6. Are these factors sufficient to determine whether an act is just?
   - the recipient's desert
   - its utility
   - the needs of the recipient
   - the rights of the recipient
   - the motive of the distributor
	
	no
	no
	no
	no
	no

7. Impartiality refers to the distributor.	
8. A just act is an act of impartiality.	
9. The issue of justice includes:	- A distributor - A distribution of objects of interest or disinterest - A recipient
10. For a person to be impartial he must favor one recipient over the other based on sound principles or reasons.	
11. A distribution which is made with impartiality may be just or unjust.	Impartiality does not ensure that an act is just.
12. It may be wrong in some cases not to discriminate.	A just distribution may require discrimination in some cases

13. For a distribution to be just, the distributor must meet the following conditions:	- have the right to make the distribution - have a duty to make the distribution - be a moral person
14. Is it possible for a just act ever to be wrong?	No
15. Is it possible for a person to deserve punishment and yet for it not to be just for someone to punish that person?	Yes
16. What is retribution?	Retribution is an act of revenge or harming someone in retaliation
17. What is retributive justice?	It is the just allocation of object of disinterest.
18. How is it possible for the allocation of an object of disinterest to be an act of impartiality?	To say that a distributor is impartial is to say that the distributor does not favor one recipient over others without sound principles or reasons.
19. How can the allocation of an object of interest or disinterest to one individual be just?	It can be just if the distributor would decide to make the same distribution of objects of interest or disinterest for all persons in similar situations.
20. What is involved in pursuing of justice?	- Act from a desire to do one's duty - Recognize a person's rights - Act from a morally good motive - Giving people what they deserve - Act with impartiality in pursuit of justice.

Chart 24. Concepts about Just[57]

To illustrate how many of these concepts about just might apply in a scenario, I have applied them in another scenario, *Palm Oil Policy*.

Palm Oil Policy

"NO DEFORESTATION, NO PEAT, NO EXPLOITATION!" (NDPE)

That sounded like a great slogan in 2014. Government, NGOs, and the largest companies in Indonesia agreed to it. Till 2015 – the worst fire season in nearly two decades in Indonesia. Why? The government had reversed its position on the pledge to honor NDPE and encouraged companies to do the same.

This reversal created a problem for Wilmar, CEO of the largest trader in Palm oil in the world. The Pledge and the government's reversal on NDPE created conflicting emotions (dissonance) for Wilmar. Should Wilmar keep the Pledge? How could it police its suppliers to cooperate? What could it do with violators? How could it operate with no government support and ramped corruption? These questions defied easy answers.

What is the just thing to do for Wilmar? Is justice with empathy possible? Towards whom should Wilmar express empathy? Why?

Justice also includes the terms *just, fair,* and *equitable*, as well as their antonyms *unjust, unfair,* and *inequitable*. These terms are frequently used in moral and legal philosophy.

Key words

People judge many things to be *just* or *unjust*. They judge actions when they say, "That was the only just thing to do." Sometimes laws are judged to be unjust. This applies to legal codes. When a person is judged to have been punished excessively, people say that the person got unjust punishment. Sometimes it is said of a person that "He received his just desert" which is to say that he got what he deserved, be it an object of interest or disinterest. Judges are sometimes accused of pronouncing unjust judgments. Members of a family sometimes feel that the disbursement of the family estate was unjust. Reformers frequently argue that the economy of a country is unjust to the poor. Historically, some religions have made a distinction between just and unjust wars. Politicians have claimed that, if elected, they will usher in a just society. Governments are sometimes accused of being unjust to certain segments of the population. Leaders of reform movements sometimes claim that their just cause warrants interference in the orderly flow of society. Appeals are sometimes made for a just distribution of the limited resources of a nation.

Applying *justice* to people introduces a usage of this term that is different from all the others. Justice as applied to a person does not refer to the same thing as applied to an action, the law, or a sentence. Justice as applied to a person refers to motive. When justice is used in this sense, it is used in a way "good" or "virtuous" are used to refer to the motive of a person. In other words, for a person to be considered a good person, it is not sufficient that he makes just or fair allocation; he must do so for a morally good motive. For example, Wilmar kept the Pledge because he wanted to do the right thing.

All the other uses of the term justice listed above do not refer to motives but only to the objective characteristics of what is judged to be just. The objective sense of the term *just* refers to the rightness of an act. When 'just' is used with reference to the distribution of goods, for example, it is used in a way that 'right' refers to 'duty.' Hence, *just* is frequently treated as being interchangeable with *right*. For example: 'What was the just thing to do for Wilmar?' However, that usage fails to consider the distinctive characteristics of *just* discussed later.

Usually, justice is used in the narrow sense where it refers to the decisions and actions of people who possess authority or the right to supervise the activities of other people. This usage is reflected in the reference to just laws, just punishment, just allocation, and so on. Most often the word 'just' is used in a less formal setting. For example, when Wilmar declared "NO DEFORESTATION, NO PEAT, NO EXPLOITATION," his action was just.

I mentioned two other terms that belong to the class of justice: *fair* and *equitable*. Fair may be used in the objective and subjective sense as is the case with just. The objective sense is reflected in the statement "He did the only fair thing." The subjective sense is meant when it is said of a person that "he is a fair person."

The only difference between *fair* and *just* is the context in which they are used. As I mentioned above, *just* is commonly used with reference to the decisions and actions made by people in authority such as government officials, CEOs, and judges. *Fair* is used in less formal situations. For example, a CEO may treat his employees unfairly by favoring some and not others. *Fair* also seems to be used in situations where the person who is making the judgment is involved in the distribution of objects in trust. For example, employees need to be able to trust their CEO that he will pay everyone fairly.

Equitable is used only in the objective sense. It is used commonly for the distribution of objects of interest or disinterest. Essentially, equitable describes the distribution. For example, an equitable pay scale should be used to determine wages for male and female staff.

In the objective sense, *just* refers to the distribution or allocation of objects of interest or disinterest. For example, an equitable pay scale is just or unjust depending on how the wages (object of interest) are distributed or allocated. Laws are just or unjust depending on how they distribute or allocate legal obligations (objects of disinterest) and legal rights (objects of interest). Governments are just or unjust depending on whether they legislate and execute just or unjust laws. Societies are just or unjust depending on how the objects of interest (property, services) and objects of disinterest (taxes, military service) are allocated or distributed. Judges make judgments for the purpose of distributing or allocating objects of interest or disinterest.

There are certain elements that must be part of the objective sense of the term 'justice.' First, there must be a *distributor* who allocates objects of interest or disinterest. For example, when a judge pronounces a sentence, the judge allocates an object of disinterest. The distributor, in this case, the judge, must be a moral person to make a just distribution.

Second, a judgment about justice requires a *recipient*. A criminal is the recipient of an object of disinterest. A recipient need not be an immoral person; he could be an actual or potential moral person. He probably has objects of interest and disinterest.

Third, there must be a *distribution*. The distribution of an object of interest or disinterest is not *just* based only on what the recipient deserves. In summary, whether a distribution is just depends on the duty of the distributor, the rights of the recipient, the motive of the distributor, and what the recipient deserves.

Key ideas

Not all right acts are considered just. For example, it might be right for Wilmar to throw a party for his staff, but it is not unjust not to do it. But all just acts are also right. It seems confusing to claim that a certain act is just even though it is wrong. One of the conditions for an act to be just is that it must be right. For example, if it is just for Wilmar to keep the Pledge, it is the right thing to do. On the other hand, if it is wrong to deny some staff to join in the party, it is also unjust.

Not all wrong acts are unjust. It may be wrong for Wilmar to play golf every afternoon, but it is unjust. But all unjust acts are wrong. If the CEO paid a bonus to some of his assistants but not to others, that would be wrong; it would also be unjust.

In short, the relationship between right and just as well as wrong and unjust can be summarized as follows:
- Not all right acts are just but all just acts are right.
- Not all wrong acts are unjust, but all unjust acts are wrong

An *act of distributing or allocating an object of interest or disinterest is not fair only from the point of view of its utility.* Some people believe that fairness includes utility. For example, they argue that promoting justice through the courts brings with it the utility of law and order for society. However, this apparent correlation between fairness and utility does not always seem to follow. For example, suppose longer sentences are an effective way of reducing crime for males ages 35-65. Should all men of this age therefore receive longer sentences? Should the father in this age range, who his children who depend on him to provide shelter and food, receive a longer sentence just because of his age? In other words, should factors other than age also be considered in the length of a sentence to be fair to everyone? These questions raise doubts about the apparent correlation between fairness and utility.

Is a distribution considered just or unjust from the point of view of the interests of the recipient? Not necessarily. Objects of needs are objects of interest, but not all objects of interests are needed. Sometimes whatever is distributed is something people want but do not need. Sometimes the distribution involves objects of disinterest. For example, the CEO may have to reprimand an employee for under-performance.

Is a distribution considered just or unjust from the point of view of the rights of the recipient? Although the rights of the recipient should be considered, rights do not offer a sufficient reason. For example, an employee may have a right to express concerns about a decision of her team leader, but that does not make her expression of concerns just or unjust.

A *distribution can affect the recipients* in one of three ways. First, a distribution does not favor one recipient over others. Second, the distribution might favor one recipient over others based on sound principles or reasons. Third, the distribution might favor one or some recipients over others without sound principles or reasons. Which of these characteristics must a distribution have for the distribution to be just? The first possibility (i.e., the distribution does not favor one recipient over others) does not involve the issue of just distribution but involves only the impartiality of the distributor which will be discussed later. The second alternative involves the issue of justice because the decision is made based on sound principles or reasons. The third option is not 'just' because a distribution is unjust if it favors one recipient over others without sound principles or sound reasons.

Is a distribution considered just or unjust from the point of view of motives? That could not be the case because any reference to motives would clearly be a reference to the distributor and not to that which is distributed. Whatever the Government's motive for withdrawing its support for NOPE may have been, the implementation of NOPE was about fairness and equity.

After all these objections to what constitutes a just distribution, I offer the following description of a just distribution: *A distribution is just or unjust from the point of view of the way it affects the interests of recipients relative to one another including those who should be considered recipients.* For example, in a case where a judge must determine what constitutes a just sentence, she must consider how people, who have committed a similar offence, were treated. Of course, the similarity between cases must consider extenuating circumstance such as the mental health of the recipient, the impact of the crime on the victims, and the context in which the crime was committed and so on. Whether in fact, a distribution affects recipients as anticipated is a different matter. What people do must not be confused with what they should do.

For a distribution to be just, a second condition must be met. The distribution must be made by a distributor who is *impartial.* Impartiality in the primary sense, applies to the person making the distribution whereas justice refers to the distribution itself. To say that a distributor is impartial is to say that the distributor does not favor one recipient over others without sound principles or reasons. Should Wilmar decide to pay a bonus to his employees, he must make sure that she does not favor one recipient over others without sound principles or reasons.

That a distribution must be done with impartiality for it to be a just distribution raises the question: *Are all distributions done with impartiality 'just'?* Not necessarily not. For example, when the CEO offered some vague replies to some employees as to why they did get a bonus, he maintained that he was unaware of it because he acted with impartiality. He refused to acknowledge that his 'impartial' action was unjust. There are no general rules for determining whether a person is impartial. Each case must be considered on its own merits. Statements about whether a distributor is impartial are descriptive and not normative.

For a distribution to be just, several conditions must be met: The distributor must have a right to make the distributions, for it is wrong for someone to distribute something if he does not have the right to do so. Also, the distributor must have a duty to make a distribution. Lastly, since only moral persons can have a duty to make a moral judgment, the distributor must be a moral person.

Did the CEO have a right to make the bonus payments? As the CEO, the answer probably is yes. Did he have a duty to make the bonus payments only to some employees? No because that would be an act of discrimination without sound reason. Was he an immoral person for paying bonuses only to some and not to others? That would depend on several factors including being fair to everyone.

If a person deserved a reward, granting it (i.e., object of interest) would be just. Similarly, it would be just to inflict punishment if it is deserved. Allocating a reward or inflicting a punishment must consider the way in which the distribution of objects of interest and disinterest affect the interests and needs of the recipients relative to one another. Hence, judgments about whether an act is just must consider what a person deserves.

When is discrimination unjust? Discrimination is unjust when a person has a duty not to discriminate or when it is wrong to discriminate. For example, since it is wrong to discriminate against a person based on color, it is unjust. However, not every act of discrimination is wrong. In fact, it may be wrong not to discriminate in some situations. It may be wrong in some situation not to discriminate in favour of the disadvantaged. John Rawls, philosopher, put it this way:

1. Society should be structured so that the greatest possible amount of liberty is given to its members, limited only by

the notion that the liberty of any one member shall not infringe upon that of any other member.

2. Inequalities either social or economic are only to be allowed if the worst off will be better off than they might be under an equal distribution.[58]

It is possible for a person to deserve punishment and yet for it not to be just for someone to mete out that punishment? That was Wilmar's concern since the government had withdrawn its support for NOPE.

I need to draw attention to the difference between *retribution* and *retributive justice*. 'Retribution' refers to acts of taking revenge or harming someone in retaliation for some harm that the person has done. 'Retributive justice' refers to the just allocation of objects of interest or objects of disinterest. A judge exercises retributive justice when he sentences a convicted person to a just sentence, an object of disinterest. Can CEO's administer retributive justice?

So far, I have defined justice in terms of two or more people. That raises the question: *How can the distribution of an object of interest or disinterest to one individual be just?* The distribution to one person could be just if the distributor decides to make the same distribution of objects of interest or disinterest to all persons in similar situations.

This concludes a review of the five categories and related concepts of the Principled Thinking Model – duty, rights, motive, desert, just - for making right and wrong moral judgments.

The final challenge is to illustrate how principled thinking coupled with a sense of fellow feeling (empathy) can help CEOs and their management teams pursue justice as they resolve conflicts of interest. I emphasize the use of the word 'pursue' because we can only strive to pursue justice; there are no guaranteed pathways to justice.' In pursuit of justice' is the purpose of Part IV.

All just acts are right but not all right acts are just.

PART IV: PRINCIPLED THINKING GROUNDED IN EMPATHY

You have just had a whirlwind tour of the components of the process for arriving at a just or fair resolution of a conflict. The process involves: exercising emotional intelligence as a primary source of energy (empathy), experiencing dissonance generated by conflicts, applying moral values principle tests, and exercising principled thinking in pursuit of justice. How can this process apply in different conflict situations that occur in companies? Let us ask a professor and his doctoral student who are paired to facilitate a hypothetical conversation about different scenarios. They are asked to suggest ways of pursuing justice grounded in empathy.

I chose to use conversation to express the emotions and reflections that are central to making decisions in pursuit of justice. Sherry Turkle in *Reclaiming Conversation: The Power of Talk in a Digital Age* put it this way:

> Face-to-face communication is the most human –
> and humanizing – thing we do. Fully present to one
> another, we learn to listen. It is where we develop the
> capacity for empathy.[59]

She captures the essence of communication by rephrasing René Descartes's (17th century philosopher) statement, 'I think, therefore I am' to, 'I share, therefore I am.'

Let us start by asking professor Small and his doctoral student, Bruno Epp, to discuss the scenario *HIV positive.*

CHAPTER 15: CONVERSATION ABOUT 'DUTY'

How did professor Small and his doctoral student, Bruno Epp, discuss duty in the scenario, *HIV positive*?

HIV positive

As the nurse for an international wholesale company, Flo encountered a range of health-related problems. Recently David brought a new case when he admitted to her that he is HIV positive. When she asked about his partner, Jack, David insisted that he was not ready to share this information with his partner.

Word gets around; Jack became uneasy about his relationship with David and wonders where he might share his unease. The company nurse of course; everyone goes to her when they need someone to talk to!

When he finally had the courage to talk to the nurse about what he regarded as an extremely sensitive and personal matter, he blurted out his concern about his partner, David. He suspected that David may have been unfaithful and consequently may be HIV positive.

Now, what should the nurse do with the information she had from both David and Jack? She realized that she was morally obligated to honor client confidentiality. On the other hand, the company's Code of Ethics states clearly that as the company nurse, she has an obligation 'to protect the health and safety of the employees.' Is she caught is a conflict of interest? She decides that, no, she is not in a conflict of interest because the company Code of Ethics states very clearly that her responsibility is to protect the health and safety of the employees. What is more, Flo was part of the company's three member HR team which interprets and applies the Code. She followed the company Code of Ethics.

CONFLICT OF INTEREST
Experiential dissonance
Universal consequences test
Cognitive dissonance
Principled thinking with empathy

Chart 25. Conflict of interest – Duty

Note how the Professor walked his student through the following process:

Conversation

Professor: Were you surprised that David was the first case of HIV positive for Flo?

Student: I certainly was. What really puzzled me was how a statement about what to do, like "to protect the health and safety of the employees" in a Code of Ethics might offer clear direction for the nurse.

Professor: What troubled me was, how quickly Flo resolved her conflict between her promise of confidentiality to David and her commitment to follow the company's Code of Ethics with Jack. Resolving that dissonance so quickly (in my opinion) ended any chance of Flo considering an alternative perspective.

Student: What do you have in mind?

Professor: Suppose you felt you should arrive at a just and fair resolution? How could a statement in a Code of Ethics guide you?

Student: You would have to think about what that statement could mean.

Professor: That is right! But we are getting ahead of ourselves. If Flo had been sensitive to the discrepancy between what she said to David and the clause in the Code of Ethics which she applied to Jack, she probably would have felt experiential dissonance. That ...

Student: What's exper... dissonance?

Professor: Experiential dissonance is felt when past habits or relationships do not align with a current situation. Flo was used to resolving conflicts by applying the company's Code of Ethics. Had she felt the discrepancy, she might have felt experiential dissonance. This might have made it difficult to simply apply the Code of Ethics.

Student: So?

Professor: Had she felt the discrepancy, she might have been open to strategies for exploring alternative resolutions. More important, if the discrepancy would have created a feeling of empathy, Flo would be searching for resolutions which could lead to justice or fairness.

Student: Is that where Festinger's strategies apply? I remember them – role exchange test, new cases test, subsumption test, and universal consequences test. Which ones or one would you apply in this case?

Professor: I would apply the universal consequences test to begin with. Had Flo explored the consequences of her two alternative responses to Bill and Jack, she might have realized the problem of applying them. She might have noticed that neither of them would necessarily lead to a just and fair resolution. No doubt, she wanted a just and fair resolution for both Bill and Jack. The discrepancy led her to feel compassionate for both.

Student: That sounds reasonable, but why did you choose universal consequences? Why not one of the other strategies?

Professor: I could have, but I thought considering the universal consequences was most applicable. If this strategy generated dissonance as I anticipated, it would urge Flo to resolve the dissonance; she might deny the dissonance, try to avoid it (as many people do). If she had felt empathic, she could be looking for a just and a fair resolution of the conflict.

Student: My guess is that now she might be open to exploring a just and fair resolution. As a nurse, she wants to be empathic towards Bill and Jack in their demanding situation. Doesn't that conflict with her commitment to be just and fair?

Professor: It should not. In fact, empathy is the first step to a just resolution. If you don not care about a person, why would you try to be just and fair towards that person?

Student: What would that look like in the case we are discussing? What would Flo have to do?

Professor: I can only imagine what that might look like. Here are a few possibilities. Listen to their thoughts and feelings including their criticism of the company's treatment of gay people. Control your own thoughts and feelings. Show that you care about their well-being. These would go a long way to build trust and a feeling of empathy.

Student: You have mapped out the dissonance and one way of dealing with it that opens the way to pursuing justice with empathy. That is a lot of stuff to be dealt with before we can get to what I wanted to do in the first place – apply principled thinking in pursuit of justice. I saw one chart which identified the concepts involved in addressing duty. That was an impressive list. So where do we start?

Professor: Let us look at the scenario again. Notice that it concentrates on Flo's responsibilities. So, I would focus on the 'duty' chart you just mentioned.

Student: The chart identifies 'duty' as "doing your duty because it is the right thing to do."

Professor: That concept of 'duty' refers to 'in pursuit of justice.' There are two other concepts of 'duty' which may not refer to justice – 'Wanting to do whatever is your duty to do' and 'do whatever is your duty to do.'

Student: What about all the other twenty-two concepts in the chart, do we have to address them for this scenario? That could be an impossible task in real life!

Professor: Are they required to deal with Flo's problem? If not, why raise them?

Student: I can think of a few in the chart. For example, I think Flo should keep in mind that a duty is right or wrong independent of ones likes or dislikes, or of one's motive. And look at this one, 'Can a person have a conflict of duties?

Professor: You are right. These are issues which Flo could keep in mind as she searches through principled thinking for a just resolution. With that, Let us stop for the day. We might look at another scenario at some other time.

Student: Thank you for taking the time to discuss ways of addressing important moral issues.

Professor: Here is a copy of a chart which identifies the major concepts about duty.

Concepts about Duty

1. Duty means:
   - following whatever is one's duty to do
 	
    - wanting to do what is one's duty to do.
 	
    - wanting to do one's duty because it is the right thing to do

2. A duty is the right thing to do independently of a person's motive or interest.
3. An action is right or wrong independent of a person's likes or dislikes.
4. One can put someone under an obligation but not under a duty.
5. If it is a person's duty to do something, then the act of doing it is morally right and it would be wrong not to do it.
6. A person is not necessarily obligated to do every morally right act.
7. Going beyond the call of duty is called an act of supererogation.
8. Doing one's duty may or may not be an object of interest.
9. Immoral must be distinguished from non-moral and amoral.
10. A morally permissible act is not morally wrong; it could be morally right or morally indifferent.
11. If a person may do an act, it is not wrong to do or not to do it.
12. Are there degrees or rightness? No.
13. Are there degrees of wrongness? Yes, there are degrees of the seriousness of wrong acts.
14. Does it follow from the fact that an act is right that not doing it is wrong? It may be wrong, but it need not be.
15. Are there morally indifferent acts? Yes.
16. What conditions must be fulfilled for an act to be right or wrong? A person must distinguish between right and wrong, have a concept of right and wrong, and understand the meaning of right and wrong.
17. A moral person can distinguish between right and wrong, have a concept of right and wrong, and understand the meaning of right and wrong.

18. Ought implies can.
19. Are people's acts determined or do people act from a free will? This question has no clear answer.
20. Is choosing determined or does it have a cause? This question has no clear answer.
21. Can a person have a conflict of duties? A person can have a *prima facia* conflict of duties but not an actual conflict of duties.
22. What may be proper duties? They must be something a person can do or refrain from doing.
23. Judgments about beliefs, attitudes feeling, emotions and thoughts are not moral judgments.

Chart 26. Concepts about Duty

CHAPTER 16: CONVERSATION ABOUT 'RIGHTS'

Chocolate Factories

Since 'rights' has come to mean human rights in the 20th century, every major violation of people's rights has alarmed consumers, CEOs, and politicians. When Jane, CEO of a major chocolate factory in Atlanta, was tipped off that the evening news would report on the widespread use of child slave labor in the production of cocoa in several African countries, she knew she had a major problem. Consumers would be incensed, and politicians would threaten immediate action. As president of the American Chocolate Association and as the CEO of a chocolate producing company, much would be expected from her. What should she do?

Primarily, she thought the industry needs time — time to develop and promote a sound course of action. Through her leadership, they got four years of grace in which to develop and test a plan. They soon encountered several obstacles that defied any implementable solution. First, cocoa was produced on countless small farms across eastern Africa. Who could ensure production in these farms would never involve child slave labor? Second, the cocoa from these farms was collected by large foreign companies. How could you make sure that a shipload of cocoa did not include cocoa produced by child slave labor?

Politicians demanded a solution. What should Jane do — pursue a government human rights plan of action at potentially a huge loss of revenue for her company or manage to delay any action by the government for as long as possible?

CONFLICT OF INTEREST
Logical dissonance
Subsumption test
Cognitive dissonance
Principled thinking with empathy

Chart 27. Conflict of interest - Rights

Note how the Professor walked his student through the following process:

Conversation

Professor Small and his doctoral candidate, Bruno Epp, met a second time to discuss another scenario, Chocolate Factory. Here is their conversation.

Student: I have learned one thing from our discussions – there is no point in rushing into principled thinking when a person involved in the conflict does not see the point of it. First you must address the dissonance felt by the person.

Professor: Of course, there are several ways of dealing with the dissonance: ignore it by pretending that it will go away, deny it, find a just or fair way of resolving it.

Student: So where should we begin with this scenario?

Professor: Since this scenario is about rights, whose rights is it about?

Student: First and foremost, it is about the rights of children. They have been denied the right to go to school.

Professor: Is it only about the rights of children? What about the rights of the farmers producing cocoa so that they can feed and clothe their families and send their children to school? Do the owners of the large marketing companies have rights?

Student: Never thought of them. The marketing companies have been able to look after themselves buying from farmers who use child slave labor. Nobody seems too concerned about the farmers who use child slave labor; some of them may need to use low-cost labor to make ends meet.

Professor: So, we have the rights of at least three groups involved. Jane with her committee was left with the task of developing and implementing ways of eliminating the use of child slave labor which was used by small and large farms. She meant well when she accepted this challenge – she wanted a fair and just solution which meant eliminating the use of child slave labor by everyone, large and small farms.

Student: She soon discovered that there was no clear solution to the demand of consumers and politicians to eliminate child slave labor. There was no practical way of enforcing the elimination of child slave labor on countless small farms across eastern Africa. Nor was there a way of monitoring the large marketing companies to make sure that their shipments did not include some cocoa produced by child slave labor. Jane was obviously blocked in her plan. It simply would not work!

Professor: This conclusion created considerable dissonance for Jane. The only way she saw out of this uncomfortable dilemma was to wait for the governments to produce a solution. In the meantime, she decided to delay any government action so that her marketing company could continue to make lucrative purchases from the farmers. After all, she had tried her best to produce a just and fair solution and failed. She did not trust the government to succeed. She feared that the government would simply put farmers using child slave labor out of business which meant there would be less cocoa available to marketing companies, including her own company.

Student: Did that put Jane at ease about this problem?

Professor: How could it? She had to block the government constantly.

Student: So, what is left for her to do?

Professor: Remember what we tried in the previous scenario. We challenged Jane to share her feeling. In this case, ask Jane to look at her feelings. Ask her to apply the subsumption test.

Student: I remember the subsumption test. It explores the interrelationship of values. For example, what is the value of the life of a person relative to that of a dog? The former would be considered more valuable. But Jane has done that already by focusing on the problem of using child slave labor.

Professor: That is the good news – she understands the test. Let us invite her to explore the relationship between cooperating with the government to find a way of eliminating the use of child slave labor and the profitability of her company.

Student: Of course, we could ask, 'What should have top priority, eliminate child slave labor, or corporate profitability, if justice and fairness is the goal?'

Professor: We could also ask, 'What is more important, children should get an education, or children should help their parents with getting the necessary food, clothing, and shelter for the family?' Since Jane is committed to a just and fair resolution, I think inviting her to explore these issues might cause sufficient dissonance for her to focus on eliminating child slave labor. She probably is ready to apply principled thinking to the problem at hand.

Student: Once again, it took a long time to arrive at this point.

Professor: I would begin with John Rawls who offered an approach that companies could adopt. He defined justice as the tension between liberty and equality.

- Society should be structured so that the greatest possible amount of liberty is given to its members, limited only by the notion that the liberty of any one member shall not infringe upon that of any other member.
- Inequality should be allowed provided that 'the worst off will be better off than they might be under an equal distribution.

As companies continue using child slave labor, the children could not go to school which would be an infringement on the children's right to an education.

But the child slaves would be worse off because they could not get an education to get out of the poverty cycle of their parents. This is unfair to the children.

Upon reflection, the solution Jane settled for does not meet her goal of a just and fair resolution.

Student: She might also be intrigued by the question in the chart, 'For every right, does a person has a corresponding duty?' In other words, if she has a right to market cocoa, does she have a duty to the people who produced the cocoa? If so, how could she claim to pursue justice and fairness if she condoned the involvement of child slave labor in producing cocoa? On the other hand, she might be prepared to take a loss in her company if that leads to being just and fair to children.

Professor: Just one more thing. As Jane thought through the questions we raised, she might have developed a sense of empathy for the children used as slaves. It felt wrong – something had to be done to end it! To her surprise, she became quite willing to risk a loss of sales if that meant putting an end to child slave labor.

Student: By-the-way here is a copy of the main concepts about rights. Thank you, Professor, for your time to discuss this issue.

Concepts about Rights
1. What is meant by the statement, Paul has a right to X?
2. How are moral rights different from legal rights?
3. What does it mean to say that 'Paul has a claim to X'?
4. Does 'to be entitled' mean the same as 'to be warranted'?
5. Is the word 'legitimate' also used in a moral sense?
6. How does ownership differ from possession?
7. Does the word 'belong' mean the same as 'ownership'?
8. What does it mean to have a prerogative?
9. What are some of the diverse ways we use the word 'have'?
10. What are some diverse ways we use the word 'earn'?
11. Is it true that for every duty a person has a corresponding right?
12. Is it true that for every right a person has a corresponding duty?
13. Is it the case that to every right there is a correlative duty?
14. Is it the case that to every duty there is a correlative right?

Chart 28. Concepts about Rights.

Let us move on to another concept, motive, and see how it applies to resolving moral dilemmas. How does it relate to duty and rights? The plot thickens as we need to consider more categories in resolving moral dilemmas.

CHAPTER 17: CONVERSATION ABOUT MOTIVE

How did the professor and the doctoral student address "motive" in the scenario, *Toxic Emission*?

Toxic Emission

Betty is the quality control supervisor for AGInc, a thriving midsize plastics company which meets all the local toxin emission regulations. She knows of innovative technology which can reduce the current emission level to protect the fish in local rivers and lakes. This would save the local recreational and commercial fishing industry for years to come.

When Betty expressed her concern about the toxic emissions at a shareholder's meeting where the Press was allowed to attend, the shareholders reminded her that AGInc was in compliance with local toxic emission limits. Hence, there was no need for the innovative technology. Of course, the Press put a different spin on Betty's concern; it expressed alarm at the potential consequences of not reducing the toxic emissions. In fact, they suspected the motive of the company – preferred increased profits vs. installing expensive technology to reduce emissions beyond current local regulations.

Although Betty took issue with the Press for imputing that the company was driven by profits, she decided not to invest in new costly technology that might risk the profitability of the company. She argued that AGInc should delay acquiring the innovative technology till the government changes the toxic emission regulations. Why? Might she be motivated by the excessive cost of the innovative technology? Did she give any thought to potential benefits of installing the innovative technology to reduce emission levels?

Why are motives so important in making decisions?

CONFLICT OF INTEREST
Cultural dissonance
New cases test
Cognitive dissonance
Principled thinking with empathy

Chart 29. Conflict of interest – Motive

Note how the Professor walked his student through the following process:

Conversation

Student: I find it interesting and surprising how quickly Betty seems to back off from her apparent concern about the limits of the current regulations on toxic emissions in local rivers and lakes. Why did she back off when she had the media supporting her concern?

Professor: Good question. Why do you think she backed off?

Student: I suspect that she may have been uncomfortable with challenging her company to go beyond local emission restrictions. Where was her loyalty – to the company or to long term sustainability of her community? That no doubt created dissonance for her which she had to deal with or deny it hoping that the feeling will go away.

Professor: Betty does not seem interested in the support she got from the Press. In fact, she questions the appropriateness of the motive they ascribed to the company. She seems to ignore that the shareholders saw no need to make the expense of installing the innovative technology till the government changes the toxicity regulations even though she seemed to ask them to consider approving the installation.

Student: Betty seemed not to show any feelings – no sense of dissonance generated by the limits of the current technology to reduce toxicity nor a concern about following the advice of the shareholders.

How can you appeal to a person who shows no emotions to consider doing what is right?

Professor: That is an exceptionally good question! Presenting more facts does not necessarily persuade people to rethink their positions – facts do not tell you what the morally right thing is. For example, suppose the cost of the innovative technology is so expensive that it would bankrupt the company. Alternatives need to be explored till a solution is found that reduces the toxicity of the emissions without destroying the company. That would be the right thing to do. Simply delaying the use of the innovative technology would not be the right thing to do.

Student: So where do you start?

Professor: Let us get back to Festinger's moral values principle tests.

Student: ... which are role exchange test, new cases test, universal consequences test, and subsumption test. I assume they are used when people experience dissonance. But Betty did not seem to experience any. Which test would you use and why?

Professor: I would try the new cases test. In preparation for the shareholders' meeting, suppose Betty had collected some case studies on different toxic emission technologies. Suppose one technology had been in place for three years and another for six years. Both showed lower levels of toxicity. In both cases, the companies showed marginal levels of profitability in the first year of using their modern technologies but by the third year they had fully recovered. As for the fish in the local rivers and lakes, they were healthy and thriving. With those kinds of stories, Betty might have become somewhat emotionally involved. As soon as that happened, she might have felt a sense of dissonance. She might have been uncomfortable when the shareholders insisted on remaining with their current less efficient technology. The technology Betty had recommended was not the same as the ones used in the case studies, but it was constructed on the same scientific principles. Now the stage is set for Betty to engage in principled thinking as she attempted to convince the shareholders to purchase the innovative technology.

Student: WOW. That was a powerful argument - capable of generating the necessary dissonance for Betty to become emotionally involved. Now it was clear to her that she wanted to pursue justice; she felt a sense of empathy towards the people who enjoyed the use of the local rivers and lakes. In fact, the media might have been so impressed that they might have focused their stories on the merit of the modern technology instead of focussing on the company's motive.

Professor: To consolidate her new course of action with the shareholders, she had to rethink several assumptions. First, for an action to be morally right, it must be done also from a morally good motive. Her original decision to comply with whatever the shareholders wanted was not made from a morally good motive. Second, the act must be right. She thought it was right to save the local rivers and lakes from further pollution.

Student: That is a 180!

Professor: Betty must be careful when friends want to help her by reminding her that 'You ought to do whatever you believe you ought to do.' That is common advice suggesting that Betty would meet her obligations by doing what she believes is the right thing to do. But that is misleading because by saying 'she ought to do whatever she believes she ought to do' is saying that her action would be morally good if she did it and morally bad if she did not do it which refers to her motive. However, 'whatever you believe you ought to do' refers to her duty. So, what is Betty's friend referring to – her motive or her duty? Every effort should be made to avoid these kinds of confusing statements.

Student: What if Betty had made her decision from a good motive, like compassion?

Professor: That is not considered a morally good motive. How could Betty's decision be morally good if it were made from a good motive?

Student: Is morally bad simply the converse of morally good?

Professor: If that were the case, morally bad would mean 'the desire to do wrong for the sake of doing wrong.' But that is not the reason given by the shareholders to stay with the current toxic emission control technology. They simply reminded Betty that the technology they were using complied with current local regulations.

I could go on, but these are some of the parameters for the pursuit of justice with a caring attitude (empathy). For your convenience, I brought a comprehensive list of concepts about motive.

Concepts about Motive	Response
1. What conditions must be fulfilled for an act to be morally good?	The act must be right. The act must be done from a morally good motive.
2. What if a person does an act which is wrong, but he believes it to be right and he does it from a morally good motive?	The act is not morally good even though the person would be regarded as a morally good person.
3. What if a person does an act which is right, but he does not believe it to be right and his motives are not good?	The person would not be regarded as a morally good person.
4. What is a morally good motive?	- believe that the act is right. - desire to do what is right.
5. 'Wanting to do one's duty' must be distinguished from 'Wanting to do the right thing.'	
6. Cynics assume that people act only from self-interest.	
7. Morally good motives must be distinguished from good motives.	Good motives include compassion and love.
8. Moral virtues must be distinguished from non-moral virtues.	Moral virtues - propensity to do what is right from a morally good motive Non-moral virtues' – intellectual motive like wit.
9. Is 'morally bad' simply the converse of 'morally good'?	No. 'Morally bad' does not refer to the desire to do wrong for the sake of doing wrong.
10. What constitutes a morally terrible act?	An act which is done with indifference to do what is right.
11. A morally weak person must be distinguished from a morally bad person.	A morally weak person yields to temptation somewhat Frequently but is not considered a morally bad person.
12. What are naturally bad motives?	Hatred, revenge, jealousy, envy, greed, lust, malice.

13. The range of stages from morally good to moral bad include the following:	- principled reasoning - misguided action - moral blind spot - unscrupulous action - not being in one's right mind
14. What about the person who desires to do his duty but is careless?	His action is not morally good.
15. The word 'ought' includes two moral senses.	- 'Ought' can refer to the motive of a person. - 'Ought' can refer to a person's duty.

Chart 30: Concepts about Motive

CHAPTER 18: CONVERSATION ABOUT DESERT

How did the professor and the doctoral student address this scenario, *Dealing with staff performance?*

Dealing with staff performance

"A woman's place is in the home," chuckled Bill as he saw Sadie, racing back to her desk late. Not only had arriving late become a common occurrence, but she had also been seen leaving her desk early rather frequently. Coming in late was of particular concern to management because by arriving late, she missed several team meetings which were scheduled at the beginning of each day. In addition, Sadie had taken a leave of absence to for seniors of limited income as was the case with her father. In fact, Sadie had to take care of her elderly father. Suitable homes for seniors were at a premium and difficult to get especially work not only for herself but also for her father.

As the Department Manager at NEWTECHIC, Nancy, appreciated Sadie's work ethic and performance. At the same time, she was concerned about the undue stress imposed on Sadie's overworked colleagues due to her frequent lates after her prolonged absence. Several colleagues were undermining Sadie, thus creating even greater stress not only for Sadie but also for management.

"Is it time for Management to intervene? But how?" mused Nancy. "First, I will have to talk to Bill."

CONFLICT OF INTEREST
Cognitive dissonance?
[test]
Cognitive dissonance
Principled thinking with empathy

Chart 31. Conflict of interest - Desert

Note how the Professor walked his student through the following process:

Conversation

Student: Since I have been a student most of my life, I do not know much about dealing with staff performance. In the part time jobs I have had, I have not been impressed with how management has dealt with staffing issues.

Professor: Dealing with staff performance is one of the most challenging aspects of being a manager. Often it is not about performance as such but more about perception. As you alluded to in your comment about management, reviewing staff performance usually involves two views – the manager's view and the employee's view. You expressed your opinion as an employee. When management assumes that their view is correct and the employee's view is inaccurate, tensions rise. Consequently, management and employees can experience different forms of dissonance. For example, when management and an employee grew up in vastly unfamiliar cultures, they may view women at work very differently.

Student: If Nancy, the manager, had had experience in the past with staff members who frequently took time off without cause, she might have been quick to assess any late comers or employees taking time off.

Maybe the performance criteria were never presented clearly in writing and consequently subject to more than one interpretation. That would be management's responsibility. Sometimes the company's Code of Ethics does not include performance criteria for all employees.

Professor: Agreed. All these situations could create a feeling of unease or dissonance between management and employees. The challenge is how could management deal with the dissonance before conducting any form of performance assessment. Without first addressing the dissonance, an employee probably does not trust management to make a fair assessment of her performance.

Student: How can management overcome the distrust, especially if it is a long-standing feeling?

Professor: Be careful not to jump to that conclusion too quickly. When the dissonance becomes personal, it is difficult to engage in any talk about an issue at hand. For example, any conversation about what Bill deserved, words of disapproval or some form of punishment, for making the rude comment to Sadie, would simply be regarded as an unfair judgement. Sadie had it coming, Bill might argue.

Student: That sounds like a stand-off. Is that the end of it? Surely Bill must be held accountable for what he did to Sadie.

Professor: Let us see. What emotions are involved? Might Bill feel singled out for the remark he made about Sadie? Does that annoy him? Does Nancy display a feeling of impatience with Bill's repeat shots at Sadie? Have these emotions lingered for some time? Given these mutually negative emotions, what is the point of discussing what Bill deserves?

Nancy must also keep in mind that punishment can be given or withheld at will, but disapprovals are not wilful.[30] An attitude of approval or disapproval is a psychological state; one either has it or does not have it. Does that make 'giving disapproval' inadequate for Bill's action?

Student: Nancy must also be sensitive to the question, does a person deserve punishment for willing to commit a harmful act but not doing it? What if Bill acknowledged what he said to Saddie, but insisted that he did not actually mean to hurt her, would he have deserved disapproval or some form of punishment?

Professor: ... to which I would add, some people would argue that he deserved some form of punishment because he acted in a manner designed to inflict harm on other people. For example, conspiracy is not just a matter of being willing to do wrong; it includes an act of planning and organizing steps to inflict harm on other people. Planning and organizing deliberate harm are part of the process of executing the harmful act. Does a person who acts with intent to harm someone deserve some form of punishment? Does that apply to Bill?

As an aside, I discovered an interesting connection between *desert* and *motives*. I have described different situations where a person might deserve approval for wanting to do what is the right thing to do (motive) and disapproval for being indifferent about doing the right thing (deserve). This shows that judgments about desert consider the motives of the person as well as what he deserves. For example, what motivated Bill to say to Saddie what he did? What did he deserve for saying it?

Student: We have side-tracked. I fail to see how the questions about punishment and reward are relevant in our discussion about what Nancy should do with Bill when there is an emotional deadlock between Nancy and Bill. Neither of them seems to be prepared to share an empathic understanding with each other – and Sadie. Will a third party have to step in?

Professor: Probably. That person will have to return to the beginning and address the emotional standoff before any of the questions that were raised should be addressed. All I can say for now, let us hope for the best!

Here is my chart on the concepts related to desert.

Concepts about Desert	Responses
1. Standard form for desert: Z deserves X on account of Y.	'Z' is the moral agent 'X' is an object of interest or disinterest 'Y' provides the reasons for allocating an object of interest or inflicting an object of disinterest.
2. Objects of disinterest	acts of disapproval or punishment.
3. Objects of interest	acts of approval or reward.
4. Awards	can be given or withheld at will.
5. Approvals and disapprovals	psychological states of being that are not wilful.
6. Acts of disapproval include the following:	a frown, words of disappointment, mild censure, or mild criticism.
7. Acts of approval include the following:	a smile, words of praise, a nod, slap on the back.
8. For what does a person deserve approval?	doing one's duty, and for doing a morally good act from a morally good motive.

9. For what does a person deserve a reward?	performing a challenging task or going beyond the call of duty – called an act of supererogation.
10. Normally, a person is not rewarded for:	- morally good action - morally good motive - not doing something wrong - being a moral agent - doing one's duty
11. A person deserves disapproval for:	- willingly doing a wrong act - being a morally bad person
12. On account of what does a person deserve punishment?	committing a morally wrong act with indifference as to the wrongness of the act.
13. Do all bad acts deserve the same degree of punishment?	The punishment should be in proportion to the seriousness of the wrong act.
14. Does a person deserve punishment for willing to do wrong?	deserves some form of disapproval.
15. What if a person planned to commit a wrong act but failed to execute it?	deserves some form of punishment.
16. Does a person deserve punishment for failure to do his duty?	Possibly, though sometimes an expression of disapproval may be appropriate.

Chart 32. Concepts about Desert

As you can see, addressing issues of desert in addition to duty, rights, and motive, adds to the complexity of resolving moral dilemmas. My challenge is to show how that can and must be done to resolve moral dilemmas in a fair and just way.

First, I must address the issue of just, the final category necessary for resolving moral dilemmas.

CHAPTER 19. CONVERSATION ABOUT JUST

How did professor Small and the doctoral student, Bruno Epp, address the scenario, *I Promised*, which I mentioned earlier illustrates overkill in applying principled thinking?

I Promised

As you no doubt have experienced many times, whenever you are confronted with right and wrong situations, your attention is quickly drawn to several concerns. It happened to me many times. For example, as a dad of a 16-year-old daughter and the CEO of a software company, KnowledgeBuilder Software Inc., I remember rescheduling a management meeting so that I could watch my daughter play in her final basketball playoff game.

Since there was tension in my team about me taking time off to see my daughter play in her team's final game, I decided to apply principled thinking to my decision to show them the wisdom of my decision. Here is how I recall my thinking process.

I asked myself, 'Do I have a primary duty to my company or my daughter? Do I honor my promise to my daughter or concentrate on my obligation to lead and protect my company?'

When challenged about my decision, I was protective of both, my rights as a parent and my shareholder's rights. Questions came to mind about rights, 'When is the right time to do one or the other? Is this the time to see my daughter play in her final playoff game?'

I imputed a questionable motive to my team leader, Peter, who insisted that my first obligation always should be to my company, but I did not acknowledge my own motive for wanting to see my daughter win in her team's playoff game. I engaged in defensive action done unconsciously – like being dismissive about what Peter had to say.

On the other hand, I felt my HR team leader, Jane, deserved approval for supporting my decision to see my daughter's final game.

Unfortunately, I was quick to judge Peter unfairly for criticizing my decision to take time out for my daughter's game.

As I reflected on the game, I thoroughly enjoyed recalling my daughter score the winning point.

Note how Professor Small and the student walked each other through the following process:

CONFLICT OF INTEREST
Cognitive dissonance?
[test]
Cognitive dissonance
Principled thinking with empathy

Chart 33. Conflict of interest - Just

Conversation

Student: This story fascinates me.

Professor Small: So, what is the tension or dissonance? Is there any since all the right questions were asked? If so, has any dissonance been resolved?

Student: Why ask those irrelevant questions – your daughter's team won! I am sure that is what you were hoping for.

Professor Small: Of course, that is what I was hoping for. But this story is more than about who won the game. It is about how I arrived at my decision and how I related to my colleagues about it.

Student: Pardon me, I got carried away about who won the game, especially about your daughter scoring the winning goal. Seriously, you felt the story was mostly about your primary duty – lead your company or watch your daughter play in the finals.

Professor Small: Some of my team leaders thought so, but not I. My tension related to Peter's and Jane's response to my decision. I was dismissive towards Peter for not supporting my decision and showed approval for Jane's support. I went one step further towards Peter – I judged Peter unfairly for criticizing my decision. That is no way to build a team; that can create tension, in fact, dissonance in a company. I did not resolve that tension but played right into it.

Student: You are too critical about yourself. I agree with you that Peter was wrong, and Jane was right.

Professor Small: That is not the point; it is the way I handled the disagreement. Why did I judge Peter and show my approval for Jane? I realize I will have to make amends.

I felt the dissonance I had created but had difficulty with what to do about it. If I chose to discuss this dilemma with a colleague on staff, would it be useful to discuss it using Festinger's moral values principle tests – role exchange test, universal consequences test, subsumption test, new cases test? The most likely test could be universal consequences by raising the question, 'What might be the consequence of ignoring the way I treated Peter? There are several possibilities: a) there may be none, b) the trust between Peter and myself may be lost to the point that Peter can no longer serve as a team leader, c) negative rumors about me favoring Jane.

Student: Why don't you go back to the beginning like you did when we discussed previous scenarios? Y insisted on addressing the emotions of the parties involved. Specifically, you invited people involved to consider the thoughts and feelings of the parties affected. In other words, you invited them to feel empathetic. Why not try it in this new case?

Professor Small: On the other hand, I could go straight to a cognitive resolution of the dissonance since I had acknowledged the dissonance and a desire to resolve the problem that generated it. I expressed sincere empathy for Peter for imputing a motive. Since I asked the kinds of questions that could lead to a just and fair resolution, it is reasonable to conclude that I was in search of a fair and just resolution of the dilemma?

Student: Professor, it probably is not enough for you to express empathy. First, you must address the relationship with Peter and yourself.

Professor Small: You are right. I will work on it. At the same time, I must remember

- all just acts are right but
- not all right acts are just but

It was right for me to take a position different from Peter's point of view, but it was not just for me to criticize Peter for expressing a different view. For an action to be just, it must meet two conditions – to act must be right and it must be done for a morally good motive. I did not act from a morally good motive when I criticized Peter for disagreeing with me. I met only the first condition.

Student: There are a few other issues you should keep in mind to make a just decision. For example, on what basis is a distribution just or unjust?

Professor Small: It depends on how the distribution affects the interests of the recipients relative to each other. Peter's trust in me was broken; approval of Jane's response was reinforced.

Student: A third issue to consider is: A distribution made with impartiality may be just or unjust. In some cases, it may be wrong not to discriminate. I had to discriminate between Peter and Jane because Peter's disagreement with me was wrong and Janes's approval was right. But the discrimination need not include criticizing Peter for disagreeing with me.

Professor Small: I need to remind myself about an issue that is disturbing to me – I fail to be mindful of the importance and power of emotional intelligence. Justice without empathy is lacking the positive emotional dimension (empathy) prompted by emotional intelligence.

Thank you, Bruno, for reminding me of the crucial importance of pursuing empathy as a prior condition for engaging in principled thinking in pursuit of justice.

By the way, here is a list of the concepts about justice.

Concepts about Justice	
1. Justice refers to the distribution objects of interest or disinterest.	
2. Justice is administered by people who exercise authority	
3. 'Fair' may be used in the objective and subjective sense	
4. What is the relationship between right acts and just acts?	- Not all right acts are just but all just acts are right - Not all wrong acts are unjust, but all unjust acts are wrong
5. On what basis is a distribution just or unjust?	The basis is how the distribution affects the interests of the recipients relative to each other.
6. Are these factors sufficient to determine whether an act is just? - the recipient's desert - its utility - the needs of the recipient - the rights of the recipient - the motive of the distrubutor	 no no no no no
7. Impartiality refers to the distributor.	
8. A just act is an act of impartiality.	
9. The issue of justice includes:	- A distributor - A distribution of objects of interest or disinterest - A recipient
10. For a person to be impartial he must favor one recipient over the other based on sound principles or reasons.	
11. A distribution which is made with impartiality may be just or unjust.	Impartiality does not ensure that an act is just.
12. It may be wrong in some cases not to discriminate.	A just distribution may require discrimination in some cases
13. For a distribution to be just, the distributor must meet the following conditions:	- have the right to make the distribution - have a duty to make the distribution - be a moral person
14. Is it possible for a just act ever to be wrong?	No

15. Is it possible for a person to deserve punishment and yet for it not to be just for someone to punish that person?	Yes
16. What is retribution?	Retribution is an act of revenge or harming someone in retaliation
17. What is retributive justice?	It is the just allocation of object of disinterest.
18. How is it possible for the allocation of an object of disinterest to be an act of impartiality?	To say that a distributor is impartial is to say that the distributor does not favor one recipient over others without sound principles or reasons.
19. How can the allocation of an object of interest or disinterest to one individual be just?	It can be just if the distributor would decide to make the same distribution of objects of interest or disinterest for all persons in similar situations.
20. What is involved in pursuing of justice?	- Act from a desire to do one's duty - Recognize a person's rights - Act from a morally good motive - Giving people what they deserve - Act with impartiality in pursuit of justice.

Chart 34: Concepts about Just

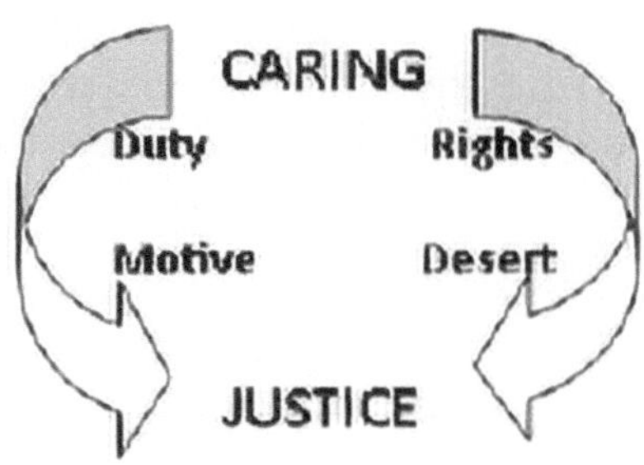

PART V. LEARNING ACTIVITIES

I have emphasized repeatedly that 'principled thinking' does not necessarily lead to moral action. Emotional intelligence is needed to deal with the emotional conflict and to generate the empathy to pursue justice. That is why all employers and employees need to be committed and able to experience a sense of fellow feeling as they exercise principled thinking to resolve conflicts in pursuit of justice. Students in business college should be introduced not only to code of ethics and the role of HR but also experience a sense of fellow feeling before they exercise principled thinking.

Whenever conflicts need to be resolved, the emotions must be dealt with first. We will see that it applies in all scenarios and conversations. When that happens, people may be willing to apply principle thinking which is referred to as slow and deliberate thinking. Since this process involves many different concepts and ideas, the learning activities address as many as possible. Since most of the time, conflicts need to be resolved immediately, intuition must and is used. Crisis situations may require any combination of the concepts involving duty (Chart 16), rights (Chart 18), motive (Chart 20), desert (Chart 22), and just (Chart 23) to arrive at just and fair decisions. Exercising principled thinking when one does not face immanent crisis can prepare oneself for crisis moments. Hence, the three sets of learning are included in this book which focus on principled thinking. In short, DNSRO (Do not shut reason out!).

For courses, programs, and learning materials on emotional intelligence as it applies to resolving the emotions generated by conflict in the workplace, google 'training sessions on emotional intelligence'[60], one of many online sources and learning activities.

Learning Activities provide refresher workshops for students, employers, and employees to enrich their emotional intelligence, resolve dissonance, and exercise principled thinking, to lead to justice or fairness.

The first set of Learning Activities, which focuses on conflicts that occur in the workplace, are built around scenarios I created based on reading a variety of scenarios and case studies. In these activities, users are asked to respond to the questions: How might principled thinking grounded in empathy lead to justice?

The second set of learning activities, which are built to address the challenges generated by climate change, are based on extensive readings about climate change. Why is this topic highlighted for companies? It probably is the single most urgent challenge facing everyone today. Massive capital will be needed to create solutions that are scalable. These conversations address the question: How can companies, in cooperation with government, mitigate or reverse climate change?

The third set of learning activities are built on the Code Moments created by Robert Chesnut in INTENTIONAL INTEGRITY[61]. I show how Chesnut's focus on customized Code of Ethics and my emphasis on principled thinking grounded in empathy can and should complement each other. The main question is: Can Chesnut's proposed Code of Ethics coupled with principled thinking grounded in empathy offer 'justice for all'?

I respond to every scenario/conversation.

First, let us go to the scenarios in Learning Activity A.

LEARNING ACTIVITY A:
COMPANY CONFLICTS OF INTEREST

Respond to each scenario and read My Response to the 'To do' questions. Take issue with my responses if you disagree with them. Give sound reasons where you agree or disagree. The following scenarios are created for Activity A.

Activity A1: Scenario – Allow low-cost generics of Zerit
Activity A2: Scenario – Industrial case study
Activity A3: Scenario – Palm oil policy
Activity A4: Scenario – Scene of an accident
Activity A5: Scenario – Company Shares
Activity A6: Scenario – Psychological Illness
Activity A7: Scenario – Improper Accounting

Activity A1: Scenario - Allow a low-cost generic Zerit

HIV/AIDS has ravaged the world, rich and poor alike. The only difference is wealthy people can afford Zerit as a treatment for people with HIV/AIDS; the poor cannot.

Yale University developed Zerit[62] and formed a partnership with BMS to market the product. This partnership was a win-win-win situation for Yale, BMS and the wealthy. The poor in places like South Africa were left to die.

Doctors Without Borders (DWB) appealed to Yale and BMS to provide a low-cost generic Zerit for poor countries but they would have none of it. Yale quickly realized that they could not afford the negative publicity, so they acknowledged the human need for a low-cost generic Zerit. This had the appearance for Yale as a humane gesture. Was it?

What does Yale deserve for having formed a partnership with a for-profit company which priced Zerit out of reach for millions suffering from HIV/AIDS. Does it deserve approval for lowering the price after widespread protests? But approval is a state of being that is not wilful. One either has it or does not. Is that a sufficient response to someone who is willing to do a wrong act? If punishment is appropriate, what form should it take? Did Yale enter the partnership knowing that they committed a wrong act? Did they commit a wrong act with indifference as to the wrongness of the act? Do they deserve some form of punishment?

Should universities like Yale enter a partnership with a for-profit company to support innovative research projects? Might it change a university's community-based mission?

To do

1. How might Yale initiate empathy? Consider the following:
   - Emotional intelligence
   - Dissonance
   - Moral values principle tests
2. How might Yale exercise principled thinking to grant people what they deserve.

3. Respond to these issues in the context of the
    scenario above:

    - Does Yale deserve approval or punishment? Explain.
    - Does Yale deserve punishment for willing to do wrong?
    - What if Yale planned to do wrong but failed to
      execute it?

My response to Activity A1: Allow a low-cost generic Zerit

1.   How might Yale proceed with empathy?[63]

- **Emotional intelligence**. Emotional intelligence is missing in this story because the people who made the decision to form a partnership are hidden behind the institution – Yale University. Did the President of Yale with his Board of Governors show some empathy when they reduced the price of Zerit under the pressure of intense protests? That's doubtful.

  There is no indication that the Yale administrators displayed any ability to understand their own emotional drives – they simply responded to the protests.

  What needs to happen for Yale to proceed with empathy? People at Yale could practice meditation concentrating on one or two specific goals. For example, they could focus on understanding the perspective of someone who may have a different view. This practice should include keeping a log on meeting the goal. This is only one example; there are many more options.

- **Dissonance**. A more thorough understanding of emotional intelligence could enable Yale administrators to recognize the implications of forming an alliance with a for-profit company which demanded a high price for Zerit. That could have created dissonance[64] for Yale. Yale seemed to justify the partnership because the increased revenue supported much-needed funding for research. Emotional intelligence could have prompted Yale to insist on lower prices for Zerit without the protests. That would have reduced the uncomfortable feeling of dissonance.

- **Moral values principle tests**[65]. Being sensitive to dissonance could drive Yale administrators to explore moral value principle tests to resolve the dissonance. Leon Festinger identified four: new cases test, role exchange test, subsumption test and universal consequences test. Had Yale administrators applied the universal consequences test, they might have realized the consequences of unaffordable prices for Zerit long before people protested demanding reduced prices.

They could have realized that millions around the world would not be able to purchase Zerit. Lowering the price would have been a true humane gesture – it would have shown that Yale administrators cared.

2.   How might Yale exercise principled thinking[66] to grant people what they deserve?

First, Yale administrators would have to be driven by a desire to do their duty because it is the right thing to do. They would want to make Zerit available to as many people who need it which means that they would have to insist that a version of Zerit would have to be affordable to the poor. Second, they would have to honor people's right to recovery by making Zerit accessible to all. Third, they would have to do their duty if it is the right thing to do. Fourth, these conditions add up to granting people what they deserve. Finally, they would have to act with impartiality - not driven by their own wishes or desires.

In this scenario, the focus should be on 'deserve' because the stakes were extremely high for the poor who could not afford Zerit. They deserve to have access to Zerit.

3.   Respond to these issues in the context of the scenario above:

-   **Does Yale deserve[67] approval or punishment?** Explain. Approval is a state of being that is not wilful. One either has it or does not. Punishment is for someone who is willing to do a wrong act. Since Yale willingly entered a marketing arrangement with a for-profit company, they were willing to do wrong to millions of poor people who could not afford the high price for Zerit. Yale deserves some form of punishment.

-   **Does Yale deserve punishment for willing to do wrong?[68]**
Yes, for the reason I offered above. They were willing to price Zerit so high that many people of limited means could not afford it and would likely die of HIV.

- **What if Yale planned to do wrong but failed to execute it?**[69]
  Suppose Yale tried to form a partnership with a for-profit company which sold Zerit for a high price but failed to conclude the partnership. A penalty would be in order because they attempted to enter into an agreement with a for-profit company which would have made Zerit unaffordable for millions of poor people. They planned to do wrong but failed.

Activity A2: Scenario - Industrial Case Study

Three former employees of an offshore manufacturing company[70], PRInc, distributed an email online claiming that there were excessive restrictions on employees' behavior in PRInc. These included the need to obtain permission before getting a drink or a snack, and strict limitations on washroom breaks. While the restrictions applied strictly to all frontline employees, they were not applied to managers.

The email also claimed that the employees had to pay compensation for any product that was stolen or went missing, even though the losses were insured. Employees had to clock out after eight hours but had to continue to work a few more hours. This created a false electronic record.

Overall, they accused the company of lacking systematic and humane management and complained that their rights and dignity were violated. The email aroused widespread critical reaction not only from PRInc employees but also from workers around the world.

To do:

1. How might PRInc proceed with empathy?
   - Emotional intelligence
   - Dissonance
   - Moral values principle tests
2. How might PRInc exercise principled thinking by acknowledging a person's rights?
3. Respond to these issues in the context of the scenario above:
   - How does ownership differ from possession?
   - What does it mean to have a prerogative?
   - Is it true that for every duty a person has a corresponding right?
   - Is it true that for every duty there is a correlative right?

My response to Activity A2: Industrial case study

1. **How might PRInc proceed with empathy?**[71]

   - **Emotional intelligence.**
   Management at PRInc needs to develop a sense of emotional intelligence to become sensitized to the wrong conditions in their workplace. For example, do they notice how they interfere with routine activities such as being required to obtain permission to get a drink of water or working within strict limitations on washroom time? One of the first steps to becoming empathic is to observe the daily life of employees. You will notice quickly what pleases employees and increases productivity and what annoys them and potentially reduces productivity. Place a reminder in your daily planner to observe – identify specific infractions and keep a record of your observations. That is a first step PRInc needs to take given the current conditions in the workplace. The observations might generate a sense of empathy for employees who must work in an intrusive environment.

   - **Dissonance.**
   One of the first results of observing the conditions in the workplace might be that management at PRInc could feel a considerable disconnect or dissonance[72] between management's perception of the workplace and what they were observing. That feeling of dissonance needs to be changed into an urgent desire to support a fair and just working environment which leads to the next step.

Moral values principle tests

One or more of the moral values principle tests identified by Festinger could help management make the transition to pursuing a fair and just workplace environment.[73] One of the obvious tests would be the universal consequences test. As management monitors what they observe, they might ask questions like, 'What might be the logical consequences of continuing current practice?' How might employees respond to fair and just working conditions where the same regulations apply to employees and management?

1. **How might PRInc exercise principled thinking[74] by respecting a person's rights?**
    If management of PRInc has a right to take a drink without requesting permission, why not respect the same right for employees? If PRInc has a right to take a washroom break as needed, why not employees? Responses to these questions might challenge management to honor the rights employees should be allowed to exercise.

2. **Respond to these issues in the context of the scenario above:**

  - **How does ownership differ from possession?[75]**
    Ownership refers to the right to use, enjoy, and dispose of something. Possession refers to someone who has the actual power to use, enjoy, or dispose of something including abstract concepts like controlling the lives of people. PRInc management had the actual power to enforce specific activities of employees. Did they have a right to treat their employees like they did? According to human rights acts, they did not have that right.

  - **What does it mean to have a prerogative?[76]**
    Prerogative refers to a right or privilege exclusive to a particular individual or class. In PRInc management exercised exclusive authority to determine the working conditions in their workplace. That was their prerogative. When management is committed to a fair and just working environment, they would collaborate with their employees on issues like working conditions.

  - **Is it true that for every duty a person has a corresponding right?[77]**
    Not necessarily. Employees at PRInc have an obligation to do their job (it's their duty). It is not clear what correlative rights they might have. Any rights would have to be established on some other ground such as a human rights act.

- **Is it true that for every duty there is a
correlative right?**[78]
It is not clear that for every duty there is a correlative
relationship with rights. Just because PRInc gave you
a job does not necessarily entitle you to certain rights
such as determining your working conditions.

Activity A3: Scenario - Palm Oil Policy

"NO DEFORESTATION, NO PEAT, NO EXPLOITATION!" (NDPE)[79]

That sounded like a great policy in 2014. Government, NGOs, and the largest companies in the Palm oil industry in Indonesia agreed to it. In 2015, Indonesia had the worst fire season in nearly two decades. Why? The government reversed its position on the pledge to honor NDPE and encouraged companies to do the same.

This reversal created a fundamental problem for Wilmar, the largest trader in Palm oil in the world. The Pledge and the government's reversal on NDPE created conflicting emotions (dissonance) for Wilmar. Should Wilmar keep its Pledge? If so, how could it police its suppliers to cooperate? What could it do with violators? How could it operate with no government support and ramped corruption? These questions defied easy answers.

What is the just thing to do for Wilmar? Is justice with empathy possible? Towards whom should Wilmar express empathy? Why?

To do

1. How might Wilmar proceed with empathy?
- Emotional intelligence
- Dissonance
- Moral values principle tests
2. How might Wilmar exercise principled thinking through acts of impartiality in pursuit of justice?
3. Respond to the following issues in the context of the scenario above:
- What is the relationship between rights act and just acts?
- On what basis is a distribution just or unjust?
- How can a person be impartial?
- What is retribution? How is it different from retributive justice?

My response to Activity A3: Palm Oil Policy

1. **How might Wilmar proceed with empathy?**[80]

    -   **Emotional intelligence.** Wilmar's heart was in the right place – no exploitation. He displayed an elevated level of emotional intelligence in his commitment to keep the pledge because it was the just thing to do. He also showed an elevated level of empathy when he committed his company to stop exploiting the poor farmers who produced the olive oil.

    -   **Dissonance.** However, Wilmar's commitment to keep the pledge created an elevated level of dissonance[81] which reflected on how to implement the pledge. He was highly motivated to keep the pledge even though the government reversed its pledge. Given his pledge to do the right thing, the dissonance he experienced prompted him to search for moral values principle tests which might provide the support he needed to do the just and fair thing.

    -   **Moral values principle tests**[82]
        He had four to choose from: new cases test, role exchange test, subsumption test, and universal consequences test. Suppose he decided to prioritize the values of 'keeping his pledge' vs 'abandoning the pledge' to support NDPE by applying the subsumption test. In other words, which value reflects the pursuit of justice – destroying the forests and peat land, and exploiting the poor farmers, or keep the pledge for NDPE? He was convinced that the latter must be subsumed under the former if justice is to be done. This reinforced his decision to keep his pledge for NDPE.

2. How might Wilmar exercise principled thinking through acts of impartiality in pursuit of justice?
    To exercise principled thinking in pursuit of justice involves a desire to do one's duty if it is the right thing to do, recognizing person's rights, act from a morally good motive, give people what they deserve, and act with impartiality in pursuit of justice. Did Wilmar address these conditions? Yes. He wanted to do his duty if it is the right thing to do. Second, in the pledge

he recognized the farmer's rights not to be exploited. Third, he acted from a morally good motive (protect the environment and the poor farmers). Fourth, through the pledge he was determined to grant poor farmers what they deserved. Fifth, he was committed to act with impartiality in pursuit of justice. Maintaining the pledge was an act of impartiality because it would be difficult to do so after the government abandoned the pledge and encouraged companies to abandon it as well.

3. **Respond to the following issues in the context of the scenario above:**

-   **What is the relationship between right act and just acts?[83]**
    Not all right acts are just but all just acts are right. Companies could be right to follow the government's advice but that may not be just. When Wilmar remained committed to the pledge, he did what is just (acted with empathy); it was also the right thing to do.

-   **On what basis is a distribution just or unjust?[84]**
    Whether a distribution is just depends on a) the duty of the distributor, b) the rights of the recipient, c) the motive of the distributor, and d) what the recipient deserves. Wilmar had a duty to do the just thing. The farmers (recipients) had a right not to be exploited. Wilmar was motivated to do the right thing. Wilmar made a pledge to protect the environment. The farmers got what they deserved (protection from exploitation).

-   **What is retribution? How is it different from retributive justice?[85]**
    Retribution refers to acts of taking revenge in retaliation for harm done by someone else.
    Retributive justice refers to the just allocation of objects of disinterest.
    Wilmar was not looking for revenge from the government for reversing its position on NDPE. He was not even looking for retributive justice – a just sentence for violators. It is not clear who are the violators since the government encouraged companies

to break the pledge. He was deliberating on how he could keep the pledge when the government reversed its commitment to the pledge.

<u>Activity A4: Scenario - Scene of an Accident</u>

"SHOOT ME! SHOOT ME," screamed the driver.[86]

Ed, the driver, had just struck a tree as he lost control of his flatbed loaded with drums of explosives. Since some of the drums were torn from their mooring and hit the cab, they exploded and burst into a ball of flames engulfing the cab, including the driver. Writhing in pain, Ed pleaded with the RCMP Officer on the scene to end his painful death by shooting him.

The Officer, realizing that she could not come close to the burning truck to remove the driver, spontaneously withdrew her revolver from its holster but just to quicky return it. As Ed continued his plea, the Officer again drew her revolver and again returned it. The Officer was caught in a dilemma of choosing between two opposite values: taking the life of a person OR ending the pain of being burnt alive. Both options were unacceptable to her.

In a matter of seconds, she recalled a third option: She removed the fire extinguisher from her RCMP cruiser, not to douse the raging flame, but to spray Ed's face which made him instantly unconscious. Seconds latter, the cab exploded killing Ed.

To do:

1. How might the officer proceed with empathy?
   - Emotional intelligence
   - Dissonance
   - Moral values principle tests
2. How might the RCMP Officer exercise principled thinking by acting from a morally good motive?
3. **Respond to the following issues in the context of the scenario above:**
   - What conditions must be fulfilled for an act to be morally good?
   - How are morally good motives distinguished from good motives?
   - Is morally bad simply the converse of morally good?
   - What constitutes a morally terrible act?
   - What are naturally bad motives?

My response to Activity A4: Scene of an accident

1. **How might the RCMP Officer proceed with empathy?**[87]

- **Emotional intelligence.**
  The Officer had a confident sense of self awareness and regulation. On first impulse, she drew her gun twice and each time returned it to its halter. Seconds later she recalled a solution which she had learned years ago. She took the fire extinguisher from her car and sprayed the truck driver's face which made him instantly unconscious. Shortly after, the truck cab exploded killing the driver.
  The Officer understood the connection between her emotions and her behavior. Her intuition told her that shooting the truck driver was wrong; her training helped her to identify a better solution to respond to the trucker's plea.

- **Dissonance.** The dissonance[88] the Officer felt seeing the trucker in flames prompted a series of quick actions. Initially her impulse was to do what the trucker asked her to do which heightened her dissonance because she knew it was wrong to kill a person. She wanted to do what is right. The dissonance was resolved, after she recalled from her past training, what to do and what not to do in a crisis like this.

- **Moral values principle tests.**[89] The Officer did not have time to explore what was the morally right thing to do. She did not have time to explore (think through) alternative moral value principle tests. So, she relied on her gut feeling and her training to arrive at an alternative solution to shooting the truck driver which she knew intuitively was wrong.

2. **How might the RCMP Officer exercise principled thinking by acting from a morally good motive?**[90]
  The Officer did not have time to exercise principled thinking. She acted from a moral good motive because she was committed to the pursuit of justice. Her gut feeling told her that taking the life of a person is wrong.

3. **Respond to the following issues in the context of the scenario above:**

- **What conditions must be fulfilled for an act to be morally good?**[91]
  The person must be capable of distinguishing right from wrong, have a concept of right and wrong, and understand the meaning of right and wrong. The Officer distinguished right from wrong – she knew it was wrong to take the life of a person, but it was not wrong to alleviate pain. That's how she showed that she had a concept of right and wrong. She also understood the meaning of right and wrong – she recognized that although it might have been good for the truck driver to be relieved from the agony of being burnt alive by shooting him, it was the wrong to take his life.

- **Morally good motives must be distinguished from good motives.**[92]
  Acting from a morally good motive refers to a commitment to justice or fairness. Good motive refers to kindness, caring, love, etc. The Officer did not want to act only from a good motive – instantly relieving the truck driver of his pain as he requested. She wanted to act from a morally good motive. That's why she could not shoot the trucker. Killing a person is the wrong thing to do. She recalled an alternative which would not kill the driver but make him unconscious.

- **Is morally bad simply the converse of morally good?**[93]
  This is a critical question. Suppose morally bad is simply the converse of morally good. If that were so, the Officer could have concluded that there is nothing she should do after she concluded that it is morally bad to shoot to kill a person. Remember morally good refers to action taken with a desire to do what's right. If morally bad action is done because the person has a desire to do wrong, that would be the converse of morally good.

  However, when the Officer pulled her gun from the halter, did she intend to shoot the truck driver with the aim of doing wrong for the sake of doing wrong? Or was she responding to the trucker's plea to end his misery? No doubt she responded to the latter as is apparent from the action she took – spray the trucker's face to make him instantly unconscious.

- **What constitutes a morally bad act?**[94]
A morally bad act is done with indifference as to whether the act is wrong. The officer was not indifferent to doing morally bad acts. That is why she stopped herself twice from shooting the trucker and recalled a morally good act to address the dissonance she experienced as the trucker pleaded to be shot to relieve his pain.

- **What are naturally bad motives?**[95]
Naturally bad motives include hatred, revenge, jealousy, envy, greed, lust, and malice. The Officer displayed none of these motives nor is there any reason she might feel that way about the trucker.

Activity A5: Scenario – Company shares

"I won't let them get away with it. That is highway robbery!" exclaimed Jake, the oldest of Len's four children. Len had been CEO of TOPInc[96] till he died suddenly of a heart attack a month ago. The company had been extraordinarily successful in the Texas oil patch since they had drilled the first well seven years ago. The shareholders had enjoyed lucrative dividends for the past five years and were looking forward to many more. Collectively, six minor shareholders owned 20% and Len owned 80%.

What will happen now that Len is gone? The company's Shareholder's Agreement states clearly that when a shareholder dies, that person's shares are assigned to the remaining shareholders. What is more, the remaining shareholders all had years of experience in the Texas oil industry. Presumably, they could continue to operate TOPInc successfully.

Len's family felt that their father's shares should remain in the family as part of the family estate. Jake felt he had to defend the family's rights. Len's shares were worth millions provided that the company could weather the loss not only of its CEO but also of its major shareholder. 'How best to move forward' pondered the remaining shareholders as they negotiated a settlement with the family. The dispute about who owns Len's rights must be resolved quickly before the company declines in value due to lack of leadership.

To Do:

1.   How might the shareholders proceed with empathy?
   - Emotional intelligence
   - Dissonance
   - Moral values principle tests
2.   How might the shareholders exercise principled thinking by acting from a desire to do one's duty?
3.   Respond to the following issues in the context of the scenario above:
   - A duty is the right thing to do independent of a person's motive or interest.
   - One can put someone under an obligation but not under a duty.

- A person is not obligated to do every morally right act.
- Going beyond the call of duty is called an act of supererogation.
- Doing one's duty may or may not be an object of interest.

My response to Activity A5: TOPInc

1. **How might the shareholders proceed with empathy?**[97]

   - **Emotional intelligences.** With the loss of their leader, Len, TOPInc will be a challenge. The six remaining shareholders will have to learn quickly how to regulate and manage their relationships to maintain and build new networks. Someone must step forward to become the new leader or they must bring someone in from outside of the company. In the short term, the latter is not an option. Initially, the new leader (call him the interim CEO) should monitor his emotions to observe their impact on his motivation and goals, learn to share them with the shareholders, log their reactions, and engage the shareholders in building a short-term plan based on clearly stated long term goals. This process could generate the necessary empathy for building trusting relationships.

   - **Dissonance.**[98] A trusting relationship is essential for addressing the dissonance that the sudden loss of the leader inevitably created. The immediate dissonance was triggered by the disagreement between the shareholders and Len's family as to who has a right to Len's 80% of the company shares. It created intense emotions for some family members. A compromise solution probably is possible if a trusting relationship is established. For that to happen, the shareholders must share consistent empathy among themselves and towards Len's family members.

   - **Moral values principle tests**[99]. Given what is at stake (shares worth millions), some specific strategies may be needed to arrive at a compromise. Leon Festinger has identified four: new cases test, role exchange test, subsumption test, and universal consequences test. The interim CEO might apply some of them and conclude that both parties (shareholders and Len's family) felt emotionally strong about each other's views through the application of role exchange. Understanding and appreciating each other's viewpoint could lead ultimately to a compromise. I must add that there are no guarantees that any of the tests lead to acceptable conclusions or just solutions.

2. How might the shareholders exercise principled thinking[100] by acting from a desire to do one's duty?

There is no doubt that the shareholders were acting from a desire to do their duty – keep the company profitable. Principled thinking goes one step further by adding 'if it is the right thing to do.' The right thing to do for the company is to keep it profitable. The shareholders and Len's family no doubt agreed on that. But what is the right thing to do with Len's shares? How can their disagreement on Len's shares be resolved using principled thinking? They need to work through the following process.

First both parties must agree that the critical issue is 'if it is the right thing to do.' If they cannot agree on this issue, they may have to fight it out in the courts. If they can agree on this issue, they are both committed to pursuing justice. They may have to work through the principled thinking process which include - a) a desire to do one's duty if it is the right thing to do, b) acknowledge every person's rights, c) act from a morally good motive, d) give people what they deserve and e) act with impartiality in pursuit of justice. Will following this process lead to a just resolution? There are no guarantees.

3. Respond to the following issues in the context of the scenario above:

- A duty is the right thing to do independent of a person's motive or interest.[101]

It may be in the interest of the shareholders to take all of Len's shares, but it may not be the right thing to do even since the Shareholder's Agreement supports the shareholder's position. Understandably, Len's family might feel that the shares really are part of the family estate, like any other property in Len's name, and therefore belong to the family. Neither of these speak to doing the right thing. The challenge for both parties is to focus on 'doing the right thing' and not on their motives or interests.

- **One can put someone under an obligation but not under a duty.**[102]
Obligation and duty have the same definition but are used in diverse ways. A person can put someone under an obligation but not under a duty. Obligation is the result of something a person has done. For example, the obligation 'to keep one's promise' follows from the fact that a person has made a promise to keep. Suppose the interim CEO promised to consult with the employees before he develops a long-term plan. He would have an obligation to keep that promise. On the other hand, a person has a duty in virtue of his position (i.e., interim CEO).

- **A person is not obligated to do every morally right act.**[103]
Suppose the interim CEO recommended that, to honour Len for his dedicated service to the company, the shareholders agree to make a $1,000.00 donation to the Heart & Stroke Foundation. Even though this gesture would be a morally good act, the shareholders would not be obligated to authorize the company to make the donation.

- **Going beyond the call of duty is called an act of supererogation.**[104]
If the shareholders had agreed to make the donation in honour of Len, they might have done it because Len often went beyond the call of duty as CEO of the company. For example, when illness struck a family, he would insist that the employee of that family take time off with pay to support his or her family for a mutually agreed upon period.

- **Doing one's duty may or may not be an object of interest.**[105]
Doing one's duty can be pleasant when it is an object of interest but doing one's duty may also involve objects of disinterest. It can be a pleasure to report at the annual shareholder's meeting that the company has once again exceeded projected revenue. On the

other hand, giving an employee termination notice for unacceptable performance is an object of disinterest. A CEO must do both.

Activity A6: Scenario - Psychiatric Illness

David, a Logistics Analyst at a thriving media company, was rumored to be abusive with his wife. He had a history of mental illness. His abusive behavior had never been extended to the workplace till last Thursday morning when suddenly he became abusive towards his co-workers. David's supervisor promptly referred this inappropriate behavior to management who requested the usual medical information from the company nurse to substantiate any necessary disciplinary action. Unfortunately, the company's Code of Ethics did not address psychiatric illness.[106]

The nurse who had conducted the psychiatric assessment felt a deep sense of fear and anxiety. What if David would have another attack a work? What if he attacked her? She decided to conduct a search on repeat abusive behavior by people with mental illness. To her surprise and relief, all the articles she located claimed that medication can prevent repeat behavior by people with similar symptoms to David's. She was confident that her company would maintain a safe workplace for her and all the employees.

To do:

1.   How might the nurse proceed with empathy?
   - Emotional intelligence
   - Dissonance
   - Moral values principle tests
2.   How might the nurse exercise principled thinking?
3.   Respond to the following issues in the context of the scenario above:
   - Justice refers to the distribution of objects of interest or disinterest.
   - 'Fair' may be used in the objective or subjective sense.
   - A distribution made with impartiality may be just or unjust.
   - How can the allocation of an object of interest or disinterest be just?

My response to Activity A6: Psychiatrics Illness

1. **How might the nurse proceed with empathy?**[107]

   - **Emotional intelligence**
     To exercise empathy requires that a person to be able to manage and control her impulses and to 'think before you act.' It is called self regulation. The nurse's initial reaction of fear and anxiety suggests that she had difficulty in managing her own emotions. She was also overly concerned about her colleagues' risk of being attacked by David.

     After a frustrating period of anxiety (dissonance), she decided to conduct research on the level of risk David displayed as a potential repeat offender. This action suggests that the nurse had moved on to a higher level of emotional intelligence. She reduced her anxiety (dissonance) by conducting the necessary research.

   - **Dissonance**
     The fear of David repeating his acts of violence at work created dissonance[108] for the nurse. Any assurances from management that David is unlikely to repeat his violent behavior sounded self-serving to her - they did not want her to leave. She wanted peace of mind more than anything else. Finally, she concluded that the only way she might get any peace of mind was to conduct a search of studies which reported on ways to prevent people suffering with mental illness from acting violently at work. She doubted there were any; she felt she would never be at ease at work when David was at work. Her research proved her wrong; medication was available for people suffering with mental illness from engaging in acts of violence, including in the workplace. This discovery reduced her feeling of dissonance substantially.

   - **Moral values principle tests.**
     The nurse wondered, 'How might I use Festinger's moral value principle tests[109] to reduce my anxiety?' She had been introduced to these tests recently in a course offered by a local university. The reference to 'new cases test' drew her interest. If she could find

refereed articles on ways of preventing people with mental illness from becoming violent at work, and if one of those treatments applied in David's case, she could continue to work with David. She conducted an extensive study and found several articles which identified several solutions. Applying the new cases test had solved her problem.

2. How might the nurse exercise principled thinking in pursuit of justice?[110]

The nurse would have to do the following to make a morally good decision: Act from a desire to do one's duty if it is the right thing to do, acknowledge a person's rights, act from a morally good motive, grant people what they deserve, and act with impartiality in pursuit of justice.

The fact that she decided to conduct a search for safe solutions that permitted people with mental illness, like David, to stay in the workplace, suggests that she was searching for 'what is the right thing to do.' It also indicated that, if possible, David should be encouraged to stay. He deserved that right. This attitude about David's well-being reflected a morally good motive. That she decided to conduct a comprehensive search showed that she wanted an impartial and just outcome.

3. Respond to the following issues in the context of the scenario above:

- **Justice refers to the distribution of objects of interest or disinterest.**[111]

This scenario involves both, distributing an object of interest and an object of disinterest. The nurse was in the process of searching for an object of interest – how to prevent an outbreak of inappropriate behavior through the administration of proper medication. The goal was an object of interest. If no medication could be identified through the research, management might dismiss David to protect staff from potentially being subjected to violent behavior. This action would be an object of disinterest for David. Both are just distributions.

- **'Fair' may be used in the objective or subjective sense.**[112]

The objective sense is reflected in the statement, 'She did the only fair thing to do.' For example, the nurse did the fair thing when she conducted a search for medication for David so that he would not act violently at work. The subjective sense is meant when it is said, 'She is a fair person.' She conducted a study to find a solution to violence in the workplace; she did not simply ask management to fire David. That made the nurse a fair person.

- **A distribution which is made with impartiality may be just or unjust[113].**
Just because a distribution was made with impartiality does not determine whether it is just or unjust. Impartial discrimination against people of color is unjust. Impartial discrimination to ensure that all people of color can enjoy a living wage is just.
Impartial discrimination to ensure that people with mental illness are employed is just. Impartial discrimination which favors white people is unjust.

- **How can the allocation of an object of interest or disinterest be just?[114]**
Other factors must be taken under consideration besides impartiality for a distribution to be just. First, the distributor must have a right to make the distribution. Second, the distributor must have a duty to make the distribution. Third, the distributor must be a moral person.
How do these conditions apply? The nurse had a right to conduct the search. As a morally good person, she probably had a duty to find a morally workable solution. She displayed the ability to distinguish between right and wrong, have a concept of right and wrong and understood the meaning of right and wrong (conduct an impartial and extensive search). This made her a morally good person.

Activity A7: Scenario - Improper Accounting Practices[115]

PAInc was an established four-person accounting firm engaged in preparing year-end accounts and tax returns. The four persons were equal shareholders and owners of the company. One of their clients, Universal Trading Company Inc (UTCInc), grew exponentially from a handful of employees to a workforce of 350. A close relationship developed between the owners of PAInc and the partners/owners of UTCInc due to their growing demands. The accounting firm got to know the inner proceedings of UTCInc which enabled the accounting firm to provide swift and efficient services. It was a win-win relationship.

Except, it disclosed some UTCInc inner practices which were conducted outside corporate regulations. For example, staff purchased goods manufactured by their company and authorized by the production manager. These purchases were processed outside the company's accounting system so that there was no record of these products. When these products were sold, the proceeds were used to throw a year-end party for the whole company. Management of PALInc was also invited.

To do:

1. How might the shareholders of PAInc proceed with empathy?
   - Emotional intelligence
   - Dissonance
   - Moral values principle tests
2. How might the shareholders of PAInc exercise principled thinking by acting from a desire to do one's duty?
3. Respond to the following issues in the context of the scenario above:
   - Does it follow from the fact that an act is right that not doing it is wrong?
   - What conditions must be fulfilled for an act to be right?
   - Ought implies can.
   - Is 'choosing' determined or does it have a cause?
   - Can a person have a conflict of duties?
   - Judgements about beliefs, attitudes, feelings, emotions, and thoughts are not moral judgements.

My response to Activity A7: Improper accounting practices

1. **How might the shareholders of PAInc proceed with empathy?**

   - **Emotional intelligence.**[116]
   PAInc, the accounting firm for UTCInc, participated in a year-end party on the invitation of Universal Trading Company Inc (UTCInc). To accept this invitation was seriously wrong because PAInc knew that the funds were fraudulent since they were the accounting firm for UTCInc. This action demonstrated that PAInc was indifferent to the wrongness of the action which suggested that their action reflected a low level of emotional intelligence. How might that change?
   Suppose UTCInc contracted James Henderson an outsider as their new president who was committed to the pursuit of justice. He soon realized that the shareholders of UTCInc needed to understand their emotions and drives. In short, he knew they needed to become self-aware of what is driving them.
   To begin with, he introduced a series of physical activities offered twice a day. He asked volunteers to keep a log of their participation and make a note of what changed. This routine made the participants aware of what needed to change – their emotional intelligence – so that they could monitor and manage their own emotions.

   - **Dissonance**
   The process I just described soon involved some intense feeling of discomfort[117] due to the disconnect between the emerging emotional intelligence and the fraudulent use of funds for the year-end party. Some shareholders simply could not continue this practice. Other needed some persuasion.

   - **Moral values principle tests.**[118]

Festinger's moral values principle tests (new cases test, role exchange test, subsumption test, universal consequences test) were introduced to encourage reluctant shareholders to revisit their views. For example, what if improper use of corporate revenue were used be various shareholders to purchase items of interest such as paid vacations, electric motorcycles, etc. What would that do to build trust among shareholders? What if the government discovered the fraud through an audit? Before long, all shareholders were on board. They decided that they personally would donate the equivalent of their fraudulent resources to a charitable organization.

2. How might the shareholders of PAInc exercise principled thinking by acting from a desire to do one's duty?[119]

Initially, when emotional intelligence was low at PLInc, some simply may have done their duty. The fraudulent use of funds for the year-end party was not a problem; it was pay-back time. Others may have wanted to their duty for the same reason or to build a successful company (a good reason). Given that nobody objected to using fraudulent funds to pay for the party, doing one's duty 'because it is the right thing to do' was not their motivation. The introduction of emotional intelligence could have drawn the shareholders to doing their duty because it is the right thing to do. That could open them to exercising principled thinking. Some of those concepts are listed below.

3. Respond to the following issues in the context of the scenario above:

- Does it follow from the fact that an act is right that not doing it is wrong?[120]

The shareholder's decision to donate funds to a charitable organization is a morally good act (right act). However, had some shareholders decided not to donate, that would not have been a wrong act.

- What conditions must be fulfilled for an act to be right?[121]

The conditions are: a person must distinguish between right and wrong, have a concept of right and wrong, and understanding the meaning of right and wrong. The shareholders seemed indifferent to these conditions for an act to be right when they used fraudulent funds to pay for a year-end party. They defended the use of fraudulent funds to throw a party by claiming 'we deserve it' which has nothing to do with right and wrong. They did not display a concept of right and wrong, and showed no understanding of the meaning of right and wrong. This is apparent when the new CEO introduced procedures for understanding the meaning of right and wrong. Some shareholders participated in these new procedures, some did not.

- **Ought implies can.**[122]
A person must be capable of what is morally expected. I have no reason to believe that the shareholders were not capable of meeting the three conditions for an act to be right. (see above)

- **Is 'choosing' determined or does it have a cause?**[123]
It is not clear whether choosing is determined or has a cause. This follows from the fact that it is not clear whether people's acts are determined or whether people act from free will. We tend to assume that people act from free will much of the time. That is why we tend to hold the shareholders responsible for using fraudulent funds to pay for a party. Suppose the shareholders of PLInc had successfully met expectations in a difficult year. They decided to use unauthorized funds to throw a year-end party. Did they choose to use unauthorized funds or was it (difficult year) the cause for using unauthorized funds? What do you think?

- **Can a person have a conflict of duties?**[124]
A person can have a *prima facia* conflict (an apparent conflict) of duty but not an actual conflict of duties. Some shareholders may have argued that they faced a conflict of duties: doing the right thing or using unauthorised funds to reward themselves for working through a difficult year. But that is a *prima facia* conflict of duties, not an actual conflict of duties. Their duty was to do the right thing.

- **Judgements about beliefs, attitudes, feelings, emotions, and thoughts are not moral judgements.**[125]

This statement raises the question, What sort of things should be judged to be right or wrong? The judgements raised above are not moral judgements.
By-the-way my mother used to say to me, 'You cannot prevent a bird from flying over your head, but you need not allow it to build a nest in your hair.'
Is that an appropriate analogy?

LEARNING ACTIVITY B: CLIMATE CHANGE

Companies need to resolve the daily conflicts they encounter in a way that is fair to everyone. These issues include staffing, performance policies, safety regulations, etc. But they also have a major responsibility for addressing global issues that require extensive cooperation among companies and all levels of government. Today one of those issues is climate change, specifically global warming. Kieran Setiya makes that point abundantly clear in a recent article in the BBC FUTURE, "Injustice is everywhere, so what are our moral duties?" As the title indicates, he challenges his readers with the question, 'so what are our moral duties?'

Learning activities were added on an emerging global issue that adversely affects millions of people. Today one of those issues is climate change, specifically global warming. This is such a massive issue that companies together with all levels of government need to deal with it. That is why business colleges and companies need to prepare students and employees to enable them to exercise principled thinking grounded in empathy about climate change. In this age of transparency, I maintain that companies have little choice but to address this issue since they are highly exposed to the consequences of climate change.

I chose to write hypothetical conversations involving college students at home and in college. Each topic on climate changa) background information, b) a scenario for group discussion and c) empathy and principled thinking strategies.

Challenge my responses and produce your own. Present your facts and reasons for the position you take.

I wrote these conversations several years ago. How might the arguments in my scenarios be different after the following books were published?

- Michael Shellenberger, APOCALYPSE NEVER: Why Environmentalisms Hurts us All, Harper, New York, 2020.[126]
- Bill Gates, HOW TO AVOID A CLIMATE DISASTER: The Solutions we have and the Breakthroughs we Need, Alfred A Knopf, New York, 2021.[127]

- Daniel Yergin, THE NEW MAP, Penguin Press, New York, 2020.[128]
- Mark Carney, VALUE(S): Building a Better World for All, Signal, Toronto, 2021[129]

Background on climate change

Current articles on climate change focus primarily on technological ways of mitigating or reversing one of the worst effects of climate change – global warming. By the beginning of the 21st century, science had convincingly established that the primary cause of climate change in the past three hundred years was the increased presence of CO_2 in the atmosphere, basically sidelining the arguments used by climate change deniers. CO_2 in the atmosphere has increased since the industrial revolution in the 18th century when coal was used to drive steam engines. The introduction of the use of oil in the 19th and 20th century significantly increased the presence of CO_2 in the atmosphere to the point where many scientists are concerned about potential apocalyptic consequences. Hence, in the 21st century scientists and many others are driving the search for ways of mitigating or eliminating CO_2 in the atmosphere through technological innovations.

The search for technological solutions is critically important, but I maintain it is not sufficient. Addressing climate change requires a foundation of values and principles. For example, who should be served first with the introduction of innovative technology for clean the air we breathe and fresh water we drink – people living in 'have countries' or 'have not countries?' That is why I think the central question should be: **What principled thinking grounded in empathy should be applied to guide scientists, politicians, academics, CEOs, and everyone else in selecting procedures for mitigating or eliminating global warming?**

'Grounded in empathy' – what does that mean? Let me explain. Sarah, who has an exam the day after Michael Shellenberger, who wrote the book APOCALYPSE NEVER: Why Environmentalisms Hurts us All, is speaking on her campus about apocalyptic futures. Should she attend Michael's address or study for the exam? Destroying all plant and animal life on earth frightens her. How could humans survive without plants and animals? Of course, they could not! What is more, it is wrong to destroy all plants and animals through global warming.

People in poor in places like Africa would suffer the most – probably long before people living in wealthy countries. That' ramped discrimination. So, what should Sarah do – prepare for the exam due the next day or listen to what Michael has to say?

As Sarah was deciding what to do, she was torn by the tension between the two options. It created intense dissonance for Sarah. At the same time, she felt a deep sense of empathy for the poor who would suffer the most even though they created the least amount of CO_2. The question is: **Would the feeling of empathy be strong enough to drive her to do what is the right thing to do?** If so, Sarah might engage principled thinking in *Learning Activity B: Climate Change* based on the following thinking process:

- You are mindful of your **duties** or responsibilities.
- When challenged, you are protective of your **rights** and sometimes the rights of people close to you.
- Sometimes you tend to impute **motives** to others for saying or acting inappropriately but fail to acknowledge your own motives.
- Whether you have the authority or not, sometimes you insist a person **deserves** criticism.
- Sometimes you are quick to judge whether a person has been fair or **just** in his action to others.

So, remember as you do the learning activities, empathy is an essential condition for engaging in principle thinking that could lead to pursuing justice.

Think about whether participants in each scenario defends 'best selfish solution' or promotes 'justice for all' where the former defends shareholder interests to maximise profits and the later is committed to the pursuit of justice energized by emotional intelligence (empathy).

Here is the list of conversations on climate change:

Activity B1: Conversation - Flooded Classroom
Activity B2: Conversation - Mistaken
Activity B3: Conversation - Big Oil
Activity B4: Conversation - The Protest Leader
Activity B5: Conversation - Consequences
Activity B6: Conversation - Deniers
Activity B7: Conversation - Ethical Responsibility
Activity B8: Conversation - Moral assumption of economic models of climate change
Activity B9: Conversation - Is 'Green energy' a charade?
Activity B10: Conversation - Economic Growth

Activity B1: Conversation - Flooded Classrooms

Nine-year-old Tiquani stands in a damaged classroom at Adrian T. Hazell Primary School located in the South Hill District on the island of Anguilla. Hurricane Irma left twelve of the school's fifteen classrooms[130] unusable and delayed the start of the school year for 325 students. UNICEF is working to set up child-friendly learning spaces so that kids can resume their education while their schools are restored.

Hurricane Irma left thousands of homes and farms in Haiti covered in mud, and damaged roads, bridges, hospitals, and schools. UNICEF is working to provide safe drinking water and sanitation in affected communities as well as child protection services.© UNICEF/UN0120004/Bradley.[131]

Conversation: Jim and his mother

"Did you see the article in the online newsfeed about the flooding in the Caribbean?" asked Jim while he and his mom were having dinner. "Anguilla was hit hard by the flooding caused by the hurricane."

"Yes," replied his mom. "Every time there is a disaster, the children suffer the most. Did you read about the school that was flooded?"

"Yes, I did," replied Jim. "Is a government obligated to make sure the children have a place to attend school? Over three hundred children lost their classrooms in one school alone!"

"Good question," said his mom as she cleared the table. "What are you referring to – moral or legal obligation?"

"I was thinking of legal obligation. Even if they have a legal obligation, who is going to force a government to do something about it?" wondered Jim. "I wonder why kids in poor districts are always neglected and ignored."

"What troubles me is the fact that the government spends millions on restoring businesses before they look after children's need for a good education," observed his mom.

"The children are our future, and we need to show that we care about them! They should come first!"

In frustration, they dropped the conversation and moved on to more immediate tasks.

To do

Was Jim offering a 'best selfish' solution or 'justice for all'? What about his mom?

How did Jim and his mom use the following concepts in this conversation?

Rights: Distinguish between moral rights and legal rights.

Duty: The right thing to do is independent of a person's motive or interest.

Deserve: Moral judgments are made about the consequences of moral or immoral acts.

Subsumption test – The relationship between principles (e.g., the value of a person vs. the value of an object).

Experiential dissonance – when two similar events seem to result in vastly different experiences.

Did Jim's mom consider the emotional intelligence that is needed to pay attention to the educational needs of the children? How might it be applied?

How might Festinger's moral values principle tests (new cases test, role exchange test, subsumption test, and universal consequences test) be applied by Jim's mom to arrive at a fair and just solution?

My response to Conversation 1 - Flooded Classrooms.

To do:

Was Jim offering a 'best selfish' solution or 'justice for all'? What about Jim's mom?[132]

- Both, Jim, and his mother expressed concern about the neglect of providing an education for the children.
  His mom added, "What troubles me is the fact that the government spends millions on restoring businesses before they look after children's need for a good education," .... "The children are our future, and we need to show that we care about them! They should come first!"

- **Rights: Distinguish between moral rights and legal rights.[133]**
  Although Jim focused more on obligations, he expressed concern about the apparent neglect of the children's rights when he says, 'I wonder why kids in poor districts are always neglected and ignored.'
  Neither seem to acknowledge a distinction between legal and moral rights even though the distinction is important. A person can have a moral right (a right as a human being) even when a government does not grant it as a legal right. Of course, a person can have a legal and moral right.
  It is interesting that Jim seems to refer to a connection between an obligation (duty) and a rights when he asks, 'Is a government obligated to make sure the children have a place to attend school? This question refers to a connection between a government's obligation and the students' right to attend school.

- **Duty: The right thing to do is independent of a person's motive or interest.[134]**
  Betty was troubled by the government's interest (motive) in spending millions restoring businesses before they make sure that children have schools (the right thing to do). She thinks that looking after the education of children is the right thing to do independent of the government's interests. She reinforced this by adding,

"The children are our future, and we need to show that we care about them! They should come first!"

- **Deserve: Moral judgments are made about the consequences of moral or immoral acts[135].**
Betty is quite aware of the challenge of determining priorities when you face competing consequences. The government realized the importance of restoring businesses; they provide employment which is what every family needs to provide for their families. But that is not the only right thing to do. The government should also consider the need for an education for all children. The government is challenged to make a moral judgment.

- **Subsumption test[136] – The relationship between principles (e.g., the value of a person vs. the value of a thing)**
Betty insisted that the government should prioritize the needs of the children. She insists that the children's need for an education should be dealt with first – before the government spends millions on a recovery program for business.

- **Experiential dissonance – when two similar events seem to result in vastly different experiences.[137]**
Probably Betty felt a sense of dissonance because she was personally aware of the importance for children to receive an education; she had experienced the challenge and rewards of making that possible for children. On the other hand, she understood the need for business to recover so that people could return to work and provide for their children. If providing schools were the priority, children could be in school sooner; if the priority is to restore businesses, families would have jobs (income) to pay for housing, food, and education for the children. Deciding between these two options could cause experiential dissonance.
The same event, the Hurricane, was the cause of both challenges – the need to restore schools so that children could continue with there education, and the need to

restore businesses so that families could provide food, housing, and an education for their children.

- **Did Jim's mom consider the emotional intelligence that might be needed to first pay attention to the educational needs of the children? How might it be applied?**[138]
Jim's mom stayed fixed on principled thinking. She failed to realize that company authorities need to feel the consequences of denying an education to children for years to come. It would be years before industry is restored. That feeling might generate an uncomfortable sense of dissonance. With appropriate coaching, company leadership might empathize with the plight of the children which could lead to prioritizing establishing appropriate schools.

- **How might Festinger's moral values principle tests (new cases test, role exchange test, subsumption test, and universal consequences test) be applied by Jim's mom to arrive at a fair and just solution?**[139]

Governments could provide training to companies to explore creative ways of determining what is the right thing to do. Company leaders could be asked to put themselves in the shoes of parents who cannot send their children to school. Company leaders could also be asked to explore the consequences for a country of having a generation of future employees who did not get an education. These initiatives could urge company leaders to review their priorities.

Email. Draft an email to your local representative about a problem created by climate change and offer a possible solution. Use some of the concepts used by Jim and Betty. Are you offering a 'best selfish' solution or 'justice for all'?

<u>**Activity B2: Conversation – Mistaken**[140]</u>

Questions raised by Jim

How much oil is consumed in the world every day? Where does it come from? How about natural gas? How about propane? How much oil is transported by ship every day? How much by pipeline? How many miles of pipeline are in the world? How many are being built as we speak? What is our home heated with? How many homes are heated with natural gas? How much food could be grown at present without petroleum?

Conversation: Jim and his mom

As Jim was collecting articles online on climate change, he compiled a random list of questions that came to mind. To his mom's (Betty) surprise, he showed her his list for a reaction. She quickly realized that all the questions were about information which could be answered quite accurately through a quick Google search. Take the first question: How much oil is consumed in the world every day? A Google search shows that the answer is 97,103,871 barrels per day in 2016. Imagine what it is today!

"WOW! That was quick and easy; I will be ready to draft my essay on Climate Change in no time," exclaimed Jim.

To which Betty responded, "How do the facts speak to climate change? What impact do the facts you have compiled have on people living in major cities? How might they affect people living in developing countries?"

Jim was quick to respond, "People in Venezuela, one of the major third world suppliers of oil, might benefit greatly from the sale of their huge oil reserves."

"Not so fast, Jim," responded his mom. "Consider the amount of CO2 dumped into the atmosphere by the consumption of that volume of oil. How will that affect us and people living in developing countries? Will the people living in Venezuela be able to have access to clean air and safe drinking water?"

"Here is the problem as I see it," said Jim. "In Venezuela, the net revenue of oil is about 20% of the country's GDP which the country depends upon. I agree that the oil generates some air pollution. But that is the trade-off we all must live with. You cannot get everything right; you must admit!"

Betty felt her son was mistaken about the trade-off. Never-the-less she believed he was driven by a morally good motive. So, she did not argue with him.

To do

Was Jim offering a 'best selfish' solution or 'justice for all'? What about his mom?

How were these concepts used in this conversation?

Duty: Can a person have a conflict of duties?

Motive: What if a person is often mistaken about what he believes to be right, but he pursues it from a morally good motive?

Universal consequences test – The interrelationship between principles - e.g., the value of a person vs. the value of a thing.

Cognitive dissonance: created when two cognitive elements do not fit together (e.g., restoring schools as a priority and restoring businesses as a priority.)

My response is on the next page.

Draft an email to your local representative about some of the problems created by climate change and some viable solutions. Are you offering a 'best selfish' solution or 'justice for all'?

My response to Activities B2: Conversation – Mistaken (page 102)

To do:

Was Jim offering a 'best selfish' solution or 'justice for all'? What about his mom?[141]

Although Jim acknowledges that the oil industry causes CO2 pollution, he defends Venezuela's opportunity to sell its oil which generates 20% of the nation's GDP. His mother refers to Jim's conclusion as a 'trade-off' which suggests that Jim is prepared to settle for the 'best selfish' solution.

His mother, on the other hand, expressed consistent concern about the impact of excessive CO2 on us and people living in developing countries. Will people living in Venezuela be able to have access to clean air and safe drinking water? She seems more concerned about 'justice for all.

How were these strategies used in this Scenario?

Duty: Can a person have a conflict of duties?[142]

A person can have a *prima facia* conflict of duty but not an actual conflict of duties. Both schools and businesses must be restored. Parents need jobs so that they can provide a home for their children and children need schools to continue their education. Children must be able to go to school while jobs are restored. A nation cannot afford to have a generation who did not receive an education.

Motive: What if a person is often mistaken about what he believes to be right, but he pursues it from a morally good motive?[143]

"Here is the problem as I see it," said Jim. "In Venezuela, the net revenue of oil is about 20% of the country's GDP which the country depends upon. I agree that the oil generates some air pollution. But that is the trade-off we all must live with. You cannot get everything right; you must admit!"

Jim seems to resolve his conflict of duties between supporting clean air and allowing Venezuela to generate revenue from oil. He did not have a *prima facia* conflict (apparent conflict). He resolved his actual conflict by viewing it as a trade-off.

That is probably why his mother was so frustrated with Jim's line of argument. She showed her sense of priorities in the questions she asked, "Consider the amount of CO2 dumped into the atmosphere by the consumption of that volume of oil. How will that affect us and people living in developing countries? Will people living in Venezuela be able to have access to clean air and safe drinking water?" For Jim's mom, there was no conflict about what should be done about dumping more CO2 into the atmosphere. Do not do it!

Universal consequences test – A person can 'test' his judgment by considering the consequences of applying his judgment to all like hypothetical or real situations.[144]

Jim's mom wanted him to consider the damage that is caused by the vast amount of CO2 released from the oil produced by Venezuela. So, she asked these questions:

"Consider the amount of CO2 dumped into the atmosphere by the consumption of that volume of oil. How will that affect us and people living in developing countries? Will people living in Venezuela be able to have access to clean air and safe drinking water?"

In other words, she asked Jim to consider the universal consequences of continuing to pump oil and increase the CO2 into the atmosphere.

Cognitive dissonance: It is an uncomfortable feeling which people try to reduce by resolving the dilemma or by trying to avoid or deny it.[145]

Jim's mother was challenging him by asking several questions. When Jim exclaimed that the fact he had assembled prepared him to draft his essay, she asked, "How do the facts speak to climate change? What impact do the facts you have compiled have on people living in the major cities? How might it affect people living in developing countries?"

Do these questions create a feeling of discomfort for Jim given that he is prepared to allow CO2 concentration in the air increase as more oil is burned? No.

When Jim responded with more facts about the benefit of producing vast quantities of oil for Venezuela, she responded by asking more tough questions:

"Consider the amount of CO2 dumped into the atmosphere by the consumption of that volume of oil. How will that affect us and people living in developing countries? Will people living in Venezuela be able to have access to clean air and safe drinking water?"

Did these questions create a feeling of discomfort (dissonance) for Jim? No.

Jim's mother was attempting to generate a feeling of discomfort or dissonance in Jim for failing to consider tough questions related to producing oil. She failed – Jim simply stayed with his facts.

Did Jim's mom consider the emotional intelligence that might be needed to first pay attention to the educational needs of the children? How might it be applied?[146]

Jim's facts did not resolve the issue of global warming, according to his mother. When she topped Jim's list of facts, that did not resolve the issue. However, Jim came closer to understanding when she asked some impact questions.

What if his mother had used a different test. Suppose she had invited Jim to put himself in the shoes of a person (role exchange test) who did not have clean air due to carbon pollution? Might that have created a feeling of empathy for the disadvantaged? If so, that could prepare Jim to consider the principled issues raised above.

How might Festinger's moral values principle tests (new cases test, role exchange test, subsumption test, and

universal consequences test) be applied by Jim's mom to arrive at a fair and just solution?[147]

Jim's mother used one of them, universal consequences but it did not work – Jim did not change his total dependence on using facts to support his position. Why? It failed to generate empathy for the people who would not have clean air and clean drinking water. What if his mother had used a different test. Suppose she had invited Jim to put himself in the shoes of a person (role exchange test) who did not have clean air due to carbon pollution? Might that have created a feeling of empathy for the disadvantaged? If so, that could prepare Jim to consider the principled issues raised above.

Email. Write an email to your local representative about some of the problems created by climate change and some possible solutions. Are you offering a 'best selfish' solution or 'justice for all'?

Activity B3: Conversation - Big Oil

Excerpts from Jim's collection of articles

Big Oil is a sinister conglomerate of multinational corporations,[148] fat middle-aged white men in pinstripe suits counting money, celebrating the pillaging of yet another 'third-world' country, and sowing "denial and doubt" about climate change.

The oil and gas industry engages millions of hard-working people, in small and large companies, that provide the world's essential fuel in a complex delivery mechanism and that care passionately about the environment. Millions work extremely hard to keep everyone alive. They take pride in saying that they enable many people to live that otherwise could not.

Conversation: Jim and his mom

"Well, what do you think? Can you have it both ways?" asked his mother.

Jim did not like the way his mom put it – implying that you cannot. So, he fired back, "Of course you can!"

Betty was getting tired of Jim's negative reaction to everything she was saying. But she tried one more time. So, she said, "Put yourself in the shoes of a poor farmer in a third world country where an oil company is pumping oil from somewhere under ground. The only source of water for your family and your cows is a local stream which was contaminated by the oil company. What would you say about that company?"

Jim refused to respond to the question. He knew where his mother was going with that line of argument, and he did not like it.

To do:

Did Jim defend a 'best selfish' solution or 'justice for all'? What about his mother?

How were these strategies used in this conversation?

Motive: What if a man does an act which is wrong, but he believes it to be right and he does it from a morally good motive?

Deserve: On account of what things does a person deserve an object of interest or disinterest?

Role exchange: Walk in the shoes of another person. Does that influence your view? Recommendation: Do not prescribe action for other people which you would find unacceptable for yourself.

Experiential dissonance – can occur when two similar events seem to result in vastly different experiences.

My response is on the following page.

Write an email to your local representative about a problem created by climate change and your solution. Are you offering a 'best selfish' solution or 'justice for all'? Try to use some of the strategies listed above.

My response to Activities B3: Conversation - Big Oil

To do:

Did Jim defend a 'best selfish' solution or 'justice for all'? What about his mother?[149]

Jim's mom is trying to help Jim see the destructive effects of Big Oil drilling for oil. When all else failed, she presented a role exchange scenario, but Jim refused to consider it. She wanted Jim to consider justice for all. Jim remained focused on a best selfish solution.

How were these strategies used in this Scenario?

> **Motive:** What if a man does an act which is wrong, but he believes it to be right and he does it from morally good motives?[150]
>
> Jim's mom posed this question to Jim, "What if a big oil company produces oil in a third world country and sows denial about climate change while at the same time claiming to be doing what is right by generating much needed revenue for them?"
>
> Jim did not like the question; he simply accused his mom of being biased against big oil. She probably understood that an act cannot be morally good if it is wrong even if it was done from a morally good motive. Does she believe that oil companies act from a morally good motive? Does Jim? In any case, Jim did not like the question.
>
> His mom tried again by asking him to put himself in the shoes of a poor farmer ... hoping that a role exchange might make Jim uncomfortable with his defence of big oil. Might this trigger some dissonance in Jim's mind? Might Jim empathize with the people living in poverty with no clean water? If his mom could generate a feeling of empathy in Jim, he might be open to engage in principled thinking.

Deserve: On account of what things judged morally does a person deserve approval?[151]

Jim takes a suspicious view of the description of the men as 'hard working men' who 'care passionately.' He disapproves of presenting them as deserving approval when they are referred to as "working very hard to keep everyone alive.' He doubts that this is the real reason they go to work every day. Hence, he does not believe that these men were acting from a morally good motive as was suggested by the statement, "working very hard to keep everyone alive." Hence, they do not deserve approval.

Role exchange: Place yourself in the shoes of another person.[152]

Betty tried one more thing. She said, "Put yourself in the shoes of a poor farmer in a third world country where an oil company is pumping oil from somewhere under-ground. The only source of water for the family and the cows is a local stream which was contaminated by the oil company. What would you say about that company?"

Betty hoped that if she could get Jim to put himself in the shoes of a person whose life is seriously impacted by the actions of Big Oil, he might reconsider his view of Big Oil. Jim refused to take up on his mom's challenge – he withdrew from the conversation.

Experiential dissonance – can occur when two similar events seem to result in vastly different experiences.[153]

Betty tried one more time by repeating her question. Did this question create sufficient dissonance for Jim to rethink his position? He refused to respond to it – he did not like the question. Although he could understand that oil companies would pump more oil which would generate more CO_2, he did not believe that the men working in the oilfields were doing it to keep everyone alive (a morally good motive). Betty and Jim were incongruent with each other – that could have created experiential dissonance. It did not for Jim.

Did Jim's mom consider the emotional intelligence as a means to open Jim's perspective on the impact of global warming? She tried to help Jim to empathize with the poor farmers in Venezuela who had access only to water from a river polluted by oil companies. Jim would have none of it.

Email. Write an email to your local representative about a problem created by climate change and your solution. Are you offering a 'best selfish' solution or 'justice for all'?

<u>Activity B4: Conversation - Protest Leader[154]</u>

Excerpt from one of Jamie's collection of articles

"Climate change will damage the world irreparably before the end of the 21st century. Some oil executives, on the other hand, maintain it is even more likely that destroying the petroleum industry will devastate the world within a year; probably within a week!"

Report: Protest Leader

Jamie, a senior high student at a Regional High School, was very upset. The regional Superintendent just announced via twitter that any student caught skipping classes to join a protest, demanding that the local oil refinery be closed in 27 months, would be suspended for two weeks. To Jamie, this protest[154] was necessary to meet the goal of zero carbon pollution by 2050. He was convinced that global warming will damage the world irreparably by 2050 if oil refineries are not closed long before that date. Without tremendous pressure on the oil companies, they will do nothing till the last minute; then they will beg national and local governments for an extension. Since high school students skipping classes to protest for a cause was a somewhat unusual happening, it might draw attention to the cause.

Jamie was quite familiar with the arguments presented by the major oil companies. In fact, they warned people of more grave consequences should the petroleum industry be destroyed. Should that happen the oil industry claims, the world will be devastated within a year – in fact much sooner they claim! Jamie was not convinced about their dire predictions.

Obviously, the Superintendent did not appreciate the urgency of the students' cause, or he would not have interfered with what young people felt compelled to do to move the cause of zero carbon emissions forward at an urgent pace.

"Given the seriousness of global warming, doesn't the Superintendent have a duty to support the students?" demanded Jamie in the Supt's office. "Does he not realize the serious consequences of not supporting the younger generations who will have to live with the consequences of global warming?"

Jamie was going to take part in the protest despite the threat of suspension. He felt strongly that he had a duty to save the world from destruction; he also felt he had a right to protest the destructive actions of the petroleum industry.

To do:

Did Jamie defend 'best selfish' solution or 'justice for all'? What about the Superintendent?

How were these strategies used in this conversation?

Duty: Doing one's duty may or may not be an object of interest.

Rights: Is it true that for every duty a person has a corresponding right?

Universal consequences – A person can 'test' his judgment by considering the consequences of applying his judgment in like hypothetical or real situation.

Cultural dissonance – A clash of cultural mores can generate dissonance which prompts people to try to reduce the uncomfortable feeling between conflicting cultural mores.

My response is on the following page.

Draft an email to your local representative about some of the problems created by climate change and some viable solutions. Are you offering a 'best selfish' solution or 'justice for all'?

My response to Activity B4: Conversation - Protest Leader

To do:

Did Jamie defend 'best selfish' solution or 'justice for all'? What about the Superintendent?[155]

Jamie seemed convinced that the only just thing to do was to meet zero carbon pollution by 2050. To meet this goal, he felt that students needed to do their part. That is why he insisted that he participate in the student protest rally on a school day.

He was disappointed with the Superintendent who warned students not to participate in the rally when he threatened students who participated with a two-week suspension. This according to Jamie, was not a just or responsible way of addressing the carbon pollution problem; he wanted justice for all.

The Superintendent thought he had to defend quality education. That is why he insisted that students should not miss classes to attend the rally.

How were these strategies used in this Scenario?

Duty: Doing one's duty may or may not be an object of interest.[156]

It is doubtful that suspending students for two weeks was an object of interest for the Superintendent. Yet, he felt obligated to apply it to any student caught skipping classes to join a protest. He felt obligated to provide the best education for his students. That is why they had to remain in class.

At the same time, Jamie felt strongly that he had a duty to save the world from destruction which was an object of interest for him.

Both felt they were doing their duty.

Rights: Is it true that for every duty, a person has a corresponding right?[157]

Jamie felt that, since he had a duty to protest, he had a right to skip classes to protest the destructive actions of the petroleum industry. A necessary connection between Jamie's duty and rights is not obvious. His right to protest does not follow from his duty to attend classes. His rights depend on a different set of facts or principles.

Jamie was not convinced about the dire predictions of the oil industry. He felt strongly that he had a duty to save the world from destruction; he also felt he had a right to protest the destructive actions of the petroleum industry. Could both be right for several reasons?

Universal consequences – A person can 'test' his judgment by considering the consequences of applying his judgment to all like hypothetical or real situations.[158]

Jamie was concerned about the universal consequences of allowing the oil industry to continue producing more oil. In fact, he was convinced that global warming will damage the world irreparably by 2050.

On the other hand, the oil industry warned people of more profound consequences should the petroleum industry be destroyed. Should that happen, the world will be devastated within a year – in fact much sooner they claim!

Cultural dissonance – A clash of cultural mores can generate dissonance which prompts people to try to reduce the uncomfortable feeling between conflicting cultural mores.[159]

The students and the superintendent reflected a clash of cultural dissonance. The students were looking forward to jobs and having a family. They wanted a clean and healthy place to live. The Superintendent on the other hand, was concerned about the immediate educational needs of the students. This difference in focus might also reflect a generational difference between the students and their superintendent.

The cultural dissonance felt by high school students and the people working in the oil industry could not have been greater. The eighteen-year-old high school students were looking into the future where they wanted a world which would support a healthy and quality lifestyle for themselves and their future families. People working in the oil industry simply needed a job so that they could meet the needs of their immediate families – including education for their children.

Jamie was concerned about allowing the oil industry to continue producing more oil. In fact, he was convinced that global warming will damage the world irreparably by 2050. On the other hand, for centuries the oil industry had been producing oil products to support society. Consequently, millions world-wide have escaped from poverty and enjoyed improvements in their lifestyle. The oil industry not only gained much wealth; they provided an essential service to sustain improved quality of life for many. That is why they warned people of more serious consequences should the petroleum industry be destroyed. Should that happen, the world will be devastated within a year – in fact much sooner, they claim!

This difference created palpable dissonance between them to the point where, I suspect, they could not see or appreciate each others point of view.

Write an email to your local representative about some of the problems created by climate change and some workable solutions. Are you offering a 'best selfish' solution or 'justice for all'?

Activity B5: Conversation – Consequences

Excerpt from Peter's collection of articles

"The consequences of changing the natural atmospheric greenhouse gas are difficult to predict, but certain effects seem likely: On average, Earth will become warmer. Some regions may welcome warmer temperatures, but others will not. Warmer conditions will probably lead to more evaporation and precipitation overall, but individual regions will vary, some becoming wetter and others dryer.

A stronger greenhouse effect will warm the oceans and melt glaciers and other ice, increasing sea levels. Ocean water also will expand if it warms, contributing further to sea level rise. Meanwhile, some crops and other plants may respond favorably to increased atmospheric CO_2, growing more vigorously, and using water more efficiently."

Report: Peter's response to the Superintendent

In his year-end speech at the Rotary Club last June, the Superintendent had made an impassioned appeal for clean air as part of an environmental renewal plan. Peter, who was looking forward to his final year in high school, was impressed. He was hopeful that the Superintendent would now be prepared to support students in their protest marches in the new year. Surely, he would acknowledge students' rights to support a just cause with the occasional protest march against air pollution by a local oil refinery. This would, Peter felt, logically follow from the Superintendent's year-end speech.

However, to Peter's disappointment, the Superintendent made the same threat of a two-week suspension when the first student protest march was announced early in the new year. When the students approached him about this inconsistency, he made the following argument. He insisted that he was faced with several competing principles. One was everyone has a right to clean air, another was students' rights, and a third was students' need for an uninterrupted education.

Students deserve the later to receive the best education possible. That is why the Superintendent believed that it was his duty to choose this principle to guide his decision not to support student protest marches during class time.

Peter and the other students were not impressed with his arguments; they had been so pleased with the Superintendent's year-end speech that they considered his position on student marches for reducing air pollution illogical. You cannot take one position on an important social issue just to make a decision that is the very opposite.

To do:

Did Peter defend 'best selfish' solution or 'justice for all? What about the Superintendent?

How were these strategies used in this conversation?

Duty: Does it follow from the fact that an act is right that not doing it is wrong?

Just: Is an act of distributing or allocating fair from the point of view of its utility?

Subsumption test: involves exploring the interrelationship of principles.

Logical Dissonance – can be generated by logical inconsistency.

My response is on the following page.

Write an email to your local representative about some of the problems created by climate change and some possible solutions. Are you offering a 'best selfish' solution or 'justice for all'?

My response to Activity B5: Conversation - Consequences

To do:

Did Peter defend 'best selfish' solution or 'justice for all? What about the Superintendent?

Peter along with many other students once again felt the need to protest air pollution. They were upset with their Superintendent who had made a strong appeal for clean air but still threatened students, who participated in student marches during class time, with a two-week suspension. They were not impressed with the superintendent's rationale for maintaining the suspension rule.

This resulted in a stand-off between the students and the Superintendent. The students felt that the Superintendent could not have it both ways – advocate for clean air and suspend students who skipped classes to participate in a march for clean air.

Maybe the Superintendent could justify his 'both and' position. He advocated for clean air for 'all' while at the same time insisting that 'all' students receive the best education possible through full-time attendance. The students along with the Superintendent wanted clean air for all – a 'just' cause. In addition, the Superintendent in his role as an education leader, wanted the best education for all students through full-time attendance – also a just cause.

How were these strategies used in this Scenario?

Duty: Does it follow from the fact that an act is right that not doing it is wrong?[160]

When the Superintendent was faced with deciding whether to allow students to miss classes to join the march, he felt he was faced with three principles: everyone is right to clean air, students' rights, and students' need for an uninterrupted education. He concluded that the students deserve the latter to receive the best education possible. That is why he believed that it was his duty to choose this principle. He did not choose one of the other two principles because they are wrong. Nor was it wrong for him not to choose one of the other two principles.

Just: Is an act of distributing or allocating fair from the point of view of its utility?[161]

Suppose the Superintendent chose the principle "students need an uninterrupted education" to protect his job as an education leader. He could be accused of applying a utilitarian solution – protect his job. That would have been insufficient reason for proclaiming the two-week suspension for the students who skipped classes to participate in a protest march. That would not have been a just decision.

Subsumption test: involves exploring the interrelationship of principles.[162]

The Superintendent explored the interrelationship of three principles – everyone has a right to clean air, students' rights, and students' need for an uninterrupted education. He had to prioritize these three principles. He chose the third option because he was convinced that students deserve the third option to receive the best education possible. Since he listed all three principles, he acknowledged everyone has a right to clean air, and students' rights. Given the year-end speech he had made in June at the Rotary Club where he appealed for clean air as part of an environmental renewal plan, he no doubt had difficulty making his decision.

Logical Dissonance – Dissonance can be generated by logical inconsistency.[163]

Peter and the other students were not impressed with the Superintendent's arguments; they had been so impressed with his year-end speech that they considered his position on student marches for reducing air pollution illogical. You cannot take one position on an important social issue just to make a decision that is the very opposite. This created considerable logical dissonance for many students, including Peter.

Write an email to your local representative about some of the problems created by climate change and some workable solutions. Are you offering a 'best selfish' solution or 'justice for all'?

<u>Activity B6: Scenario – Deniers</u>

Excerpt from Sarah's collection of articles

Climate change deniers argue that we should not rush into changing things.[164] They maintain that climate change is not as bad as scientists make it out to be. We will be much richer in the future and better able to fix climate change they argue. They also play on our emotions as many of us do not like change and feel we are living in the best of times – especially if we are rich or in power.

Similar hollow arguments were used in the past – to delay ending slavery, granting the vote to women, ending colonial rule, ending segregation, decriminalizing homosexuality, bolstering worker's rights and environmental regulations, allowing same sex marriages, and banning smoking.

Why are we allowing people with the most privilege and power convince us to delay saving our planet from climate change?

In the 18th century, the primary focus on energy was on the search for and use of fossil fuels. By the end of the 19th century the debate on the use of fossil fuels centered on the effects on the environment and on people. The 20th century is focused on procedures for mitigating or reducing global warming. The polarization of the debates is reflected in the following conversation.

Conversation: Sarah with her Dad and Uncle

Sarah was looking forward to her Uncle David's visit. He had just arrived from Exxon headquarters in Irving, Texas where he served as Vice President, Research and Development. She loved to listen in on the discussions her dad, a dedicated environmentalist who teaches at a local college, and her uncle engage in spirited discussions on many different issues including global warming.

After a sumptuous dinner, her dad could not resist challenging her uncle one more time by referring to a recent article published by Exxon on the environmental impact of global warming. Simply stated, the article questioned the impact of human activities on global warming. My dad could not resist reminding my uncle about Exxon's behavior. So, he started the conversation with the following reminder:

"Exxon knew since the late 1970's about changes in the climate" asserted my dad. "Yet they refused to acknowledge it. In fact, they have spread misinformation for decades. Why? Were they afraid that the truth about climate change would hurt their bottom line?"

"That accusation is based on old information," retorted my uncle. "You know full well that at that time there was a lot of uncertainty about climate change. We were not alone in raising doubts about the facts environmentalists screamed about based on questionable information."

"Why did Exxon continue to spread disinformation about a probable cause of global warming? Your scientists confirmed as far back as the 1980's that carbon dioxide was released into the air when fossil fuels were burned?" argued my dad.

"You are quite right," replied my uncle. "We conducted research on probable causes of climate change. But we did not try to bury any information based on continuous research. Why would we? Do not forget, we even tried to determine how much CO2 was captured in oceans."

At the same time," retorted my dad, "when NASA presented a report on global warming to congress in the late 1980's, Exxon continued to question the scientific basis for climate change. Why?"

"I think you will agree with me that we must constantly subject every idea or action to scientific scrutiny," replied my uncle."

"But we cannot afford to ignore the effect of global warming as we continue to conduct scientific research," insisted my dad. "Recall what global warming did to many people around the world. For example, on the island of Anguilla, hurricane Irma left twelve of one of the school's fifteen classrooms unusable and delayed the start of the school year for 325 students." (See Scenario 1 about hurricane Irma)

"You can't prove that the hurricane was caused by global warming!" exclaimed my uncle.

"True," acknowledged my dad, "but the ferocity of the hurricane was quite unusual – probably the result of global warming which raised the temperature of the ocean."

"Sorry, you can't build a case for global warming on one case study," insisted my uncle.

With that, both my dad and my uncle decided to change the subject to something much lighter and enjoyable for both – fishing.

To do:

Did Sarah's dad appeal to 'best selfish' solution or 'justice for all'? What about her uncle?

How were these strategies used in this conversation? Try to use some of them in your email to a local representative.

- Motive: People who often mistakenly believe something to be right when it is, in fact, wrong.
- Just: Is it possible for a just act ever to be wrong?
- New cases test: Consider the value of the tentative value decision in a similar new case.
- Experiential dissonance: when two similar events seem to result in different experiences or when past experiences do not align with current experiences.

My response is on the following page.

Write an email to your local representative about some of the problems created by climate change and some viable solutions. Are you offering a 'best selfish' solution or 'justice for all'?

My response to Activity B6: Conversation – Deniers

To do:

Did Sarah's Dad appeal to 'best selfish' solution or 'justice for all'? What about her uncle?[165]

The difference in the arguments defended by Sarah's Dad and her uncle is quite clear. Her Uncle defended actions taken by Exxon, a major oil company while her dad insisted that the evidence is sufficiently convincing that the CO_2 emitted into the air is causing havoc. He referred to hurricane Irma which left twelve of one of the school's fifteen classrooms unusable and delayed the start of the school year for 325 students. Her Uncle rightly points out that one case study does not prove a point.

This exchange suggests that her uncle attempts to give the appearance that Exxon has been conducting climate research like anyone else who might be concerned about the impact of global warming. Her Dad challenges this position and suspects that Exxon is merely defending its commercial interest. In other words, her dad suspects that Sarah's Uncle is defending a 'best selfish' solution to global warming. Her Dad maintains he is presenting evidence that global warming is hurting people around the world which must be stopped. He maintains he is defending 'justice for all.'

What is Sarah's dad trying to achieve? If he wants David to switch from defending Exon to pursuing justice, he will have to change his approach. Unless he can persuade David to empathize with the people suffering from breathing polluted air, no amount of collecting 'evidence' is likely to change his attitude. Nor will he be interested in principled thinking as is applies to the pursuit of justice.

How were these strategies used in this Scenario?

Motive. How would you describe people who frequently mistakenly believe something to be right when it is, in fact, wrong?[166]

Sarah's Uncle David insisted throughout the conversation with Sarah's dad that Exxon was not wrong in their research about climate change. Imputing a selfish motive (Were they afraid that the truth about climate change would hurt their bottom line?) did not seem to phase David. He challenged the research conducted by environmentalists based on questionable information. He defended the constant need for scientific scrutiny and challenged arguments based on one case study. Does all this suggest that David believed in the research Exon conducted? It would seem that way. Yet, all major current research studies strongly support the destructive impact on climate change by the oil industry.

This suggests that the actions defended by David are not morally good, but we should not conclude that David is a morally bad person. He might be misguided by the studies conducted by Exon. Should David persist in his views after years of research challenging it, we might have to conclude that David is not only misguided but is unscrupulous.

Just: Is it possible for a just act ever to be wrong?[167]

If it is just not to ignore the effect of global warming on the lives of people, then it is not wrong. It would be self-contradictory to say that a just act is wrong. Every act that is just is also right and every act that is unjust is also wrong. If it is just not to ignore the effect of global warming, then it is also the right thing to do. Similarly, if it is unjust to build a case on a single study, it is also wrong.

New cases test: Consider the tentative value in a similar new case.[168]

Sarah's Dad presented what he described as a case to show the effect of global warming by referring to hurricane Irma in Anguilla. David pointed out that one case does not prove a point. Most scientists would agree with David. Sarah's dad would have to research several new cases to convince David of the potential damage of global warming.

Experiential dissonance: when two similar events seem to result in vastly different experiences or when current experiences do not align with past experiences.[169]

Sarah's dad and her uncle had vastly different careers. Her Uncle David was Vice President, Research and Development, at Exxon in Irving, Texas. Her Dad was a dedicated environmentalist teaching at a local college. Their conversations on global warming reflected their divergent experiences based on their careers which sometimes created experiential dissonance for Sarah's dad; he was frustrated by her uncle's weak counter arguments.

Draft an email to your local representative about some of the problems created by climate change and some viable solutions. Are you offering a 'best selfish' solution or 'justice for all'?

Activity B7: Conversation - Ethical Responsibility[170]

Excerpt from Sarah's collection of articles

Given the historic legacy of greenhouse gas pollution, developed countries have an ethical responsibility to lead the way in cutting emissions. But ultimately, all countries need to act because if we want to eliminate the effects of climate change, the entire world must go carbon zero.

Conversation: Sarah challenges her dad and uncle

Ten years later Sarah came home for her dad's birthday party. Uncle David along with her other uncles and aunts had been invited to her dad's birthday celebrations. After an evening of dining and laughter, everyone left except Uncle David, her favorite. Her dad and Uncle David had so much to talk about – which included their disagreements about climate change. Sarah's dad, whom she sometimes calls by his first name, Ed, led the conversation back to climate change.

"I'm really concerned about the future of our kids," expressed Ed with a heavy heart. "We are leaving a terrible mess for them to live with. I am not sure they can survive in the world we are leaving for them."

"Why are you so pessimistic about the future?" queried David. "Do not forget the rich culture and heritage we are leaving for the next generation thanks to cheap carbon-based energy – less poverty, higher literacy, better health services, and more educational opportunities, in just a few centuries. Just look at what is happening; the world has gotten better for millions."

"That's fine and good," retorted Ed, "but how will our children be able to enjoy our cultural legacy when the violent weather we are experiencing gets a lot worse? See what is happening around the world right now – frequent and extreme heat, excessive rainfall, hurricanes, floods, drought, and gigantic wildfires just to mention a few."

"We can imitate much of the extreme weather," insisted David, "by pursuing the many steps we are already taking to reduce carbon in the atmosphere including wind energy, solar energy, nuclear energy, reforestation, capturing CO_2 from the atmosphere, - the list goes on. Unfortunately, we likely will have to live with some extreme weather. In fact, we have always had to live with some of it."

"The fact is," insisted my dad, "that all these initiatives in developing and implementing alternative sources of energy collectively will reduce the disaster, but they cannot avoid disaster."

Finally, Sarah could not be silent any longer. Ed and David were not addressing the principles underlying what should be done as she saw it. So, she interjected the conversation by asking, "Who should be held ethically responsible for the climate crisis you are arguing about? Which values and principles should those responsible pursue?"

"Principles don't stop violent weather; they don't feed children or provide them with an education," retorted David. "We have to be practical in our efforts of addressing new challenges."

To Sarah, David's response sounded like a put-down; she would have none of that. She replied, "Let me be practical as well. How are you going to respond to thousands of people who live daily with hopelessness, inequality or as migrants who have no country to call home?"

Realizing Sarah's view of his sense of being practical, David tempered his response, "Free and open markets will, over time, deliver social services to more people. Just look at China, they have pulled over 500,000,000 million people out of poverty and India is not far behind."

This was too much for Sarah, so she fired back, "Too often we have been led by market values. That certainly applies to China even though they claim to be governed by a 'people's party.' Are they driven by people's values? I don't think so.

Whenever people's values compete with market values, the later trump people's values every time!"

"What kind of principles – universal principles – are you talking about?" asked Ed hoping that his question might tone down the exchange between his daughter and his brother."

Without hesitation, Sarah replied, "Yes, I am thinking about universal principles which should be applied to all people, rich and poor. They include, we should act from a desire to do our duty; we should recognize every person's rights; we should act from a morally good motive, we should give people what they deserve and finally, we should always act with impartiality in pursuit of justice."

"So where does technological innovations fit?" asked David.

"Let me answer that question with questions. Have you applied your decision to yourself before prescribing it to others? Have you prioritized competing principles? Have you considered the consequences of applying your decision to similar hypothetical or real situations?

To which Sarah's dad replied to Sarah, "Maybe we should take a step back from your lofty principles. Why? Because principles tend not to prompt people to change their minds. Let us talk about people who do not have access to clean drinking water. Let us place ourselves in their position. Do we empathize with them?

Sarah's interjections had disrupted the polarized conversation between Ed and David. It had become obvious to both, Ed, and David, that addressing climate change would require some major rethinking. Had Ed started that process?

To do:

Did Sarah defend the 'best selfish' solution or 'justice for all'? What about her dad? Her uncle?

How were these strategies used in this conversation? Try to use some of them in your email to a local representative.

Just: Is it possible for a just act ever to be wrong?

Motive: What if a person does an act which is wrong, but he believes it to be right and he does it from morally good motives?

Universal consequences: A person can be invited to 'test' his judgment by considering the consequences of applying his judgment to like hypothetical or real situations.

Cognitive dissonance: cognitive dissonance refers to situations where two cognitive elements do not fit together; they may be inconsistent or contradictory. Dissonance generated through applying a cognitive process (i.e., principled thinking with empathy) might offer the most promising approach to reducing dissonance.

My response is on the following page.

Draft an email to your local representative about some of the problems created by climate change and some viable solutions. Are you offering a 'best selfish' solution or 'justice for all'?

My response to Activity B7: Conversation - Ethical Responsibility

To do:

Did Sarah defend the 'best selfish' solution or 'justice for all'? What about her Dad? Her Uncle?[171]

David is optimistic that the free and open market will continue to bring cheap carbon-based energy to millions which has already led to less poverty, higher literacy, better health services, and more educational opportunities. In just a few centuries, the world has gotten better for millions. When Sarah entered the conversation, David was quite skeptical about Sarah's 'universal principles.' David's approach could be described as 'best selfish' solution' in that he is defending Exxon's right to continue to produce oil. His defense rests on the prosperity and the quality of life that the oil industry has made available for millions.

In contrast, Sarah defended her position by applying principled thinking about duties, rights, motives, and desert in pursuit of justice. She also appealed to David to engage in role exchange or universal consequences as he reflects on the impact of global warming on millions. She was concerned about achieving justice for all. Did David experience empathy for those who do not have clean drinking water and clean air to breathe?

As for her Dad, he was anxious about the kind of future his generation was leaving for the next generation, but he did not engage in the spirited exchange between Sarah and David. Would he have supported his daughter's emphasis on the principal place of universal principles in any discussion on global warming? He might have; we do not know. More important, did he experience a sense of empath for those suffering due to elevated levels of carbon pollution. If you fail to empathize, why would you change your lifestyle?

How were these strategies used in this conversation? Try to use some of them in your email to a local representative.

Just: Is it possible for a just act ever to be wrong?[172]

Sarah maintains it is unjust that we allow 'thousands of people, who live daily with hopelessness, inequality or as migrants who have no country to call home,' suffer as we let the free and open market determine when they will 'over time, deliver social services to more and more people'. It is also wrong. The reverse position would be right; it could not be wrong.

Motive: What if a person does an act which is wrong, but he believes it to be right and he does it from a morally good motive?[173]

David insists that a 'free and open markets will, over time, deliver social services to more people. He supports this view by referring to China, which has pulled over five hundred million people out of poverty and India is not far behind.' David seems to be driven by a morally good motive – improve the quality of life for millions through Exxon's best selfish solution.

But what if David is wrong about scientists being able to mitigate much of the extreme weather? He continues to believe 'oil' offers the right solution and he does it from a morally good motive. His claim is not morally good because one of the conditions for being morally good is missing - the claim is not right. If it is true that the increasing presence of CO_2 in the atmosphere will destroy life, an apocalypse might be inevitable.

In short, an action cannot be morally good if the action itself is wrong because one of the conditions of a morally good act is absent.

Universal consequences: A person can be invited to 'test' his judgment by considering the consequences of applying his judgment to all like hypothetical or real situations.[174]

What would be the universal consequences of adding more CO_2 to the atmosphere each year? According to the record of the past 100 years, life on earth as we know it would collapse. The test provides essential information needed to plan.

Cognitive dissonance: cognitive dissonance refers to situations where two cognitive elements do not fit together; they may be inconsistent or contradictory. It can help to clarify or resolve moral issues.[175]

Sally tries to create cognitive dissonance for David by asking the question, "Who should be held ethically responsible for the climate crisis you are arguing about? Which values and principles should those responsible pursue?" Obviously, it did not work.

David replies, "Principles do not stop violent weather; they do not feed children or provide them with an education. We must be practical in our efforts of addressing new challenges."

Sally tried again by saying, "Let me be practical as well. How are you going to respond to thousands of people who live daily with hopelessness, inequality or as migrants who have no country to call home?"

To which David responded, "Free and open markets will, over time, deliver social services to more people. That is our experience."

To which Sarah responded, "Too often we have been led by market values that didn't work."

Finally, her Dad joined in by asking, "What kind of principles – universal principles – are you talking about?"

Enthusiastically, Sally listed the principles she thought should be applied.

Did that create the cognitive dissonance which Sally wanted her uncle and her dad experience? Maybe. It had become obvious to both Ed and David that addressing climate change would require some major rethinking. That is uncertain.

Sarah tried to persuade her Uncle with principled thinking by referring to the five categories – duty, rights, motive, desert, and just. She failed because she had not addressed the emotions that separated Ed and David.

Draft an email to your local representative about some of the problems created by climate change and some viable solutions. Are you offering a 'best selfish' solution or 'justice for all'?

Activity B8: Conversation - Moral responsibilities for economic models[176]

Excerpts from Sarah's collection of articles

Climate change is many problems in one. Developing and deploying zero-carbon technologies is a formidable challenge. So is the politics of coordinating disparate groups to achieve a necessary collective action. For example, policymakers met in Katowice, Poland, to discuss implementing the climate deal signed three years ago in Paris, from which America withdrew under President Donald Trump.

Behind all this, however, lies an economic problem. Humanity must work out how many resources should be diverted from other valuable uses—from life-enriching consumer goods to funding for pensions—to the task of limiting global warming. These calculations may look bloodless, but they are built on weighty moral assumptions, namely, *how to value other people's lives*. Though it is hard to know what might finally impel humanity to take the threat of climate change seriously, speaking more plainly about its moral costs might help.[48]

Intense conversations: Environmental Club at a University

In Sally's first year at a distinguished university, she was eager to join the Environment Club to do her part in promoting renewable energies. The Club organized weekly noon hour open forums where any student could raise concerns or advance strongly held opinions about any issue related to climate and the environment. Of course, Sally was a regular at these events.

No sooner had the informal forum begun, Bill an economics student, pointed out the economic implications of quickly transitioning to deploying zero-carbon technologies.

"What happens to the millions of investments made by pension funds and countless wage-earning people in traditional energy companies when these companies file for bankruptcy?" Bill demanded. "How will pension funds be able to meet their obligations to retirees who bank on their pensions?"

"And who is coordinating countless interest groups and countries to work together towards achieving and sustaining zero-carbon environment?" added Mary. "I don't think that will ever happen!"

" So, what might finally compel humanity to take the threat of climate change seriously?" asked Nancy.

"Good questions," replied Sarah. "I might come across like a purist, but ..."

Before Sarah could finish her thought, Bill chimed in, "I know what you are going to say about morality, but you are naive about the place of moral issues, to say the least. Everything depends on economics. Everything depends on the ability to pay the bills ... in a household or ...."

"What I was about to say is this," interrupted Sarah. "Every action is based on moral assumptions, including financial actions, Billy. That is why I believe that we should keep in mind how we value other people's lives as we deal with climate change issues. It affects everyone – rich and poor."

It was obvious from the frown on Bill's face that he did not appreciate what he took to be a 'lecture' from a first-year student.

As for Mary, who was clearly surprised that Sarah dared to speak up so confidently on matters of morality, responded, "That is an interesting thought. I never quite thought of it that way. You got me thinking. Thanks."

To do:

Did Sarah defend the 'best selfish' solution or 'justice for all'? What about Bill? Mary?

How were these strategies used in this conversation?

Duty: Ought implies can.

Justice: Not all right acts are just but all just acts are right.

Subsumption test – This test involves exploring the interrelationship of principles. When there is strong disagreement about a value decision due to disagreement over the applicability of a principle, it might be necessary to prioritize the principles.

Cognitive dissonance – refers to situations where two cognitive elements do not fit together; they may be inconsistent or contradictory.

- **Dissonance** - generated through applying a cognitive process of principled thinking might offer the most promising approach to pursuing justice.

My response is on the following page.

Draft an email to your local representative about some of the problems created by climate change and some viable solutions. Are you offering a 'best selfish' solution or 'justice for all'?

My response to Activity B8: Conversation – Moral responsibilities for economic models

To do:

Did Sarah defend the 'best selfish' solution or 'justice for all'? What about Bill? Mary?[177]

Sally's commitment to justice for all is quite clear in this statement: "Every action is based on moral assumptions, including financial actions, Billy. That is why I believe that we should keep in mind how we value other people's lives as we deal with climate change issues. It affects everyone – rich and poor. We should appeal for empathy?"

Bill's trust and commitment to carbon-based companies is quite clear when he said: Everything depends on economics. Everything depends on the ability to pay the bills … in a household or …." This sounds more like a 'best selfish' solution except that he acknowledges the improvements to the quality of life for many through pensions provided by oil companies.

Mary is sceptical about who is coordinating countless interest groups and countries to work together towards achieving and sustaining zero-carbon environment." That seems to be an expression of a desire for justice for all.

How were these strategies used in this Scenario? Try to use some of them in your email to a local representative.

Duty: Ought implies can.[178]

Bill suggests that only carbon-based companies can meet the challenge. "How will pension funds be able to meet their obligations to retirees who bank on their pensions?" This is an important question because if the bankrupt companies must be able to pay the pensions, they must have the means to do it. Ought implies can.

"And who is coordinating countless interest groups and countries to work together towards achieving a zero-carbon environment?" Does Mary suggest that it cannot be done when she adds, "I don't think that will ever happen."

Justice: Not all right acts are just but all just acts are right.[179]

It may be right to coordinate all the interest groups to collaborate with each other to reduce carbon emissions, but it has nothing to do with justice because their action need not be just. However, all just acts are right – inherent in just acts is that it is also right. That is why Sarah insists that any action on climate change must focus on just.

Subsumption test

The subsumption test[180] involves exploring the interrelationship of principles. When there is strong disagreement about a value decision due to disagreement over the applicability of a principle, it might be necessary to prioritize the relationship of the principles.

The group of students produced several competing principles. Bill defended 'everything depends on economics.' Mary presented the principle of 'collective effort to achieve and sustain a zero-carbon environment.' Sarah maintained that the over-riding principle should be 'how we value other people's lives.' How should they be prioritized? Bill was clear about his priority. Sarah insisted that how we value other people's lives should have top priority. What do you think?

Cognitive dissonance: Cognitive dissonance[181] refers to situations where two cognitive elements do not fit together; they may be inconsistent or contradictory.

Two conflicting thoughts were defended by this group of college students. Sarah represented one and Bill the other. Before Sarah could finish her thought, Bill chimed in, "I know what you are going to say about morality, but you are quite naive about the place of moral issues, to say the least. Everything depends on economics. Everything depends on the ability to pay the bills … in a household or …."

"What I was about to say is this," interrupted Sarah. "Every action is based on moral assumptions, including financial actions, Billy. That is why I believe that we should keep in mind how we value other people's lives as we deal with climate change issues. It affects everyone – rich and poor."

What was the group to make of these two students defending vastly different ideas? As for Mary, who was clearly surprised that Sarah dared to speak up so confidently on matters of morality, responded, "That is a good thought. I never quite thought of it that way. You got me thinking." Did she experience any dissonance when she reflected on the two vastly different ideas advocated by Sarah and Bill? If so, she might have set the stage for ways of resolving the dissonance so that the group could go on to apply principled thinking in pursuit of justice.

Write an email to your local representative about some of the problems created by climate change and some practical solutions. Are you offering a 'best selfish' solution or 'justice for all'?

Activity B9: Conversation - Is 'Green energy' a charade?[182]

Excerpts from Scot's Internet searches.

A single wind tower requires over sixty truckloads of concrete at the base and needs its own acre to operate in. One tower takes hundreds of tons of steel and several tons each of copper, aluminum, and rare earth elements. It takes around $4 million to install one. The net energy savings of wind projects are very much in doubt.

Folks tell you that solar panels are made of "sand"—easy to come by, cheap as dirt! Yet it is not the sand of vacant lots or empty backwoods that goes into solar panels, but rather highly refined quartz, plus the sodium hydroxide and hydrofluoric acid required in manufacturing the panels. And how much space does a solar array require? The Ivanpah Solar Power Facility, which opened in 2014 at a cost of $2 billion, required 3,500 acres and was supposed to power 140,000 homes, but already shows ominous signs of wear and tear.

Solar and wind projects have clear environmental advantages over coal-fired and nuclear power plants as well as fracking and tar sands mining. The point, though, is that the "green" energy industry is a charade if we think it will solve the sustainability problem without ever addressing the unsustainable demands of the human economy.

Conversation: Environment Club

It was the first forum in the Sarah's second year with the Environment Club; she felt confident about her influence in the Club forums. She felt like a veteran on environmental issues; nobody could trip her up any more on the benefits of wind energy or solar energy. So, right off the bat, she launched into the energy efficiencies of wind towers. Before Sarah could get into the details on wind energy, a sophomore student, Betty, asked in a hesitant voice, "What is involved in building a wind tower? They seem big to me. What does it cost?"

Confidently, Sarah acknowledged that she did not have the facts at her fingertip, but she would look it up for the next forum. She asked Betty for her name and email address and assured her that she would get back to her ASAP.

To Sarah's surprise, another student, Scot, spoke up to say that he had just googled the question and received a comprehensive answer and promptly went ahead to read it aloud, "A single wind tower requires over sixty truckloads of concrete at the base and needs its own acre to operate. One tower takes hundreds of tons of steel and several tons each of copper, aluminum, and rare earth elements. It takes around $4 million to install one."

Everyone was stunned at the complexity and cost of building a single wind tower. "Furthermore," Scot added, "The net energy savings of wind projects are very much in doubt given the energy needed to mine and ship the raw products to the site where the tower is built."

Sarah was at a loss for words; she had never seen a breakdown of building a wind tower, nor the cost of it. So, she quickly switched the conversation to solar power; she felt quite confident about its clean energy value; it was not possibly in dispute. The solar panels are made of 'sand' – easy to come by and cheap as dirt!

No sooner had Sarah finished her assuring words, Scot practically shouted to say that he had just identified the ingredients for manufacturing solar panels and the acres required to set up a solar farm. "Here it is," he said. "It requires highly refined quartz, plus the sodium hydroxide and hydrofluoric acid required in manufacturing the panels."

"And how much space does a solar farm require?" he asked. To answer this question, he quoted the statistics about one solar farm: "The Ivanpah Solar Power Facility, which opened in 2014 at a cost of $2 billion, required 3,500 acres. It was supposed to power 140,000 homes."

Then came the downer when he added, "Already it shows ominous signs of wear and tear", according to the google report he found online.

Sarah was stunned by these revelations. She had been a dedicated environmentalist since grade school. "How come this information had never been discussed in all the meetings and forums?" she asked herself. She was also annoyed at herself; why had she blindly accepted that 'green energy means clean energy.' She wondered how much energy is needed to produce and deliver the parts required to produce green energy for the entire world. As a responsible citizen, she realized that she would have to do ongoing independent research.

To do:

Did Sarah defend a 'best selfish' solution or 'justice for all'?

How were these strategies used in this conversation?

Desert. Why do people take the question of desert very seriously?

Just: How is 'fair' used in the subjective sense?

Universal consequences: A person can be invited to 'test' his judgment by considering the consequences of applying his judgment to all like hypothetical or real situations.

Cognitive dissonance: cognitive dissonance refers to situations where two cognitive elements do not fit together; they may be inconsistent or contradictory.

Subsumption test: This test involves exploring the interrelationship of principles. When there is strong disagreement about a value decision due to disagreement over the applicability of a principle, it might be necessary to prioritize the principles.

My response is on the following page.

Write an email to your local representative about some of the problems created by climate change and some viable solutions. Are you offering a 'best selfish' solution or 'justice for all'?

My response to Activity B9: Conversation - Is 'Green energy' a charade?

To do:

Did Sarah defend a 'best selfish' solution or 'justice for all'?[183]

Sarah favored clean energy. She was annoyed at herself; why had she blindly accepted that green energy means carbon-free energy. She wondered how much energy is required to produce and deliver the parts required to produce green energy for the entire world. As a responsible citizen, she realized that she would have to do ongoing independent research.

Sarah experienced dissonance because she encountered information that raised questions about her steadfast views of generating clean energy. Will this intensify her empathy for people suffering from breathing contaminating air? If so, she may be on a path to pursuing justice for all.

How were these strategies used in this Scenario?

Desert. Why do people take the question of desert very seriously?[184]

Sarah acknowledged that she did not have the facts at her fingertip, but she would look them up for the next forum. She asked Betty for her name and email address and assured her that she would get back to her ASAP. She felt Betty deserved no less. When Sarah discovered from others at the forum about the seriousness of the damage and cost of wind and solar energy, she decided that she would have to do ongoing independent research. Her audience deserved to hear about the damages and cost of her favorite sources of renewable energies if she was going to advocate for them.

Just: How is 'fair' used in the subjective sense?[185]

Sarah presented herself as a fair person. She offered to make information about the cost of building wind towers available to Betty ASAP. This illustrates the use of 'fair' in the subjective sense. 'Fair' can also be used in the objective sense. Then we would say about Sarah, 'Sarah did the only fair thing to do when she offered a quick reply to Betty.'

Universal consequences: – Consider the consequences of applying a decision to all like hypothetical or real situations.[186]

After receiving the added information about the production and cost of wind towers and solar panels, Sarah produced another disturbing question: 'How much energy is required to produce and deliver the parts required to produce green energy for the whole world.' Sarah was immediately sensitive to the universal consequences of her latest information.

Cognitive dissonance: refers to situations where two cognitive elements do not fit together; they may be inconsistent or contradictory. It can help to clarify or resolve moral issues.[187]

Sarah was disturbed when she discovered from members of the forum that her confidence in wind and solar energy was shattered by the cost of producing and installing wind towers and solar panels. How could she be so convinced that wind and solar energy was the way forward? This dissonance prompted her to research the facts to resolve the dissonance.

Did it also encourage Sarah to search for alternative forms of clean energy that cost less and were more readily available? In other words, are viable sources of clean energy available for people living in poor parts of the world?

Write an email to your local representative about some of the problems created by climate change and some viable solutions. Are you offering a 'best selfish' solution or 'justice for all'?

<u>Activity B10: Conversation - Economic growth[188]</u>

Excerpts from Sarah's collection of articles

Gore teamed up with David Blood (who spent 18 years at Goldman Sachs) to set up Generation Investment Management, known most notoriously for its investment in Brazilian sugar cane, where the industry created severe pollution problems and pushed indigenous Amazonians straight out of their very cultures. Gore was also one of the world's leading proponents of "sustainable growth," the oxymoronic bane of the steady-state program. Along with Bill and Hillary Clinton, Gore favored the win-win rhetoric that "there is no conflict between growing the economy and protecting the environment."

Not to be judgmental and not to play God, we have to deal with population growth and sustainable resources. We have all got to cut back. That is the most terrifying realization I have ever had. We can lament population growth until we are blue in the face, but if the fiscal and monetary levers are all set for GDP growth, incentives will be devised, installed, and maintained for population and consumption growth[188].

There is a fundamental conflict between economic growth and environmental protection. Sustainability is not some newfangled energy technology but rather a steady state economy with stabilized population and per capita consumption.

The reason we are not talking about overpopulation, consumption, and economic growth, is that it would be bad for business, especially the cancerous form of capitalism that rules the world.

Conversation: Population and consumption

While the members of the Environment Club continued to focus on current novel ways of direct-air-capture of CO_2 and sequestration of CO_2 in underground pockets where oil and gas had been pumped to meet the growing demand for energy by the transportation industry and factories, Sarah was on a completely different thought path. After she had been caught blindly accepting the mythology of renewable energies like wind energy and solar energy, she had done a lot of reading. Quietly, she listened as Scot, who had inundated her with 'facts' about wind and solar energy, raved on, saying, "The future of clean air lies with capturing CO2 directly from the air. We have already polluted the air – reducing our polluting habits is not enough!" concluded Scot.

"So where are you suggesting we store the CO2 which we can remove from the air?" asked Mary.

"We have vast storage capacity in the underground cavities created by the gas and oil we have pumped the last few centuries," assured Scot. In fact, the pressure of injecting CO2 into these cavities would enable us to extract even more oil from existing oil fields."

"Innocently, Mary asked, "Who is funding the carbon capture and sequestration you are talking about?"

Immediately Scot realized where Mary was going with her 'innocent' question. So, he replied, "Many different investors including apparently some oil companies who are very concerned about air pollution and how it may affect thousands."

Mary let him get away with this generalized response.

Sarah took this awkward moment to interject what had been bothering her ever since she read about the need for 'first principles,' "I think we need to shift our attention to first principles before we settle on solutions to our environmental problems."

"There she goes again!" chimed in Scot with a smirk on his face.

"Let me finish, Scot," Sarah responded. "I believe we should first rethink our obsession with 'growth' – population growth and consumption growth."

Scot realized that Sarah had raised a sensitive issue – containing population growth. So, he asked, "Which population do you suggest that should be contained – American, African, European, China, or some other nations?"

Sarah was aware of the challenge presented by containing the population of the world. She replied, "You asked a great question for which there is no easy answer. Never-the-less, I am not sure that this planet can support the demand for additional energy generated by a growing population."

"Let me switch to 'consumption growth'," Sarah continued. "Consumers in the developed countries seem to crave for every new gadget which generates increasing consumer demand, while people in the developing world want the basics for a better life – shelter, food, jobs, and education just to mention a few. This, of course, generates huge and growing demands for consumer goods. Can these demands be contained or met without generating more consumer goods? That is the question, we need to focus on."

Scot could not resist his strong disagreement with Sarah, so he fired back, "That would put a damper on the opportunities created by a free capitalist society. Capitalism is, after all, the supreme engine of growth. The essence of being human is to grow and develop – we must not take that away from people."

They ended up in a stand-off. Sarah remained firm in her conviction; Scot was convinced that Sarah's question flew in the face of what it means to be 'human.' At the same time, it left Sarah struggling with how to address the fundamental principles she had identified. Scot not so much.

To do:

Did Sarah defend the 'best selfish' solution or 'justice for all'?

How were these strategies used in this conversation?

Desert: Does a person deserve punishment for "sins of omission"?

Just: Not all wrong acts are unjust, but all unjust acts are wrong.

Subsumption test: This test involves exploring the interrelationship of principles. When there is strong disagreement about a value decision due to disagreement over the applicability of a principle, it might be desirable to prioritize the principles.

Cognitive dissonance – refers to situations where two cognitive elements do not fit together; they may be inconsistent or contradictory.

My response is on the following page.

Draft an email to your local representative about some of the problems created by climate change and some viable solutions. Are you offering a 'best selfish' solution or 'justice for all'?

My response to Activity B10: Conversation - Economic growth

To do:

Did Sarah defend the 'best selfish' solution or 'justice for all'?[189]

Sarah was struggling with trying to be just with her appeal for 'first principles' when she said, "I think we need to shift our attention to first principles before we settle on solutions for our environmental problems." Then she gets more specific about 'growth; population growth and consumption growth which must be reconsidered. She has no easy answer about population growth when she was asked the question, "Which population do you suggest should be contained – American, African, European, China, or some other nations?" She switched to 'consumption growth' where she stressed the importance of addressing the basic needs of people in the developing countries including shelter, food, jobs, and education as well as the demands of consumers in the developed world.

Sarah seems to vacillate on the concept of growth. On the one hand, she suggests that growth need to be contained. This sounds like 'justice for all' till she is faced with the question, 'which population needs to be contained.' Then she suggests that we need to meet the needs of the people in the developing world and the developed world. It is not clear whether she is committed to 'justice for all.'

As for Scot, he was off to a good start when he said, "We have already polluted the air – reducing our polluting habits is not enough!" But he showed his bias when he added, "In fact, the pressure of injecting CO_2 into empty oil wells would enable us to extract even more oil from existing oil fields." He threw a smart comment at Sarah when he asked, "Which population do you suggest should be contained – American, African, European, China, or some other nations?"

When Sarah shifted the conversation to 'consumer growth, Scot fired back, "That would put a damper on the opportunities created by a free capitalist society. Capitalism is, after all, the supreme engine of growth. The essence of being human is to grow and develop – we must not take that away from people." By this time, Scot had no interest in discussing population or consumer growth; he was convinced that humans need 'growth.' 'Justice for all' had to take second place to 'growth.'

How were these strategies used in this conversation?

Desert: Does a person deserve punishment for committing "sins of omission"?[190]

Sarah acknowledged that she had never paid attention to the cost of construction and the land required to instal sola panels and wind towers. Is this a sin of omission? If so, what punishment does Sarah deserve? It is not clear that it is her duty to know this information. That makes it difficult to determine whether Sarah deserves any form of punishment.

Just: Not all wrong acts are unjust, but all unjust acts are wrong.[191]

Suppose Sally was wrong to claim that the planet cannot support more population growth. That claim would not be unjust. However, if Scot had insisted that only the people in Europe should reduce their family size, that would be unjust and wrong because it would discriminates against people living in Europe.

Subsumption test – This test involves exploring the interrelationship of principles. When there is strong disagreement about a value decision due to disagreement over the applicability of a principle, it might be desirable to explore related principles."[192]

There is a conflict of principles between Sarah's empathic concern about placing limits on 'growth' – population growth and consumer growth, and Scot's commitment to capitalism in this statement – "That would put a damper on the opportunities created by a free capitalist society. Capitalism is, after all, the supreme engine of growth.

The result was a standoff. as is evident from this concluding statement – Sarah was left 'struggling with how to address the fundamental principles she had identified; Scot not so much.' This statement also suggests that Sarah had her own struggle – how to pursue justice in addressing population growth and consumer growth.

So how might the interrelationship between these two principles be resolved? Determine the impact of growth on the quality of life. Sarah's empathic concern was about how growth affects people and Scot was committed to capitalism as the supreme engine of growth.

Cognitive dissonance – refers to situations where two cognitive elements do not fit together; they may be inconsistent or contradictory. It can help to clarify or resolve moral issues.[193]

Sarah and Scot represented two conflicting cognitive elements – limits to growth and the need for capitalism which thrives on growth.

Sarah was left 'struggling with how to address the fundamental principles she had identified; Scot not so much.' Scot was convinced that Sarah's question flew in the face of what it means to be 'human.'

Sarah also had her own struggle – how to deal with the clash between population growth and consumer growth. This struggle created considerable dissonance for Sarah which needed to get resolved to give Sarah a sharp vision going forward based on principled thinking grounded in empathy in pursuit of justice.

Write an email to your local representative about some of the problems created by climate change and some possible solutions. Are you offering a 'best selfish' solution or 'justice for all'?

LEARNING ACTIVITY C: CODE OF ETHICS AND PRINCIPLED THINKING

The learning activities demonstrate the relationship between code of ethics, HR, and principled thinking. This is accomplished by demonstrating how these factors can support each other. To that end, I draw on INTENTIONAL INTEGRITY by Robert Chesnut for a framework for a code of ethics and the need for a human resource (HR) department. I draw on this book for principled thinking and the condition needed to open people to engage in principle thinking. That prior condition is 'empathy' which is needed to deal with the emotions surrounding conflicts.

Read INTENTIONAL INTEGRITY by Robert Chesnut Part I-VI about Code Moments as you prepare your responses to the following Code Moments. Respond to each Activity and read My Response. Take issue if you disagree with them. Give sound reasons where you agree or disagree.

> Code Moment 1: Who's your customer, Charlie? (# 2)
> Code Moment 2: The game is on, the vibe is off (# 5)
> Code Moment 3: Just another tequila coffee break (# 6)
> Code Moment 4: Blame it on Rio (# 12)
> Code Moment 5: Password piracy (# 13)
> Code Moment 6: Three blind mice (# 14)

<u>Activity C1: Code Moment - Who's your customer, Charlie? (# 2)</u>

Read about this Code Moment in **INTENTIONAL INTEGRITY** (page 235) by Robert Chesnut.

Respond to the following questions using **INTENTIONAL INTEGRITY** and this book.

Questions

1. **How did Chesnut respond to this code moment?**

   Should Charlie bend the account privacy rule?

   Should Charlie rationalize his action for the common good?

   Should Charlie be sympathetic to the commission member who is asking for a special favor?

2. **Respond to the following prompts.**

   Why did Larry's logical argument not seem to persuade Charlie?

   Did Larry create a conflict of duties for Charlie by asking him to relax the company rules to please the commission member?

   A morally weak person must be distinguished from a morally bad person.' Explain considering Larry's request.

   What does Larry deserve – disapproval or punishment?

3. How do the following approaches complement each other or not?

   Code of ethics and HR

   Principled thinking with empathy

My response to Activity C1: Code Moment - Who is your customer, Charlie?[194] [Chesnut # 2]

Questions

1.   **How did Chesnut respond to this Code Moment?**

     Should Charlie bend the account privacy rule?[195]

     No, he should not bend the account privacy rules because that would be a breach of the rule of law, which is a fundamental principle of a code of ethics. Chesnut points out that a breach could lead to a variety of complications such as:

     request for more favors

     customer service might become suspicious

     husband could accuse the company of violating his privacy

     feed the rumor mill

     tempt reps to peek at emails

     Should Charlie rationalize his action 'for the common good'?[196]

     Rationalizing 'for the common good' is a breach of the law which makes it a violation of the code of ethics.

     Should Charlie be sympathetic to the commission member who is asking for a special favor?

     Yes, he should call the commission member, explain why he cannot accommodate her request and suggest possible courses of action she might consider.

2.   **Respond to the following prompts**

     Why did Larry's logical argument not persuade Charlie?[197]

     The Code Moment does not tell us how Charlie responds to Larry's request. We can assume that Charlie was not happy with the request. His company had experienced several regulatory setbacks and certainly cannot afford another one. Larry's request is illegal. In fact, his logic is false. Relaxing the rules to accommodate a commission member might help her but not the company. This no doubt caused some logical dissonance for Charlie. He wanted to be fair to the commission member and to Larry. How could he change the logical dissonance to cognitive dissonance so that Larry might realize his logical error?

Charlie might have felt that Larry would be sensitive to any consequences of the breach of privacy law by relaxing the rules to accommodate the commission member's request. He could use the universal consequences test to help Larry understand the cognitive dilemma his request was creating. If Larry did, he could be ready to engage in principled thinking and potentially be ready for a fair resolution of the commission member's request.

Did Larry create a conflict of duties for Charlie when he asked Charlie to please the commission member by relaxing company rules?[198]

Larry possibly created a *prima facie* conflict but not an actual conflict because Charlie knew it is against the law to disclose privacy information. He knew what not to do.

A morally weak person must be distinguished from a morally bad person. How does this apply to Larry's request?[199]

If Larry is a law-abiding citizen who erred in one request with the aim of looking after the need of a commission member, he may have a blind spot or possibly be a morally weak person. He would not be regarded a morally bad person (act with indifference to doing the right thing.) That's probably why he requested Charlie's approval before he responded to the commissioner.

What does Larry deserve – disapproval or punishment?[200]

Since 'approval' and 'disapproval' are a psychological state of mind, they are involuntary. Charlie could not conceal his disapproval from Larry. Since Larry made a request and would act on it only if Charlie gave his approval, any form of punishment would be unnecessary. If Larry had read Charlie's disapproval instantly, he probably would have withheld his request.

3. **How do these two approaches complement each other?**

Chesnut offers the following:[201]

Some parameters of right conduct are clear and distinct – they can be stated in a code of ethics and serve as a foundation for moral conduct. Violating the law is one of them.

Thoughtful and caring communication is needed even when a request is denied. Sometimes it is needed to make a decision in pursuit of justice.

Principled thinking grounded in empathy[202]

We don't know Charlie's initial response to Larry's request – he might have felt logical dissonance due the logical flaw in Larry's request. This had to be replaced with cognitive (thinking) dissonance in search for a just resolution. Charlie could have thought of several approaches. What struck him most was the possible consequences of approving Larry's request. These include the ones mentioned by Chesnut - Request for more favors, customer service might become suspicious, husband could accuse the company of violating his privacy, feed the rumor mill, reps peeking at emails.

In short, thinking through the implications of Larry's request created the dissonance. Wanting to be fair to the commissioner generating an empathic desire. Principled thinking provided the reflection in the context of a caring attitude which could lead to a just resolution.

Chesnut's emphasis on the importance of thoughtful and caring communication describes the setting for principled thinking. This is a positive application of emotional intelligence which is needed to understand and apply empathy.

Principled thinking in pursuit of justice requires that the negative emotions generated by conflict must be replaced with empathy.

<u>Activity C2: Code Moment - The game is on, the vibe is off[203] (# 5)</u>

Read this Code Moment in **INTENTIONAL INTEGRITY** (page 244) by Robert Chesnut.

Respond to the following questions using **INTENTIONAL INTEGRITY** and this book.

Questions

1. **How did Chesnut respond to this code moment? Consider the following:**

    Is this code moment about an overly sensitive employee?

    Things to consider in team building

    Proposed decision and action plan.

2. **Respond to the following prompts.**

    Restoring a sense of fellow feeling

    Is 'morally bad' the converse of 'morally good'?

    For what does a person deserve punishment?

3. **How do the following approaches complement each other or not?**

    Code of ethics and HR

    Principled thinking with empathy

My response to Activity C2: Code Moment - The game is on, the vibe is off. [Chesnut # 5]

To do:

1. **How did Chesnut respond to this Code Moment? Consider the following:**

   Is this code moment about an overly sensitive employee?[204]

   The purpose of the outing was team building. One of the team members felt isolated since she declined to participate in 'the game is on' – a sexually sensitive game. How can this activity promote team building? It is a mistake to view the person who declined to play the game as being overly sensitive. The incident should be investigated before any decision or action is taken.

   Things to consider in team building[205]

   Chesnut acknowledged the importance of teambuilding. It is not just engaging employees in 'fun' activities. They require careful planning considering the values and principles of the company. When individuals feel their values are not in line with colleague's values, they need to be treated with respect.

   Proposed decision and action plan[206]

   Certainly, the 'game' is not appropriate for a work outing. In fact, this incident shows that it is time for the company to review outings. They can provide opportunities for sexual harassment, drinking too much alcohol, and sleeping in close quarters which may lead to the need for a therapist. Remember, you are a team manager, not a therapist. That leads to the question, "should work outings be encouraged for important developments like team building?"

   Responsibilities[207]

   Should an event like the one described in this Code Moment happen in your company, what should you do? First, thank the employee for alerting you to the incident – do not wait for further confirmation of the incident. Express that you care by appreciating her discomfort. Should she request a transfer, take it seriously. Do not stop at this point – you have a larger challenge in front of you - avoiding a repeat of similar incidents. Discuss the incident with the manager in charge but also with all your managers to ensure that these kinds of incidents are not repeated. Raise the question again, "Should work outings be used for teambuilding or other important staff developments?" Put in another way, "Are offsite bonding events uniting or dividing?"

I am surprised that there is no mention of the consequences for the manager or the person who promoted the 'game.' In Robert Chesnut's code of ethics, every rule is matched with specific consequences.

2. **Respond to the following prompts.**

Restoring a sense of fellow feeling[208]

Management and the person responsible for introducing the 'game' created a toxic setting for one of the team members who declined to participate in the 'game.' The team showed a lack of empathy for her in the way they snickered about her. Management defended playing the 'game.' Were there other team members who felt like the person who resisted to play the 'game' but did not object to participate? Certainly, this event did not facilitate teambuilding which was the main purpose of this off-site trip.

To amend the damage done by the 'game,' team members must change their attitudes and their behavior. They must develop a sense of fellow feeling for each other as opposed to snickering about those who are uncomfortable with what the team is engaged in. That must start with management. How? The CEO or his HR have several options. What might be most promising is role exchange. Invite the team manager to put himself in the shoes of the person who declined to participate in the 'game' and imagine the rest of the team snickering about you. You might feel the absence of fellow-feeling and wish that you could return to be part of the team. Restoring that sense of fellow feeling (empathy) opens a path to principled thinking and a commitment to pursuing a just resolution of conflict.

Introduce ways of creating a fair resolution of the conflict[209]

I applied role exchange that could lead to fair resolution of conflicts. HR has a few more options:

Use the New cases test to explore how your proposed resolution matches resolutions in similar case. HR could have cited another example where a team discriminated against one member.

Apply the subsumption test.[210]

When more than one principle is involved, HR could begin by prioritizing the principles. Since in this Code Moment, one issue was dominant, this strategy was not applicable.

Universal consequences test: [211]

Identify potential consequences of a proposed plan of action[211]. Since there were several potential consequences such as loss of morale and loss of trust within the team and across the company, this strategy could have been used to lead the team to a fair resolution of the conflict created by the 'game.'

On account of what does a person deserve punishment?[212]

A person who is indifferent to doing what is wrong deserves punishment. The manager and his team were indifferent to the discomfort of one of the team. The manager deserved some form of punishment; so also, the person who introduced the 'game.'

3. **How do these two approaches complement each other or not?**[213]

    Both emphasize the emotional tension of the Code Moment. Moral values principle tests can generate the empathy to create the setting for thinking about fair or just action.

    Both recommend engaging the manager in a discussion of the benefits and pitfalls of using offsite functions for team building. Principled thinking includes an organized discussion of the duties, rights, motive, desert to pursue justice.

    Chesnut does not place sufficient emphasis on emotional intelligence, specifically empathy although it is implied in several indirect observations.

<u>Activity C3: Code Moment – Just another tequila coffee break [# 6]</u>

Read this Code Moment in **INTENTIONAL INTEGRITY** (page 247) by Robert Chesnut.

Respond to the following questions using **INTENTIONAL INTEGRITY** and this book.

Questions

1. **How did Chesnut respond to this Code Moment?**

    Is this a Code Moment about management?

    Use of alcohol in the workplace

2. **Respond to the following prompt.**

    A morally permissible act is not morally wrong; it could be morally right or morally indifferent.

3. **How do the following approaches complement each other or not?**

    Code of ethics and HR

    Principled thinking with empathy

My response to Activity C3: Code Moment - Just another tequila coffee break[214] [# 6]

To do:

1. **How did Chesnut respond to this Code Moment?**

   Is this a Code Moment for management?[215]

   Yes. Once again, this points to the importance for companies to have a customised code of ethics which identifies the core values and principles of a company. It should include values related to the business mission such as providing excellent customer service and respecting employees.

   The use of alcohol creates potential problems in the workplace. These include:[216]

   Other teams may want to use the bar or have their own.

   It could create divisions within a department and within the company.

   It could lead to improper use of the bar.

   Some might drink too much.

   Partners of employees may not appreciate the smell of alcohol on their breath causing strained family life.

2. **Respond to the following prompts.**

   Since this Code Moment takes place at the planning phase, it creates an opportunity to discuss ideas and related details. Its also a time to look ahead at possible implications including possible breach of the company's code of ethics or moral principles. Principled thinking offers practical ways of thinking through moral dilemmas. For example, the team might have to determine their position on the following:

A morally permissible act is not morally wrong; it could be morally right or morally indifferent.[217]

The planning team probably would conclude that setting up a pub per say is not morally wrong; it could be morally indifferent. However, when they discussed alcohol-related issues they identified moral issues. For example, how the pub might be used by some team members could be a problem for other members of the team.

They might prompt each other to discuss a range of moral related issues. In response to Meredith, the team manager, they discussed who is responsible for how the pub is used. Others might ask questions about who has a right to use the pub. Someone who objects to having it in their workplace, might ask, 'What is the real motive for setting up a pub in the workplace?' Still others might demand to know what consequences (meaning punishment) would there be for violators? Finally, someone is sure to ask who and how would this 'perk' be managed on a day-to-day basis? Would everyone on the team be committed to an intense sense of fellowfeeling so that everyone is treated fairly including those who would not stay back for a quick drink? Complicated but fair questions.

Meredith and her team are clearly exploring the greatest possible amount of liberty for everyone on the team. But as I indicated above, some people might object to having a pub located in the workplace. Does the proposed pub infringe on the liberty of those members? If so, what is fair about introducing a pub in the workplace? Some members might argue that inequalities should be allowed. What if the objection to having a pub in the workplace isolates those who objected to it? Is it still a fair proposal? John Rawls would say 'NO' for two reasons: The liberty to have a pub in the workplace would infringe upon the person(s) objecting to it. Second, the inequality might lead to discrimination against those who objected to it.

3. **How do these two approaches complement each other or not?**[118]

Both emphasize the importance to think through the idea of installing a pub in the workplace. Chesnut identifies the pitfalls of having a pub in the workplace and recommends against it.

Principled thinking provides a process for arriving at a just resolution. Hence, the focus is on a just and fair conclusion for all members of the team and the company about having a pub in the workplace. To do so, principled thinking includes the five questions I listed above. The concerns mentioned by Chesnut are addressed within the principled thinking framework. In short, both approaches deal with the details identified by Chesnut, but only principled thinking provides a reflective process for arriving at a just and fair decision.

Chesnut would also address justice as part of his format of a code of ethics, but in this Code Moment, he does not address specifically the pursuit of justice. Nor does he address the need for an empathic approach to those who object to installing a pub in the workplace. This should have been the first order of business in deciding whether a pub should be installed.

<u>Activity C4: Code Moment - Blame it on Rio[219] (# 12)</u>

Read this Code Moment in **INTENTIONAL INTEGRITY** (page 261) by Robert Chesnut.

Respond to the following questions using **INTENTIONAL INTEGRITY** and this book.

Questions

1. **How did Chesnut respond to this code moment?**

   The line between 'person life' and 'work life' is not that simple. Explain.

   Actual or possible 'conflicts of interest' complicate leadership. Explain.

   Customers want to be able to trust company leadership.

2. **Respond to the following prompts.**

   An action is morally right or wrong independent of a person's likes or dislikes.

   What is involved in the pursuit of justice?

   How might the CEO apply the moral values principle tests to help Elliot take whatever necessary steps to resolve this Code Moment?

3. **How do the following approaches complement each other or not?**

   Code of ethics and HR

   Principled thinking with empathy

My Response is on the next page.

My response to Activity C4: Code Moment - Blame it on Rio [# 12]

To do:

1. **How did Chesnut respond to this Code Moment?**

   The line between 'person life' and 'work life' are not that obvious.[220]

   A code of ethics concentrates on work life including on and off campus. However, life is not that simple; personal life can complicate work life and therefore cannot be ignored by company leadership. Hence, Elliot's personal life must be investigated, and appropriate action taken.

   Actual or possible 'conflicts of interest' complicate leadership.[221]

   'Conflicts of interest' can have disastrous results for a company and therefore must be addressed. Elliot's conflict of interest was obvious; he was living with two families in two countries. He had a personal interest in both, his family life and vital corporate growth. Whether abuse of company funds is involved is a secondary though prominent issue.

   Other complications can develop when an 'in group' covers for a person involved in a conflict of interest. Even hiding a possible conflict of interest is ultimately a defeating strategy. Management needs to take prompt action upon a careful investigation. Dismissal may be an appropriate course of action.

   Customers want to be able to trust company leadership.[222]

   Chesnut maintains that 'trust' is what the world demands of leadership. The double life led by Elliot makes it difficult for employees and customers to trust the leadership of a company. They question the motive of its management.

2. **Respond to the following prompts.**

An action is morally right or wrong independent of a person's likes or dislikes.[223]

Whether Elliot wants to look after both families does not make it right for him to support both possibly at the expense of the company. This secret life might interfere with his ability to make clear judgments about company matters such as expanding the company's business in Brazil or somewhere else. This is one of many issues addressed through principled thinking.

What is involved in the pursuit of justice? How does it apply in this code moment?

Doing one's duty if it is the right thing to do.[224]

Elliot may have convinced himself that it is his duty to look after both families. However, his first duty in Brazil is to look after his company which makes it the right thing to do.

Defending the rights of people[225]

This Code Moment is not about defending Elliot's rights - his affair in Brazil was wrong. The rights of the pharmaceutical company must be defended by terminating Elliot's employment with the company.

Act from a morally good motive[226]

Elliot did not act from a morally good motive by secretly having a second family in Brazil where he was attending to company business. It compromised his motive. His primary obligation should not be to his family in Brazil but to the company.

Give people what they deserve[227]

Because Elliot broke the trust of the company, he could no longer represent the company's interest in Brazil or anywhere else where the company is operating. He deserves to be dismissed.

Act with impartiality in pursuit of justice[228]

Elliot did not act with impartiality in pursuit of justice when he supported a second family in Brazil. Selfish interests drove him possibly using company funds to see his second family.

3. **How might the CEO apply the moral values principle tests to help Elliot understand why he cannot work in the company?[229]**

The CEO had two choices – fire Elliot OR help him understand why he cannot work with the company. To show that you care and are committed to fair treatment of all employees, the CEO should choose the later option. This process should begin with a careful investigation of all relevant facts. Next, the CEO should consider which of the moral values principle tests might help Elliot understand the course of action the company needs to take and why. His options include new cases test, role exchange test, subsumption test, and universal consequences test. He might choose to start with a universal consequences test. The CEO might acknowledge that companies usually do not address personal matters in a code of ethics. However, when an employee's conduct directly affects the welfare of a company, the CEO must address the personal conduct. In this case, Elliot's conduct negatively affects the trust relationship between Elliot and the company owners and employees. That is an unacceptable situation. Just imagine for a moment the impact of the absence of trust among employees of a company when anyone in a company could freely engage in secret affairs. Before long, not only would the absence of trust prevail among employees but could spread to vendors, shareholders, and customers. A company probably could not survive this spread of distrust for long.

Elliot might realise the significance of his action on the company and see how his conduct affects many in the network of his company which might cause significant discomfort or dissonance. He might realize that for his sake and the company, he must leave the company. No need for the CEO to fire him. What is more, the other employees are likely to show respect and confidence in the CEO in the way he showed that he cared for Elliot even though he caused damage to the company.

How do these two approaches complement each other?[230]

There are several ways in which the two approaches complement each other. Both emphasize the importance of a trusting relationship. Hiding possible conflicts of interest from colleagues as well as customers can be devastating for a company. Both emphasize the importance of addressing conflict of interest immediately.

Chesnut correctly identifies the complications that arise with conflicts of interests. This includes personal conflicts of interest such as multiple marriage relationships because they cause a breakdown of trust at many levels.

Principled thinking addresses the dissonance experienced by the violator. This can happen only if HR can help Elliot feel empathic towards the company where his secret family arrangement compromises company trust. Principled thinking can build on the Chesnut framework for a code of ethics by helping violators realize the source of the discomfort. It can lead to a fair and just resolution even when that turns out to be a negative resolution like a dismissal for Elliot. In short, Chesnut stresses the value of sensitively thinking through conflicts of interest and principled thinking offers some of the conceptual tools for doing it in pursuit of justice.

<u>Activity C5: Code Moment - Password piracy[231] (# 13)</u>

Read this Code Moment in **INTENTIONAL INTEGRITY** (page 264) by Robert Chesnut.

Respond to the following questions using **INTENTIONAL INTEGRITY** and this book.

Questions

1. **How does Chesnut respond to this Code Moment?**

   How should Terry handle this mission?

   The foundation of any legitimate code of ethics is 'obey the law.' How does Chesnut apply it in this Code Moment?

2. **Respond to the following prompts.**

   Can a person have a conflict of duties?

   What constitutes a morally bad act?

   Describe Terry's feeling of discomfort (dissonance). What prompted it?

3. **How do the following approaches complement each other?**

   Code of ethics and HR

   Principled thinking with empathy

My Response is on the next page.

My response to Activity C5: Code Moment - Password piracy [# 13]

To do:

1. **How did Chesnut respond to this Code Moment? How should Terry handle this mission?**[232]

   Knowingly logging into a private data base with a username that is not yours is a criminal act. Information posted on Blind is not evidence; it could be an internal leak or simply false information created by someone.

   Terry should refuse to do what Tina asked him to do and say that he does not want to work in a place where he is asked to perform illegal acts. Following orders is no excuse for committing a crime.

   The foundation of any legitimate code of ethics is 'obey the law.'[233]

   Terry should obey the law. Loyalty is no excuse for illegal behavior.

2. **Respond to the following prompts.**

   Can a person have a conflict of duties?[234]

   A person can have a *prima facie* conflict of duties but not an actual conflict of duties. Terry did not have a conflict of duties between what Tina asked him to do and obeying the law even though he might have felt torn between them. Terry's duty is clear – he had a duty to obey the law. Tina was asking Terry to commit corporate espionage which is a crime. It is not a path in pursuit of justice.

   No sense of empathy towards Terry, a new hire, is reflected in Tina's manner. How could she ask a new staff member to commit a crime for the company?

   What constitutes a morally bad act?[235]

   A morally bad act is not the converse of a morally good act. It is not a desire to do wrong for the sake of doing wrong. A morally bad act is done with indifference to do what is right. For example, If Terry would have done what Tina told him to do, he would have followed orders. There is no reason he would do it for the sake of doing wrong. Terry had an obvious choice – follow an order to commit a crime OR refuse the order and take the consequences. There was nothing in it for him to do wrong for wrong's sake.

Describe Terry's feeling of discomfort (dissonance). What prompted it?[236]

Terry signalled his discomfort about Tina's request by the question he asked, "Have we called the FBI?" It was prompted by Tina's instructions for Terry to engage in an illegal act. If Terry's question was also prompted by a feeling of cognitive dissonance, he was aware of the morality of the request – that it was more than a breech of a code of ethics; it was a breach of the law. In other words, he displayed a desire to do what is right.

This feeling of discomfort (dissonance) set the stage for Terry to do what is right. Probably, it was prompted by a desire to do what is the right thing to do.

3. **Do these two approaches complement each other or not?[237]**

Chesnut emphasized the illegality of Tina's plan for Terry. By signing on to the company's code of ethics, Terry was committed to 'obey the law.' His choice was clear; he had to say, "No, I know this is illegal, and if you want me to engage in illegal acts, I don't want to work here." This decision eliminated any conflict of interest for Terry.

Terry followed the company code of ethics, but did he make a morally sound decision? Unfortunately, a code of ethics does not necessarily answer the question of how to make a morally sound decision. A decision made based on a code of ethics may or may not be morally good.

Let me explain. In *Paul, Serena and dead duck*, Paul's membership in the NRA is not in violation of the company's code of ethics. The code only prohibits bringing guns to the workplace. In fact, there is no code violation in this code moment. So how might the conflict of interest be resolved? I submit that the only morally sound approach is through principled thinking in the context of a sense of fellow feeling which I have explained above.

The two approaches to resolve conflicts of interest provide a comprehensive approach to resolving dilemmas. Terry was open and honest about obeying the law through his commitment to the company's code of ethics. To ensure, to the extent possible, to do the morally right thing, he could have applied principled thinking in the context of a sense of fellow feeling. Both approaches emphasized the importance 'that we care' about the parties involved in the conflict.

Activity C6: Code Moment - Three blind mice[238] (# 14)

Read this Code Moment in **INTENTIONAL INTEGRITY** (page 266) by Robert Chesnut.

Respond to the following questions using **INTENTIONAL INTEGRITY** and this book.

Questions

1. **How does Chesnut respond to this Code Moment?**

   Can you afford to 'bury your head in the sand'?

   Is it better to follow the saying 'What you don't know won't hurt you'?

   Should any of these issues be dealt with? If so, how?

   Weed distribution

   Recycling issue

   Problem in the IT department

2. **Respond to the following prompts.**

   Is it true that for every right, a person has a corresponding duty? Apply this to Rick.

   What if a person planned to commit a wrong act (i.e., use a fake email to spread a false rumor) but did not execute it? What does he deserve?

   How might a general counsel lead Rick to realize the problem of spreading false rumors?

3. **How do the following approaches complement each other or not?**

   Code of ethics and HR

   Principled thinking with empathy

My Response is on the next page.

My response to Activity C6: Code Moment - Three blind mice [# 14]

To do:

Questions

1. **How did Chesnut respond to this Code Moment?[239]**

   Can you afford to 'bury you head in the sand' on this one? NO!

   Is it better to follow the saying 'what you don't won't hurt you'? You are better off knowing about problems and dealing with them.

   Should any of the following issues be dealt with? If so, how?

   Marijuana distribution[240]

   You must investigate this allegation; it may be legal in some states but not in others. Chesnut points out that it could have implications for the company. In any case, a company's code of ethics should be clear about the use of drugs on company premises which could be monitored through the installation of a video camera or some surprise site visitations during off hours.

   Recycling issue[241]

   Chesnut recommends that management follow up on this rumor even though it probably does not involve a criminal offence. Not to follow up could tarnish the company's 'green' image which could raise questions about 'trust' in the company's leadership.

   Problem in the IT department[242]

   Recognize that you have a problem in the IT department if fake emails are being created. Take whatever legitimate necessary steps to trace who is using those accounts and who is behind the anonymous posts.

Chesnut draws attention to the age of transparency. Although transparency makes it more difficult to hide violations, it can also create a challenge for tracing some violations. This Code Moment illustrates the latter.

2. Respond to the following prompts.

The charts on the Principled Thinking Model identify numerous ways of thinking through conflicts of interest. Here are a few that apply to this Code Moment.

Is it true that for every right, a person has a corresponding duty? How might this apply to Rick?[243]

Rick has a right to freedom of speech, but he also has a duty to do the right thing independent of his motive or interests. Just because he has a right to free speech, does not give him a right to malign other employees or senior management in his company. In other words, there is not a necessary correspondence between rights and duties.

What if a person planned to commit a wrong act (i.e., use a fake email to spread false rumors) but failed to execute it? What does he deserve?

Suppose Rick had tried to post inappropriate comments under different usernames but failed to do so, what does he deserve? He would deserve some form of punishment because he acted like a person who intends to harm others. Planning and organizing steps to inflict deliberate harm on others is part of the process of executing the harmful act and therefore deserves some form of punishment.

How might a general counsel lead Rick to realize the problem of spreading false rumors?[244]

Suppose general counsel regards Rick as a highly performing employee, how might general counsel help Rick appreciate the potential damage he might do to his company by spreading false rumors. What could general counsel do? Primarily, Rick must acknowledge the problem. To accomplish this, general counsel has several options. As I mentioned in a previous Code Moment, general counsel could use a new cases test, role exchange test, subsumption test, or a universal consequences test. Suppose she used role exchange test. Suppose an anonymous person spread false rumors about you (e.g., you are always late for work). How would you feel about that? Suppose Rick replied, "I don't care."

She could try another test – new cases test. Your friend, Betty, who works in an IT company spread a false rumor about senior management. What happened to her? She was dismissed with no discussion about whether it was a fair dismissal. Could that happen to you? Rick got the point; he certainly did not want to be dismissed – he loves his work.

Rick appears ready to mend his ways – prepared to work on ways of changing what had become a bad habit. Management did not need to dismiss him.

3. **How do these two approaches complement each other or not?**[245]

Once again, I agree with Chesnut that the issues raised in this Code Moment need to be investigated promptly to avoid any damage to leadership caused by rumors. If Rick has some whistle-blower protection, they should be respected. Efforts should be made to open communication so that Rick is free to report infractions through normal channels. Both approaches stress the need to attend to the emotional stress created by Rick's conduct. The challenge is to help Rick see the impact his conduct has on the company and management. If he can learn to empathize with them, he could be open to resolving the conflict through principled thinking in pursuit of justice.

Principled thinking offers two procedures to ensure that every effort is made to be fair towards Rick.

First, it offers four ways of helping a person realize his/her indiscretions: new cases test, role exchange test, subsumption test, or a universal consequences test. Second, it, presents five categories of thinking in pursuit of justice: duty, rights, motive, desert, and justice. These two procedures extend the basic framework for a code of ethics outlined by Chesnut by providing specific ways of addressing the dissonance generated by conflicts of interest.

CONCLUSION

I have presented a global framework for justice grounded in empathy to encourage CEOs to use the necessary conceptual tools (principle thinking) and emotions (empathy) to resolve conflicts with a firm commitment to pursuing justice. It could complement a customised code of ethics which every company should have. This framework of principled thinking grounded in empathy should serve an HR well to resolve the dissonance generated by conflict.

At the same time, applying this framework raises many questions. For example, which of the concepts under 'duty' apply to a particular scenario? The same applies to rights, motive, desert, and just. This was particularly evident to me when I wrote My Response to the questions, I raised in the Learning Activities in Part IV.

Second, I listed four types of dissonance – experiential, cultural, logical, cognitive. Why only four? Why is cognitive dissonance the only feeling of dissonance that sets the emotional stage for principled resolution of conflicts?

Third, what should be included in a customized code of ethics? Does Chesnut offer a sufficient framework? Does it require the additional support of 'principled thinking grounded in empathy to resolve conflicts, as I recommend?

Fourth, do all employees need to exercise principled thinking or does it apply only to the CEO and senior administrators?

No doubt there are more questions that need to be raised. The problem is that there are few standard resolutions of conflicts that can be coded in a code of ethics. That is why principled thinking grounded in empathy is essential.

I conclude with the fundamental principled thinking grounded in empathy with which I opened this book because they are essential to using a code of ethics to pursue justice. Here they are again:

- We are mindful of our **duties** in specific situation.
- When challenged, we are protective of our **rights**.
- Sometimes we impute a **motive** to an employee for acting inappropriately.
- Sometimes we feel an employee **deserves** an approval or punishment.
- Sometimes we are challenged to make **just (fair)** decisions.

I close with this question: Should the combination of a code of ethics and principled thinking grounded in empathy become the foundation for companies to resolve conflicts in pursuit of justice?

In other words, can you have justice without empathy? You know my answer. What is yours?

POSTSCRIPT

"Transparency could lead companies to pursue justice for all," I argued in one of my conversations with a senior executive friend of mine who spent his life in the oil industry.

"Don't be so sure," he replied. "Companies have creative ways of beating the system. Shareholders expect them to make money. Period!"

This conversation went for hours. Fortunately, we remained friend's despite of our differing views.

This conversation took place during the COVID–19 pandemics. Here is what the International Finance Corporation (IFC) had to say about what corporations needed to do during the pandemic.

> In this period of high uncertainty, it is important for businesses to proactively communicate how they are responding to the crisis to their investors and stakeholders—including their employees, their customers, and the communities in which they are operating.[246]

The IFC goes on to say that there is

> a growing demand for higher standards of corporate disclosure and transparency about environmental, social, and governance matters. This could set the stage for companies of the future.[247]

The critical question is, 'Might increased disclosure and transparency lead companies increasingly to pursue justice for all'?

Could it? Will it?

ACKNOWLEDGEMENTS

I agree with Meg Whitman, CEO of HP, and eBay, when she says about Robert Chesnut, "No one has wrestled with more difficult business integrity challenges over the last 20 years than Rob. His insights will instruct you how to drive integrity into your culture. Now, more than ever, we need someone to lead a constructive, direct conversation about integrity in business – Rob delivers."[77]

To that end, Chesnut concludes in his book, INTENTIONAL INTEGRITY, that companies should contribute to 'creating a better world for everyone." That statement, to my mind, includes 'justice grounded in empathy' which is the focus of this book. Justice grounded in empathy should be the foundation of a Code of Ethics.

The Principled Thinking framework developed in this book, I developed through a philosophy class conducted by Professor Glassen and as part of my doctoral dissertation under the guidance of Dr. Tony Riffle. Thank you for your, challenges, patience, and support.

A special thanks to the graphic artist, Gordon Gemmell, who created a final version of the title page. This invites/challenges new readers to read CAN YOU HAVE JUSTICE WITHOUT EMPATHY? Thank you, Gordon for creating the elegant graphics for the cover page. Your artistic talents and patient coaching resulted in a clear and focused statement.

Many thanks go to Leslie Wurtak (M. Ed.) who devoted hours to edit and proofread the manuscript along with others. Your editing and suggestions on diverse ways to present my arguments improved the clarity of the book. Thank you.

Thank you, George Wurtak (M. Ed.), for coaching me when I encountered technical difficulties.

Thank you to Gregg and Lisa for attending to many routine tasks from providing transportation to ensuring that the necessary documents were accurately completed in a timely manner during my wife's illness and my concentration on writing this book. Your support is much appreciated.

Thank you, Eleanor Toews (MBA), for raising interesting and challenging ideas about the book and its title. Try applying her concept "evocative of justice" to CAN YOU HAVE JUSTICE WITHOUT EMPATHY? That stirs up issues of social justice.

A special thanks go out to all who took the time to offer feedback. I humbly appreciate the insights representing a range of formal and informal backgrounds.

The book would not have an empathic focus without the persistent challenge and support of my wife, Joan McCreath. A special THANK YOU to you. Unfortunately, you are not able to read this book which I have dedicated to you.

This book is truly a tribute to my whole family! Thank you. Otto

END NOTES

1. Otto B. Toews, **SO YOU THINK YOU CAN THINK.** Thinking through moral dilemmas in pursuit of justice. FriesenPress, Victoria, BC. 2017.
2. *KIRKUS* REVIEW. A debut work of psychology recommends a system to make readers more adept at solving moral dilemmas.

Introduction

3. Daniel Kahneman THINKING, FAST AND SLOW. Toronto, Anchor Canada, 2011.
4. William Burr, ONE DAM THING AFTER ANOTHER.
5. KnowledgeBuilder Software Inc. Winnipeg, 1994
6. Bret Fox, Fmr CEO @ Touchstone Semiconductor," What is a (working) day in the life of a CEO like?" https://www.quora.com/What-is-a-working-day-in-the-life-of-a CEO-like
7. Tom Nault, Managing Partner at Middlerock Partners LLC (2016-present)
8. *Discretion and Justice in Educational Administration: Towards a Normative Conceptual Framework, University of Manitoba, Winnipeg, 1981*
9. Otto B. Toews, **SO YOU THINK YOU CAN THINK**, Thinking through moral dilemmas in pursuit of justice.
10. Robert Chesnut with Joan O'C. Hamilton, *INTENTIONAL INTEGRITY*, St. Marin's Press, New York, 2020.
11. Maynard Keynes. British economist who

spearheaded a revolution in economic thinking that overturned the then-prevailing idea that free markets would automatically provide full employment—that is, that everyone who wanted a job would have one as long as workers were flexible in their wage demands. https://www.google.com/searc h?gs_ssp=eJzj4tDP1TewTM_C1CHBF_61j0j15&sourceid=chrome&ie=UTF-8

12. Milton Freedman was an American economist and statistician. He was the most prominent advocate of free markets in the 20th century. the twentieth century. https://www.econlib.org/library/Enc/bios/Friedman.html.

13. In the twenty-first century, Robert Chesnut developed standard elements for a basic code of ethics. He set the stage for the evolution of the code of ethics to 'create a better world for everyone

14. Code Moments developed by Robert Chesnut in INTENTIONAL INTEGRITY.

Part I. Recent History On How We Got Here

15. The first step in moral thinking. It will be to the 21st century what 'rights' was to the 20th century and 'equality' was to the 19th century.

16. John Maynard Keynes[16] challenged the current understanding of economics that the free market was perfectly capable of generating full employment.

17. Milton Freedman. He revived the reliance on free markets to address the difficulties of the market in his famous 1970 address, "*The Social Responsibility of Business Is to Increase Its Profits*".

18. I need only look out the window to see the results of libertarian economic ideology.

19. In the past 20 years, Robert Chesnut has led an ethical revolution in companies.

20. [Chesnut] maintained that 'stakeholder value' should be the basis for companies to develop their own code of ethics. To that end, he named five basic elements

for a standard code of ethics.

21. Robert Chesnut, *INTENTIONAL INTEGRITY*
22. … the wealthiest 1 percent of people in this country have 40 percent of the wealth.
23. The notion of linking corporations to explicit social goods is resurfacing.
24. Several employees surfaced the idea of donating their credits to hosts, and on their own, unprompted by management, over 2000 employees donated over $1 million to hosts in need.
25. Chignell, "As we will see, this approach provides the necessary foundation for moral action."
26. Golman[26], stated, "The interest in emotional intelligence in the workplace stems from the widespread recognition that these abilities – self-awareness, self-management, empathy, and social skill – separate the most successful workers and leaders from the average."
27. It has been convincingly presented by Daniel Kahneman in THINKING, FAST AND SLOW where 'fast' refers to intuitive thinking and 'slow' refers to deep thinking.
28. . Read what David Brooks, columnist for the *New York* describe *Times*, reported in 2011 on how young people answered questions about "right" and "wrong."
29. "when asked to describe a moral dilemma they had faced, two-thirds of the young people either couldn't answer the question or [shifted to] problems that were not moral at all.
30. When asked about wrong or evil, the respondents agreed that rape and murder qualified as such. But, aside from agreeing on these two extreme examples, moral thinking (e.g., thinking about right and wrong) did not enter the picture for them, even when they considered issues like drunk driving, cheating in school, or cheating on a partner.
31. Brooks concluded that "they [the young people] don't

have the categories or concepts to answer questions about right and wrong.

Part II. Emotional Intelligence

32. David Hume, "Reason is...the slave of the passions."
33. [Festinger] identified four types of dissonance - logical dissonance, cultural dissonance, experiential dissonance, and cognitive dissonance.
34. Experiential dissonance is felt when past habits or relationships do not align with a current incident or when two similar events seem to result in different outcomes.
35. Logical inconsistencies can create dissonance when what appears to be logical isn't.
36. A clash of cultural mores can generate dissonance which prompts people to try to reduce or block the uncomfortable feeling created by the incongruity between conflicting cultural mores or customs.
37. Cognitive dissonance refers to a situation where two cognitive elements do not fit together – they may be inconsistent or contradictory.
38. According to Leon Festinger[38], moral values principle tests (see Chart 8) can assist in reframing dilemmas and possibly changing the dissonance into cognitive dissonance.
39. Can applying the universal consequences test create the situation where the people involved are prepared to exercise principle thinking? Can the test generate empathy?
40. How can applying the subsumption test create the situation where the people involved are prepared to exercise principle thinking? First, can the test generate empathy?
41. Does John Rawls offer a way of solving this challenge? Here is what he has to say. He identified the fundamental meaning of justice as 'the tension between liberty and equality.
42. How can the new cases test create the situation

where the people involved are prepared to
exercise principle thinking? How can the test
generate empathy?

43. Can the role exchange test create the situation where
the people involved are prepared to exercise principle
thinking? How can the test generate empathy?

44. In the article, *The Dark Side of Emotional Intelligence*,
Adam Grant points out some of the abuses of
emotional intelligence.

Part III: Principled Thinking

45. John Rawls, a moral philosopher, identified the
fundamental meaning of justice.

46. As Robert Chesnut says, a twenty first century
company needs to contribute to "creating a better
world for everyone."

47. quick review of each of the five categories: duty,
rights, motive, desert, just.

48. Duty

49. Concepts about Duty

50. Rights

51. Concepts about Rights

52. Motive

53. Concepts about Motive

54. Desert

55. Concepts about Desert

56. Just

57. Concepts about Just

58. John Rawls, philosopher, put it this way:

Part IV. In Pursuit Of Justice Grounded In Empathy

59. Sherry Turkle in *Reclaiming Conversation: The
Power of Talk in a Digital Age* put it this way:" Face-
to-face communication is the most human – and
humanizing – thing we do. Fully present to one
another, we learn to listen. It is where we develop the
capacity for empathy."

60. For courses, programs, and learning materials on

emotional intelligence as it applies to resolving the emotions generated by conflict in the workplace, google 'training sessions on emotional intelligence', one of many online sources and learning activities.

61. The third set of learning activities are built on the Code Moments created by Robert Chesnut in INTENTIONAL INTEGRITY

Part V. Learning Activities

62. Yale University developed Zerit and formed a partnership with BMS to market the product.
63. How might Yale proceed with empathy?
64. That could have created dissonance
65. Moral values principle tests
66. How might Yale exercise principled thinking to grant people what they deserve?
67. Does Yale deserve approval or punishment?
68. Does Yale deserve punishment for willing to do wrong?
69. What if Yale planned to do wrong but failed to execute it?[69]
70. Three former employees of an offshore manufacturing company, PRInc, distributed an email online claiming that there were excessive restrictions on employees' behavior in PRInc.
71. How might PRInc proceed with empathy?
72. One of the first results of observing the conditions in the workplace might be that management at PRInc could feel a considerable disconnect or dissonance between management's perception of the workplace and what they were observing.
73. One or more of the moral values principle tests identified by Festinger could help management make the transition to pursuing a fair and just workplace environment.
74. How might PRInc exercise principled thinking by respecting a person's rights?
75. How does ownership differ from possession?

76. What does it mean to have a prerogative?
77. Is it true that for every duty a person has a corresponding right?
78. Is it true that for every duty there is a correlative right?
79. "NO DEFORESTATION, NO PEAT, NO EXPLOITATION!" (NDPE)
80. How might Wilmar proceed with empathy?
81. Wilmar's commitment to keep the pledge created an elevated level of dissonance which is reflected in how to implement the pledge.
82. Moral values principle tests
83. What is the relationship between rights act and just acts?
84. On what basis is a distribution just or unjust?
85. What is retribution? How is it different from retributive justice?
86. SHOOT ME! SHOOT ME," screamed the driver.
87. How might the RCMP Officer proceed with empathy?
88. The dissonance the Officer felt seeing the trucker in flames prompted a series of quick actions.
89. Moral values principle tests.
90. How might the RCMP Officer exercise principled thinking by acting from a morally good motive?
91. What conditions must be fulfilled for an act to be morally good?
92. Morally good motives must be distinguished from good motives.
93. Is morally bad simply the converse of morally good?
94. What constitutes a morally bad act?
95. What are naturally bad motives?
96. Len had been CEO of TOPInc till he died suddenly of a heart attack.
97. How might the shareholders proceed with empathy?
98. Dissonance. A trusting relationship is essential for addressing the dissonance that the sudden loss of the

leader inevitably created.

99. Moral values principle tests.
100. How might the shareholders exercise principled thinking by acting from a desire to do one's duty?
101. A duty is the right thing to do independent of a person's motive or interest.
102. One can put someone under an obligation but not under a duty.
103. A person is not necessarily obligated to do every morally right act.
104. Going beyond the call of duty is called an act of supererogation.
105. Doing one's duty may or may not be an object of interest.
106. David had a history of mental illness
107. How might the nurse proceed with empathy?
108. The fear of David repeating his acts of violence at work created dissonance for the nurse
109. The nurse wondered, 'How might I use Festinger's moral value principle tests to reduce my anxiety?'
110. How might the nurse exercise principled thinking in pursuit of justice?
111. Justice refers to the distribution of objects of interest or disinterest.
112. 'Fair' may be used in the objective or subjective sense.
113. A distribution which is made with impartiality may be just or unjust.
114. How can the allocation of an object of interest or disinterest be just?
115. Improper Accounting Practices
116. Emotional intelligence
117. The process I just described soon involved some intense feeling of discomfort due to the disconnect between the emerging emotional intelligence and the fraudulent use of funds for the year-end party
118. Moral values principle tests.
119. How might the shareholders of PAInc exercise

principled thinking by acting from a desire to do
one's duty

120. Does it follow from the fact that an act is right that
not doing it is wrong?

121. What conditions must be fulfilled for an act
to be right?

122. Ought implies can.

123. Is 'choosing' determined or does it have a cause?

124. Can a person have a conflict of duties?

125. Judgements about beliefs, attitudes, feelings,
emotions, and thoughts are not moral judgements.

126. Michael Shellenberger, APOCALYPSE NEVER:
Why Environmentalisms Hurts us All, Harper, New
York, 2020.

127. Bill Gates, HOW TO AVOID A CLIMATE
DISASTER: The Solutions we have and the
Breakthroughs we Need, Alfred A Knopf, New
York, 2021.

128. Daniel Yergin, THE NEW MAP, Penguin Press,
New York, 2020.

129. Mark Carney, VALUE(S): Building a Better World
for All, Signal, Toronto, 2021.

Learning activities B: Conversations about climate change

130. Hurricane Irma left twelve of the school's 15
classrooms unusable and delayed the start of the
school year for 325 students.

131. UNICEF is working to provide safe drinking
water and sanitation in affected communities as
well as child protection services. © UNICEF/
UN0120004/Bradley

132. Was Jim offering a 'best selfish' solution or 'justice for
all'? What about Jim's mom?

133. Rights: Distinguish between moral rights and
legal rights.

134. Duty: The right thing to do is independent of a
person's motive or interest.

135. Deserve: Moral judgments are made about the

consequences of moral or immoral acts.

136. Subsumption test – The relationship between principles (e.g., the value of a person vs. the value of a thing)

137. Experiential dissonance – when two similar events seem to result in vastly different experiences.

138. Did Jim's mom consider the emotional intelligence that might be needed to first pay attention to the educational needs of the children? How might it be applied?

139. How might Festinger's moral values principle tests (new cases test, role exchange test, subsumption test, and universal consequences test) be applied by Jim's mom to arrive at a fair and just solution?

140. Mistaken: Questions raised by Jim

141. Was Jim offering a 'best selfish' solution or 'justice for all'? What about his mom?

142. Duty: Can a person have a conflict of duties?

143. Motive: What if a person is often mistaken about what he believes to be right, but he pursues it from a morally good motive?

144. Universal consequences test – A person can 'test' his judgment by considering the consequences of applying his judgment to all like hypothetical or real situations.

145. Cognitive dissonance: It is an uncomfortable feeling which people try to reduce by resolving the dilemma or by trying to avoid or deny it.

146. Did Jim's mom consider the emotional intelligence that might be needed to first pay attention to the educational needs of the children? How might it be applied?

147. How might Festinger's moral values principle tests (new cases test, role exchange test, subsumption test, and universal consequences test) be applied by Jim's mom to arrive at a fair and just solution?

148. Big Oil is a sinister conglomerate of multinational

corporations.

149. Did Jim defend a 'best selfish' solution or 'justice for all'? What about his mother?

150. Motive: What if a man does an act which is wrong, but he believes it to be right and he does it from morally good motives?

151. Deserve: On account of what things judged morally does a person deserve approval?

152. Role exchange: Place yourself in the shoes of another person.

153. Experiential dissonance – can occur when two similar events seem to result in vastly different experiences.

154. To Jamie, this protest[154] was necessary to meet the goal of zero carbon pollution by 2050.

155. Did Jamie defend 'best selfish' solution or 'justice for all'? What about the Superintendent?

156. Duty: Doing one's duty may or may not be an object of interest.

157. Rights: Is it true that for every duty, a person has a corresponding right?

158. Universal consequences – A person can 'test' his judgment by considering the consequences of applying his judgment to all like hypothetical or real situations.

159. Cultural dissonance – A clash of cultural mores can generate dissonance which prompts people to try to reduce the uncomfortable feeling between conflicting cultural mores.

160. Duty: Does it follow from the fact that an act is right that not doing it is wrong?

161. Just: Is an act of distributing or allocating fair from the point of view of its utility

162. Subsumption test: involves exploring the interrelationship of principles.

163. Logical Dissonance – Dissonance can be generated by logical inconsistency

164. Climate change deniers argue that we should not rush into changing things.
165. Did Sarah's Dad appeal to 'best selfish' solution or 'justice for all'? What about her uncle?
166. Motive. How would you describe people who frequently mistakenly believe something to be right when it is, in fact, wrong?
167. Just: Is it possible for a just act ever to be wrong?
168. New cases test: Consider the tentative value decision in a similar new case
169. Experiential dissonance: when two similar events seem to result in quite different experiences or when current experiences do not align with past experiences.
170. Ethical Responsibility
171. Did Sarah defend the 'best selfish' solution or 'justice for all'? What about her Dad? Her Uncle.
172. Just: Is it possible for a just act ever to be wrong?
173. Motive: What if a man does an act which is wrong, but he believes it to be right and he does it from a morally good motive?[173]
174. Universal consequences: – A person can be invited to 'test' his judgment by considering the consequences of applying his judgment to all like hypothetical or real situation
175. Cognitive dissonance – cognitive dissonance refers to situations where two cognitive elements do not fit together; they may be inconsistent or contradictory. It can help to clarify or resolve moral issues.
176. Moral responsibilities for economic models
177. Did Sarah defend the 'best selfish' solution or 'justice for all'? What about Bill? Mary?
178. Duty: Ought implies can.
179. Justice: Not all right acts are just but all just acts are right.
180. The subsumption test involves exploring the interrelationship of principles. When there is

strong disagreement about a value decision due to disagreement over the applicability of a principle, it might be necessary to prioritize the relationship of the principles.

181. Cognitive dissonance refers to situations where two cognitive elements do not fit together; they may be inconsistent or contradictory.

182. Is 'green energy' a charade?

183. Did Sarah defend a 'best selfish' solution or 'justice for all'?

184. Desert. Why do people take the question of desert very seriously?

185. Just: How is 'fair' used in the subjective sense

186. Universal consequences: – Consider the consequences of applying a decision to all like hypothetical or real situations.

187. Cognitive dissonance – cognitive dissonance refers to situations where two cognitive elements do not fit together; they may be inconsistent or contradictory. It can help to clarify or resolve moral issues.

188. … if the fiscal and monetary levers are all set for GDP growth, incentives will be devised, installed, and maintained for population and consumption growth.

189. Did Sarah defend the 'best selfish' solution or 'justice for all'?

190. Desert: Does a person deserve punishment for committing "sins of omission"?

191. Just: Not all wrong acts are unjust, but all unjust acts are wrong.

192. Subsumption test – This test involves exploring the interrelationship of principles. When there is strong disagreement about a value decision due to disagreement over the applicability of a principle, it might be desirable to explore related principles.

193. Cognitive dissonance – refers to situations where two cognitive elements do not fit together; they may be

inconsistent or contradictory. It can help to clarify or resolve moral issues.

Learning activities C: Applying Code of Ethics and Principled Thinking

194. Who is your customer, Charlie?
195. Should Charlie bend the account privacy rule? Should Charlie rationalize his action
196. for the common good'?
197. Why did Larry's logical argument not persuade Charlie?
198. Did Larry create a conflict of duties for Charlie when he asked Charlie to please the commission member by relaxing company rules?
199. A morally weak person must be distinguished from a morally bad person. How does this apply to Larry's request?
200. What does Larry deserve – disapproval or punishment?
201. Chesnut offers the following:
202. Principled thinking grounded in empathy
203. The game is on, the vibe is off.
204. Is this code moment about an overly sensitive employee?
205. Things to consider in team building
206. Proposed decision and action plan
207. Responsibilities
208. Restoring a sense of fellow feeling
209. Introduce ways of creating a fair resolution of the conflict
210. Apply the subsumption test.
211. Identify potential consequences of a proposed plan of action.
212. On account of what does a person deserve punishment?
213. How do these two approaches complement each other or not?
214. Just another tequila coffee break.

215. Is this a Code Moment for management?
216. The use of alcohol creates potential problems in the workplace.
217. A morally permissible act is not morally wrong; it could be morally right or morally indifferent.
218. How do these two approaches complement each other or not?
219. Blame it on Rio
220. The line between 'person life' and 'work life' are not that obvious
221. Actual or possible 'conflicts of interest' complicate leadership.
222. Customers want to be able to trust company leadership
223. An action is morally right or wrong independent of a person's likes or dislikes.
224. Doing one's duty if it is the right thing to do.
225. Defending the rights of people
226. Act from a morally good motive
227. Give people what they deserve
228. Act with impartiality in pursuit of justice
229. How might the CEO apply the moral values principle tests to help Elliot understand why he cannot work in the company?
230. How do these two approaches complement each other?
231. Password Piracy
232. How should Terry handle this mission?
233. The foundation of any legitimate code of ethics is 'obey the law.'
234. Can a person have a conflict of duties?
235. What constitutes a morally terrible act?
236. Describe Terry's feeling of discomfort (dissonance). What prompted it?
237. Do these two approaches complement each other or not?
238. Three Blind Mice.

239. How did Chesnut respond to this Code Moment?
240. Marijuana distribution
241. Recycling issue
242. Problem in the IT department
243. Is it true that for every right, a person has a corresponding duty? How might this apply to Rick?
244. How might a general counsel lead Rick to realize the problem of spreading false rumors?
245. How do these two approaches complement each other or not?

Postscript

246. In this period of high uncertainty, it is important for businesses to proactively communicate how they are responding to the crisis to their investors and stakeholders—including their employees, their customers, and the communities in which they are operating.
247. The IFC goes on to say that there is a "growing demand for higher standards of corporate disclosure and transparency about environmental, social, and governance matters. This could set the stage for companies of the future."

REFERENCES

1. Armstrong, Allison, & Casement, Charles, *the child and the Machine*, Key Porter, Toronto, 198.

2. Baier, Kurt, *A MORAL POINT* OF VIEW, Random House, Canada, 1966.

3. Brooks, David, *Road to Character*. New York: Random House, 2015.

4. Carney, Mark, VALUE(S): Building a Better World for All, Signal, Toronto, 2021.

5. Chesnut, Robert, with Joan O'C. Hamilton, *INTENTIONAL INTEGRITY*, St. Marin's Press, New York, 2020.

6. Damasio, Antonio, *Self Comes to Mind*, (Vintage, New York, 2012).

7. Daniel Kahneman, *Thinking, Fast and Slow* (Toronto: Anchor Canada, 2013).

8. Empathy: Tap It or Teach It, but Definitely Integrate It, https://justicerequiresempathy.com/tag/empathy-and-social-justice/, April 30, 2012.

9. Fox, Bret, Fmr CEO @ Touchstone Semiconductor, 'What is a (working) day in the life of a CEO like?' https://www.quora.com/What-is-a-working-day-in-the-life-of-a CEO-like.

10. Freedman, Milt, https://www.econlib.org/library/Enc/bios/Friedman.html.

11. Friedman, Milt, https://www.nytimes.com/2020/10/03/opinion/letters/milton-friedman-capitalism.html.

12. Friedman, Milt, https://www.nytimes.com/2020/10/03/opinion/letters/milton-friedman-

capitalism.html.

13. Gates, Bill, HOW TO AVOID A CLIMATE DISASTER: The Solutions we have and the Breakthroughs we Need, Alfred A Knopf, New York, 2021.
14. Keynes, Maynard, https://www.google.com/search?gs_1j0j15&sourceid=chrome&ie=UTF-8.
15. Michael Shellenberger, APOCALYPSE NEVER: Why Environmentalisms Hurts us All, Harper, New York, 2020.
16. Nault, Tom, Managing Partner at Middlerock Partners LLC (2016-present).
17. Rawls, John, A Theory of Justice, Harvard University Press, Cambridge, 1971.
18. Setiya, Kieran, Injustice is everywhere, so what are our moral duties? BBC FUTURE, November 2, 2022.
19. Simmons Aaron, In Defense of the Moral Significance of Empathy, *Ethic Theory Moral Practice*, https://doi.org/10.1007/s10677-013-9417-4.
20. Sorokin, David, "The Corporation: Its History and Future." Washington
21. Toews, Otto, Can you be JUST without EMPATHY? The foundation for a Code of Ethics, pre-published.
22. Toews, Otto, *Discretion and Justice in Educational Administration: Towards a Normative Conceptual Framework, University of Manitoba, Winnipeg, 1981.*
23. Toews, Otto, and Cross, Robert, KnowledgeBuilder, KnowledgeBuilder Software Inc. Winnipeg, 1991.
24. Toews, Otto, SO YOU THINK YOU CAN THINK, FriesenPress, Victoria, 2017
25. Turkle, Sherry, Reclaiming Conversation; The Power of Talk in a Digital Age, Penguin Press, New York, 2015.
26. Yergin, Daniel, THE NEW MAP, Penguin Press, New York, 2020.

INDEX

PART III: PRINCIPLED THINKING, 49

PART V: Learning Activities, 143

Learning Activity A: Conflicts in companies, 145
Activity A1: Scenario - Allow a low-cost generic Zerit, 146